THE OFFICIAL PATIENT'S SOURCEBOOK

on

HEMORRHOIDS

JAMES N. PARKER, M.D.
AND PHILIP M. PARKER, PH.D., EDITORS

ICON Health Publications
ICON Group International, Inc.
4370 La Jolla Village Drive, 4th Floor
San Diego, CA 92122 USA

Last digit indicates print number: 10 9 8 7 6 4 5 3 2 1

Publisher, Health Care: Tiffany LaRochelle
Editor(s): James Parker, M.D., Philip Parker, Ph.D.

Publisher's note: The ideas, procedures, and suggestions contained in this book are not intended as a substitute for consultation with your physician. All matters regarding your health require medical supervision. As new medical or scientific information becomes available from academic and clinical research, recommended treatments and drug therapies may undergo changes. The authors, editors, and publisher have attempted to make the information in this book up to date and accurate in accord with accepted standards at the time of publication. The authors, editors, and publisher are not responsible for errors or omissions or for consequences from application of the book, and make no warranty, expressed or implied, in regard to the contents of this book. Any practice described in this book should be applied by the reader in accordance with professional standards of care used in regard to the unique circumstances that may apply in each situation, in close consultation with a qualified physician. The reader is advised to always check product information (package inserts) for changes and new information regarding dose and contraindications before taking any drug or pharmacological product. Caution is especially urged when using new or infrequently ordered drugs, herbal remedies, vitamins and supplements, alternative therapies, complementary therapies and medicines, and integrative medical treatments.

Cataloging-in-Publication Data

Parker, James N., 1961-
Parker, Philip M, 1960-

    The Official Patient's Sourcebook on Hemorrhoids: A Revised and Updated Directory for the Internet Age/James N. Parker and Philip M. Parker, editors
        p.   cm.
    Includes bibliographical references, glossary and index.
    ISBN: 0-597-83279-X
    1. Hemorrhoids-Popular works.   I. Title.

Disclaimer

This publication is not intended to be used for the diagnosis or treatment of a health problem or as a substitute for consultation with licensed medical professionals. It is sold with the understanding that the publisher, editors, and authors are not engaging in the rendering of medical, psychological, financial, legal, or other professional services.

References to any entity, product, service, or source of information that may be contained in this publication should not be considered an endorsement, either direct or implied, by the publisher, editors or authors. ICON Group International, Inc., the editors, or the authors are not responsible for the content of any Web pages nor publications referenced in this publication.

Copyright Notice

If a physician wishes to copy limited passages from this sourcebook for patient use, this right is automatically granted without written permission from ICON Group International, Inc. (ICON Group). However, all of ICON Group publications are copyrighted. With exception to the above, copying our publications in whole or in part, for whatever reason, is a violation of copyright laws and can lead to penalties and fines. Should you want to copy tables, graphs or other materials, please contact us to request permission (e-mail: iconedit@san.rr.com). ICON Group often grants permission for very limited reproduction of our publications for internal use, press releases, and academic research. Such reproduction requires confirmed permission from ICON Group International Inc. **The disclaimer above must accompany all reproductions, in whole or in part, of this sourcebook.**

Dedication

To the healthcare professionals dedicating their time and efforts to the study of hemorrhoids.

Acknowledgements

The collective knowledge generated from academic and applied research summarized in various references has been critical in the creation of this sourcebook which is best viewed as a comprehensive compilation and collection of information prepared by various official agencies which directly or indirectly are dedicated to hemorrhoids. All of the *Official Patient's Sourcebooks* draw from various agencies and institutions associated with the United States Department of Health and Human Services, and in particular, the Office of the Secretary of Health and Human Services (OS), the Administration for Children and Families (ACF), the Administration on Aging (AOA), the Agency for Healthcare Research and Quality (AHRQ), the Agency for Toxic Substances and Disease Registry (ATSDR), the Centers for Disease Control and Prevention (CDC), the Food and Drug Administration (FDA), the Healthcare Financing Administration (HCFA), the Health Resources and Services Administration (HRSA), the Indian Health Service (IHS), the institutions of the National Institutes of Health (NIH), the Program Support Center (PSC), and the Substance Abuse and Mental Health Services Administration (SAMHSA). In addition to these sources, information gathered from the National Library of Medicine, the United States Patent Office, the European Union, and their related organizations has been invaluable in the creation of this sourcebook. Some of the work represented was financially supported by the Research and Development Committee at INSEAD. This support is gratefully acknowledged. Finally, special thanks are owed to Tiffany LaRochelle for her excellent editorial support.

About the Editors

James N. Parker, M.D.

Dr. James N. Parker received his Bachelor of Science degree in Psychobiology from the University of California, Riverside and his M.D. from the University of California, San Diego. In addition to authoring numerous research publications, he has lectured at various academic institutions. Dr. Parker is the medical editor for the *Official Patient's Sourcebook* series published by ICON Health Publications.

Philip M. Parker, Ph.D.

Philip M. Parker is the Eli Lilly Chair Professor of Innovation, Business and Society at INSEAD (Fontainebleau, France and Singapore). Dr. Parker has also been Professor at the University of California, San Diego and has taught courses at Harvard University, the Hong Kong University of Science and Technology, the Massachusetts Institute of Technology, Stanford University, and UCLA. Dr. Parker is the associate editor for the *Official Patient's Sourcebook* series published by ICON Health Publications.

About ICON Health Publications

In addition to hemorrhoids, *Official Patient's Sourcebooks* are available for the following related topics:

- The Official Patient's Sourcebook on Appendicitis
- The Official Patient's Sourcebook on Autoimmune Hepatitis
- The Official Patient's Sourcebook on Bacteria and Foorborne Illness
- The Official Patient's Sourcebook on Barrett's Esophagus
- The Official Patient's Sourcebook on Celiac Disease
- The Official Patient's Sourcebook on Cirrhosis of the Liver
- The Official Patient's Sourcebook on Constipation
- The Official Patient's Sourcebook on Crohn Disease
- The Official Patient's Sourcebook on Cyclic Vomiting Syndrome
- The Official Patient's Sourcebook on Diarrhea
- The Official Patient's Sourcebook on Diverticular Disease
- The Official Patient's Sourcebook on Fecal Incontinence
- The Official Patient's Sourcebook on Gallstones
- The Official Patient's Sourcebook on Gas
- The Official Patient's Sourcebook on Gastritis
- The Official Patient's Sourcebook on Gastroparesis
- The Official Patient's Sourcebook on Hemolytic Uremic Syndrome
- The Official Patient's Sourcebook on Hepatitis A
- The Official Patient's Sourcebook on Hepatitis B
- The Official Patient's Sourcebook on Hepatitis C
- The Official Patient's Sourcebook on Hiatal Hernia
- The Official Patient's Sourcebook on Hirschsprung
- The Official Patient's Sourcebook on Indigestion
- The Official Patient's Sourcebook on Inguinal Hernia
- The Official Patient's Sourcebook on Intestinal Pseudo-obstruction
- The Official Patient's Sourcebook on Irritable Bowel Syndrome
- The Official Patient's Sourcebook on Lactose Intolerance
- The Official Patient's Sourcebook on Ménétrier
- The Official Patient's Sourcebook on Pancreatitis
- The Official Patient's Sourcebook on Peptic Ulcer
- The Official Patient's Sourcebook on Porphyria
- The Official Patient's Sourcebook on Primary Biliary Cirrhosis
- The Official Patient's Sourcebook on Primary Sclerosing Cholangitis
- The Official Patient's Sourcebook on Proctitis
- The Official Patient's Sourcebook on Rapid Gastric Emptying

- The Official Patient's Sourcebook on Short Bowel Syndrome
- The Official Patient's Sourcebook on Ulcerative Colitis
- The Official Patient's Sourcebook on Whipple Disease
- The Official Patient's Sourcebook on Wilson's Disease
- The Official Patient's Sourcebook on Zollinger-ellison Syndrome

To discover more about ICON Health Publications, simply check with your preferred online booksellers, including Barnes & Noble.com and Amazon.com which currently carry all of our titles. Or, feel free to contact us directly for bulk purchases or institutional discounts:

ICON Group International, Inc.
4370 La Jolla Village Drive, Fourth Floor
San Diego, CA 92122 USA
Fax: 858-546-4341
Web site: **www.icongrouponline.com/health**

Table of Contents

INTRODUCTION

Overview

Dr. C. Everett Koop, former U.S. Surgeon General, once said, "The best prescription is knowledge."[1] The Agency for Healthcare Research and Quality (AHRQ) of the National Institutes of Health (NIH) echoes this view and recommends that every patient incorporate education into the treatment process. According to the AHRQ:

> Finding out more about your condition is a good place to start. By contacting groups that support your condition, visiting your local library, and searching on the Internet, you can find good information to help guide your treatment decisions. Some information may be hard to find — especially if you don't know where to look.[2]

As the AHRQ mentions, finding the right information is not an obvious task. Though many physicians and public officials had thought that the emergence of the Internet would do much to assist patients in obtaining reliable information, in March 2001 the National Institutes of Health issued the following warning:

> The number of Web sites offering health-related resources grows every day. Many sites provide valuable information, while others may have information that is unreliable or misleading.[3]

---

[1] Quotation from **http://www.drkoop.com**.
[2] The Agency for Healthcare Research and Quality (AHRQ):
http://www.ahcpr.gov/consumer/diaginfo.htm.
[3] From the NIH, National Cancer Institute (NCI):
http://cancertrials.nci.nih.gov/beyond/evaluating.html.

Since the late 1990s, physicians have seen a general increase in patient Internet usage rates. Patients frequently enter their doctor's offices with printed Web pages of home remedies in the guise of latest medical research. This scenario is so common that doctors often spend more time dispelling misleading information than guiding patients through sound therapies. *The Official Patient's Sourcebook on Hemorrhoids* has been created for patients who have decided to make education and research an integral part of the treatment process. The pages that follow will tell you where and how to look for information covering virtually all topics related to hemorrhoids, from the essentials to the most advanced areas of research.

The title of this book includes the word "official." This reflects the fact that the sourcebook draws from public, academic, government, and peer-reviewed research. Selected readings from various agencies are reproduced to give you some of the latest official information available to date on hemorrhoids.

Given patients' increasing sophistication in using the Internet, abundant references to reliable Internet-based resources are provided throughout this sourcebook. Where possible, guidance is provided on how to obtain free-of-charge, primary research results as well as more detailed information via the Internet. E-book and electronic versions of this sourcebook are fully interactive with each of the Internet sites mentioned (clicking on a hyperlink automatically opens your browser to the site indicated). Hard copy users of this sourcebook can type cited Web addresses directly into their browsers to obtain access to the corresponding sites. Since we are working with ICON Health Publications, hard copy *Sourcebooks* are frequently updated and printed on demand to ensure that the information provided is current.

In addition to extensive references accessible via the Internet, every chapter presents a "Vocabulary Builder." Many health guides offer glossaries of technical or uncommon terms in an appendix. In editing this sourcebook, we have decided to place a smaller glossary within each chapter that covers terms used in that chapter. Given the technical nature of some chapters, you may need to revisit many sections. Building one's vocabulary of medical terms in such a gradual manner has been shown to improve the learning process.

We must emphasize that no sourcebook on hemorrhoids should affirm that a specific diagnostic procedure or treatment discussed in a research study, patent, or doctoral dissertation is "correct" or your best option. This sourcebook is no exception. Each patient is unique. Deciding on appropriate options is always up to the patient in consultation with their physician and healthcare providers.

Organization

This sourcebook is organized into three parts. Part I explores basic techniques to researching hemorrhoids (e.g. finding guidelines on diagnosis, treatments, and prognosis), followed by a number of topics, including information on how to get in touch with organizations, associations, or other patient networks dedicated to hemorrhoids. It also gives you sources of information that can help you find a doctor in your local area specializing in treating hemorrhoids. Collectively, the material presented in Part I is a complete primer on basic research topics for patients with hemorrhoids.

Part II moves on to advanced research dedicated to hemorrhoids. Part II is intended for those willing to invest many hours of hard work and study. It is here that we direct you to the latest scientific and applied research on hemorrhoids. When possible, contact names, links via the Internet, and summaries are provided. It is in Part II where the vocabulary process becomes important as authors publishing advanced research frequently use highly specialized language. In general, every attempt is made to recommend "free-to-use" options.

Part III provides appendices of useful background reading for all patients with hemorrhoids or related disorders. The appendices are dedicated to more pragmatic issues faced by many patients with hemorrhoids. Accessing materials via medical libraries may be the only option for some readers, so a guide is provided for finding local medical libraries which are open to the public. Part III, therefore, focuses on advice that goes beyond the biological and scientific issues facing patients with hemorrhoids.

Scope

While this sourcebook covers hemorrhoids, your doctor, research publications, and specialists may refer to your condition using a variety of terms. Therefore, you should understand that hemorrhoids is often considered a synonym or a condition closely related to the following:

- Lump in the Rectum
- Piles
- Rectal Lump

In addition to synonyms and related conditions, physicians may refer to hemorrhoids using certain coding systems. The International Classification of Diseases, 9th Revision, Clinical Modification (ICD-9-CM) is the most commonly used system of classification for the world's illnesses. Your physician may use this coding system as an administrative or tracking tool. The following classification is commonly used for hemorrhoids:[4]

- 455 hemorrhoids
- 455.0 internal hemorrhoids without mention of complication
- 455.1 internal thrombosed hemorrhoids
- 455.2 internal hemorrhoids with other complication
- 455.3 external hemorrhoids without mention of complication
- 455.4 external thrombosed hemorrhoids
- 455.5 external hemorrhoids with other complication
- 455.6 hemorrhoids
- 455.6 hemorrhoids, nos
- 455.6 unspecified hemorrhoids without mention of complication
- 455.7 unspecified thrombosed hemorrhoids
- 455.8 unspecified hemorrhoids with other complication
- 455.9 residual hemorrhoidal skin tags

For the purposes of this sourcebook, we have attempted to be as inclusive as possible, looking for official information for all of the synonyms relevant to hemorrhoids. You may find it useful to refer to synonyms when accessing databases or interacting with healthcare professionals and medical librarians.

Moving Forward

Since the 1980s, the world has seen a proliferation of healthcare guides covering most illnesses. Some are written by patients or their family members. These generally take a layperson's approach to understanding and coping with an illness or disorder. They can be uplifting, encouraging, and highly supportive. Other guides are authored by physicians or other

---

[4] This list is based on the official version of the World Health Organization's 9th Revision, International Classification of Diseases (ICD-9). According to the National Technical Information Service, "ICD-9CM extensions, interpretations, modifications, addenda, or errata other than those approved by the U.S. Public Health Service and the Health Care Financing Administration are not to be considered official and should not be utilized. Continuous maintenance of the ICD-9-CM is the responsibility of the federal government."

healthcare providers who have a more clinical outlook. Each of these two styles of guide has its purpose and can be quite useful.

As editors, we have chosen a third route. We have chosen to expose you to as many sources of official and peer-reviewed information as practical, for the purpose of educating you about basic and advanced knowledge as recognized by medical science today. You can think of this sourcebook as your personal Internet age reference librarian.

Why "Internet age"? All too often, patients diagnosed with hemorrhoids will log on to the Internet, type words into a search engine, and receive several Web site listings which are mostly irrelevant or redundant. These patients are left to wonder where the relevant information is, and how to obtain it. Since only the smallest fraction of information dealing with hemorrhoids is even indexed in search engines, a non-systematic approach often leads to frustration and disappointment. With this sourcebook, we hope to direct you to the information you need that you would not likely find using popular Web directories. Beyond Web listings, in many cases we will reproduce brief summaries or abstracts of available reference materials. These abstracts often contain distilled information on topics of discussion.

While we focus on the more scientific aspects of hemorrhoids, there is, of course, the emotional side to consider. Later in the sourcebook, we provide a chapter dedicated to helping you find peer groups and associations that can provide additional support beyond research produced by medical science. We hope that the choices we have made give you the most options available in moving forward. In this way, we wish you the best in your efforts to incorporate this educational approach into your treatment plan.

The Editors

PART I: THE ESSENTIALS

ABOUT PART I

Part I has been edited to give you access to what we feel are "the essentials" on hemorrhoids. The essentials of a disease typically include the definition or description of the disease, a discussion of who it affects, the signs or symptoms associated with the disease, tests or diagnostic procedures that might be specific to the disease, and treatments for the disease. Your doctor or healthcare provider may have already explained the essentials of hemorrhoids to you or even given you a pamphlet or brochure describing hemorrhoids. Now you are searching for more in-depth information. As editors, we have decided, nevertheless, to include a discussion on where to find essential information that can complement what your doctor has already told you. In this section we recommend a process, not a particular Web site or reference book. The process ensures that, as you search the Web, you gain background information in such a way as to maximize your understanding.

CHAPTER 1. THE ESSENTIALS ON HEMORRHOIDS: GUIDELINES

Overview

Official agencies, as well as federally-funded institutions supported by national grants, frequently publish a variety of guidelines on hemorrhoids. These are typically called "Fact Sheets" or "Guidelines." They can take the form of a brochure, information kit, pamphlet, or flyer. Often they are only a few pages in length. The great advantage of guidelines over other sources is that they are often written with the patient in mind. Since new guidelines on hemorrhoids can appear at any moment and be published by a number of sources, the best approach to finding guidelines is to systematically scan the Internet-based services that post them.

The National Institutes of Health (NIH)[5]

The National Institutes of Health (NIH) is the first place to search for relatively current patient guidelines and fact sheets on hemorrhoids. Originally founded in 1887, the NIH is one of the world's foremost medical research centers and the federal focal point for medical research in the United States. At any given time, the NIH supports some 35,000 research grants at universities, medical schools, and other research and training institutions, both nationally and internationally. The rosters of those who have conducted research or who have received NIH support over the years include the world's most illustrious scientists and physicians. Among them are 97 scientists who have won the Nobel Prize for achievement in medicine.

---

[5] Adapted from the NIH: **http://www.nih.gov/about/NIHoverview.html**.

There is no guarantee that any one Institute will have a guideline on a specific disease, though the National Institutes of Health collectively publish over 600 guidelines for both common and rare diseases. The best way to access NIH guidelines is via the Internet. Although the NIH is organized into many different Institutes and Offices, the following is a list of key Web sites where you are most likely to find NIH clinical guidelines and publications dealing with hemorrhoids and associated conditions:

- Office of the Director (OD); guidelines consolidated across agencies available at **http://www.nih.gov/health/consumer/conkey.htm**

- National Library of Medicine (NLM); extensive encyclopedia (A.D.A.M., Inc.) with guidelines available at **http://www.nlm.nih.gov/medlineplus/healthtopics.html**

- National Institute of Diabetes and Digestive and Kidney Diseases (NIDDK); guidelines available at **http://www.niddk.nih.gov/health/health.htm**

Among these, the National Institute of Diabetes and Digestive and Kidney Diseases (NIDDK) is particularly noteworthy. The NIDDK's mission is to conduct and support research on many of the most serious diseases affecting public health.[6] The Institute supports much of the clinical research on the diseases of internal medicine and related subspecialty fields as well as many basic science disciplines. The NIDDK's Division of Intramural Research encompasses the broad spectrum of metabolic diseases such as diabetes, inborn errors of metabolism, endocrine disorders, mineral metabolism, digestive diseases, nutrition, urology and renal disease, and hematology. Basic research studies include biochemistry, nutrition, pathology, histochemistry, chemistry, physical, chemical, and molecular biology, pharmacology, and toxicology. NIDDK extramural research is organized into divisions of program areas:

- Division of Diabetes, Endocrinology, and Metabolic Diseases

- Division of Digestive Diseases and Nutrition

- Division of Kidney, Urologic, and Hematologic Diseases

The Division of Extramural Activities provides administrative support and overall coordination. A fifth division, the Division of Nutrition Research Coordination, coordinates government nutrition research efforts. The Institute supports basic and clinical research through investigator-initiated

---

[6] This paragraph has been adapted from the NIDDK: **http://www.niddk.nih.gov/welcome/mission.htm**. "Adapted" signifies that a passage is reproduced exactly or slightly edited for this book.

grants, program project and center grants, and career development and training awards. The Institute also supports research and development projects and large-scale clinical trials through contracts. The following patient guideline was recently published by the NIDDK on hemorrhoids.

What Are Hemorrhoids?[7]

Hemorrhoids are swollen but normally present blood vessels in and around the anus and lower rectum that stretch under pressure, similar to varicose veins in the legs. The increased pressure and swelling may result from straining to move the bowel. Other contributing factors include pregnancy, heredity, aging, and chronic constipation or diarrhea. Hemorrhoids are either inside the anus (internal) or under the skin around the anus (external).

What Are the Symptoms of Hemorrhoids?

Many anorectal problems, including fissures, fistulae, abscesses, or irritation and itching (pruritus ani), have similar symptoms and are incorrectly referred to as hemorrhoids.

Hemorrhoids usually are not dangerous or life threatening. In most cases, hemorrhoidal symptoms will go away within a few days.

Although many people have hemorrhoids, not all experience symptoms. The most common symptom of internal hemorrhoids is bright red blood covering the stool, on toilet paper, or in the toilet bowl. However, an internal hemorrhoid may protrude through the anus outside the body, becoming irritated and painful. This is known as a protruding hemorrhoid.

Symptoms of external hemorrhoids may include painful swelling or a hard lump around the anus that results when a blood clot forms. This condition is known as a thrombosed external hemorrhoid.

In addition, excessive straining, rubbing, or cleaning around the anus may cause irritation with bleeding and/or itching, which may produce a vicious cycle of symptoms. Draining mucus may also cause itching.

---

[7] Adapted from the National Institute of Diabetes and Digestive and Kidney Diseases (NIDDK): **http://www.niddk.nih.gov/health/digest/pubs/hems/hemords.htm.**

How Common Are Hemorrhoids?

Hemorrhoids are very common in men and women. About half of the population have hemorrhoids by age 50. Hemorrhoids are also common among pregnant women. The pressure of the fetus in the abdomen, as well as hormonal changes, cause the hemorrhoidal vessels to enlarge. These vessels are also placed under severe pressure during childbirth. For most women, however, hemorrhoids caused by pregnancy are a temporary problem.

How Are Hemorrhoids Diagnosed?

A thorough evaluation and proper diagnosis by the doctor is important any time bleeding from the rectum or blood in the stool lasts more than a couple of days. Bleeding may also be a symptom of other digestive diseases, including colorectal cancer.

The doctor will examine the anus and rectum to look for swollen blood vessels that indicate hemorrhoids and will also perform a digital rectal exam with a gloved, lubricated finger to feel for abnormalities.

Closer evaluation of the rectum for hemorrhoids requires an exam with an anoscope, a hollow, lighted tube useful for viewing internal hemorrhoids, or a proctoscope, useful for more completely examining the entire rectum.

To rule out other causes of gastrointestinal bleeding, the doctor may examine the rectum and lower colon (sigmoid) with sigmoidoscopy or the entire colon with colonoscopy. Sigmoidoscopy and colonoscopy are diagnostic procedures that also involve the use of lighted, flexible tubes inserted through the rectum.

What Is the Treatment?

Medical treatment of hemorrhoids initially is aimed at relieving symptoms. Measures to reduce symptoms include:

- Warm tub or sitz baths several times a day in plain, warm water for about 10 minutes.

- Ice packs to help reduce swelling.

- Application of a hemorroidal cream or suppository to the affected area for a limited time.

Prevention of the recurrence of hemorrhoids is aimed at changing conditions associated with the pressure and straining of constipation. Doctors will often recommend increasing fiber and fluids in the diet. Eating the right amount of fiber and drinking six to eight glasses of fluid (not alcohol) result in softer, bulkier stools. A softer stool makes emptying the bowels easier and lessens the pressure on hemorrhoids caused by straining. Eliminating straining also helps prevent the hemorrhoids from protruding.

Good sources of fiber are fruits, vegetables, and whole grains. In addition, doctors may suggest a bulk stool softener or a fiber supplement such as psyllium (Metamucil) or methylcellulose (Citrucel).

In some cases, hemorrhoids must be treated surgically. These methods are used to shrink and destroy the hemorrhoidal tissue and are performed under anesthesia. The doctor will preform the surgery during an office or hospital visit.

A number of surgical methods may be used to remove or reduce the size of internal hemorrhoids. These techniques include:

- Rubber band ligation--A rubber band is placed around the base of the hemorrhoid inside the rectum. The band cuts off circulation, and the hemorrhoid withers away within a few days.

- Sclerotherapy--A chemical solution is injected around the blood vessel to shrink the hemorrhoid.

Techniques used to treat both internal and external hemorrhoids include:

- Electrical or laser heat (laser coagulation) or infrared light (infrared photo coagulation)--Both techniques use special devices to burn hemorrhoidal tissue.

- Hemorrhoidectomy--Occasionally, extensive or severe internal or external hemorrhoids may require removal by surgery known as hemorrhoidectomy. This is the best method for permanent removal of hemorrhoids.

How Are Hemorrhoids Prevented?

The best way to prevent hemorrhoids is to keep stools soft so they pass easily, thus decreasing pressure and straining, and to empty bowels as soon as possible after the urge occurs. Exercise, including walking, and increased fiber in the diet help reduce constipation and straining by producing stools that are softer and easier to pass.

More Guideline Sources

The guideline above on hemorrhoids is only one example of the kind of material that you can find online and free of charge. The remainder of this chapter will direct you to other sources which either publish or can help you find additional guidelines on topics related to hemorrhoids. Many of the guidelines listed below address topics that may be of particular relevance to your specific situation or of special interest to only some patients with hemorrhoids. Due to space limitations these sources are listed in a concise manner. Do not hesitate to consult the following sources by either using the Internet hyperlink provided, or, in cases where the contact information is provided, contacting the publisher or author directly.

Topic Pages: MEDLINEplus

For patients wishing to go beyond guidelines published by specific Institutes of the NIH, the National Library of Medicine has created a vast and patient-oriented healthcare information portal called MEDLINEplus. Within this Internet-based system are "health topic pages." You can think of a health topic page as a guide to patient guides. To access this system, log on to **http://www.nlm.nih.gov/medlineplus/healthtopics.html**. From there you can either search using the alphabetical index or browse by broad topic areas. Recently, MEDLINEplus listed the following as being relevant to hemorrhoids:

- Guides On hemorrhoids

  Hemorrhoids
  http://www.nlm.nih.gov/medlineplus/ency/article/000292.htm
  Hemorrhoids
  http://www.nlm.nih.gov/medlineplus/hemorrhoids.html

- Guides on Human Anatomy and Systems

  Digestive System Topics
  http://www.nlm.nih.gov/medlineplus/digestivesystem.html

- Other Guides

  Anal/Rectal Diseases
  http://www.nlm.nih.gov/medlineplus/analrectaldiseases.html

  Digital rectal exam
  http://www.nlm.nih.gov/medlineplus/ency/article/007069.htm

Within the health topic page dedicated to hemorrhoids, the following was recently recommended to patients:

- General/Overviews

  Hemorrhoids: Reducing the Pain and Discomfort
  Source: American Academy of Family Physicians
  http://familydoctor.org/healthfacts/090/

  What are Hemorrhoids?
  Source: Mayo Foundation for Medical Education and Research
  http://www.mayoclinic.com/invoke.cfm?id=DS00096

- Diagnosis/Symptoms

  Elimination Problems: Self-Care Flowcharts
  Source: American Academy of Family Physicians
  http://familydoctor.org/flowcharts/532.html

- Treatment

  Hemorrhoid Surgery
  Source: Patient Education Institute
  http://www.nlm.nih.gov/medlineplus/tutorials/hemorrhoidsurgeryloader.html

  Hemorrhoidectomy
  Source: Animation Education Group
  http://www.yoursurgery.com/ProcedureDetails.cfm?BR=7&Proc=25

- Nutrition

    Fiber: How To Increase the Amount in Your Diet
    Source: American Academy of Family Physicians
    http://familydoctor.org/handouts/099.html

- From the National Institutes of Health

    Hemorrhoids
    Source: National Digestive Diseases Information Clearinghouse
    http://www.niddk.nih.gov/health/digest/pubs/hems/hemords.ht
    m

- Organizations

    American Gastroenterological Association
    http://www.gastro.org/index.html

    National Digestive Diseases Information Clearinghouse
    http://www.niddk.nih.gov/health/digest/nddic.htm

- Pictures/Diagrams

    Hemorrhoids
    Source: Mayo Foundation for Medical Education and Research
    http://www.mayoclinic.com/popupinvoker.cfm?objectid=64E2E8AE
    -D57F-4432-BEB8135A51DEF7CD

If you do not find topics of interest when browsing health topic pages, then you can choose to use the advanced search utility of MEDLINEplus at **http://www.nlm.nih.gov/medlineplus/advancedsearch.html**. This utility is similar to the NIH Search Utility, with the exception that it only includes material linked within the MEDLINEplus system (mostly patient-oriented information). It also has the disadvantage of generating unstructured results. We recommend, therefore, that you use this method only if you have a very targeted search.

The Combined Health Information Database (CHID)

CHID Online is a reference tool that maintains a database directory of thousands of journal articles and patient education guidelines on hemorrhoids and related conditions. One of the advantages of CHID over other sources is that it offers summaries that describe the guidelines available, including contact information and pricing. CHID's general Web site is **http://chid.nih.gov/**. To search this database, go to **http://chid.nih.gov/detail/detail.html**. In particular, you can use the advanced search options to look up pamphlets, reports, brochures, and information kits. The following was recently posted in this archive:

- **Hemorrhoids: Steps to Finding Relief**

  Source: San Bruno, CA: StayWell Company. 1999. [2 p.].

  Contact: Available from StayWell Company. Order Department, 1100 Grundy Lane, San Bruno, CA 94066-9821. (800) 333-3032. Fax (650) 244-4512. E-mail: email@staywell.com. Website: www.staywell.com. Price: $17.95 for pack of 50; plus shipping and handling.

  Summary: This patient education brochure describes hemorrhoids and their treatment. Written in nontechnical language, the brochure first defines hemorrhoids as cushions of swollen veins in the anal canal. Hemorrhoids are a very common problem and can affect all kinds of people, including those who sit for long periods, pregnant women, and others. Symptoms of hemorrhoids can include pain, itching, irritation, burning, and bleeding of the rectal area. Constipation (dry, hard to pass stool) is a major cause of hemorrhoids. Other causes include heavy lifting, lack of exercise, too much strenuous exercise, chronic cough, and poor bowel habits (such as sitting on the toilet for long periods of time). Diagnosis is important to rule out more serious diseases and will include the patient's medical history and some diagnostic tests, such as sigmoidoscopy. Most treatment plans focus on steps that the patient can follow at home, including sitz baths, nonprescription medications, and good bowel habits. The brochure reminds readers that steps to ease constipation include increasing fluid intake and undertaking regular exercise. One section of the brochure illustrates and describes the physiology of the anal canal and the types of hemorrhoids that can occur (external or internal). The last page of the brochure summarizes the recommendations for increasing dietary fiber. The brochure is illustrated with full color line drawings. 6 figures.

- **Hemorrhoid Book: A Look at Hemorrhoids, How They're Treated and How You Can Prevent Them from Coming Back. [Folleto de las Hemorroides: Information Sobre las Hemorroides: Tratamiento y Prevencion]**

  Source: San Bruno, CA: StayWell Company. 1999. 15 p.

Contact: Available from Staywell Company. Order Department, 1100 Grundy Lane, San Bruno, CA 94066-9821. (800) 333-3032. Fax (650) 244-4512. Price: $1.25 per copy; plus shipping and handling.

Summary: This patient education brochure describes hemorrhoids and problems that can occur with swollen hemorrhoids. Written in nontechnical language, the brochure first defines hemorrhoids as normal cushions of tissue that swell gently to aid in the process of elimination (defecation). Hemorrhoids become a problem only when they swell too much, at which point they may cause pain, itching, irritation, burning, and bleeding. The primary cause is a low fiber diet, leading to constipation and straining on the toilet. Other causes include a sedentary lifestyle, too much strenuous exercise, pressure on the rectum from pregnancy or from standing a lot, regulating bowel habits by the clock, and medications that cause diarrhea or constipation. Because symptoms of hemorrhoids can mimic symptoms of a more serious disease such as colorectal cancer, prompt evaluation and diagnosis is important. Once the doctor confirms a diagnosis of bleeding or swollen hemorrhoids, treatment options can be explored. For many people, a change in diet and level of activity is the only treatment that may be needed. For others, treatment at the doctor's office or surgery may be necessary. Maintaining a healthy, high fiber diet, which relieves constipation and eases the digestive process, is the best way to prevent bleeding or swollen hemorrhoids. The brochure describes and illustrates external and internal hemorrhoids, and other anal problems, including fissures and fistulae. Treatment options reviewed include injection therapy, infrared coagulation, banding, cryosurgery, laser therapy, and hemorrhoidectomy (surgical removal of the hemorrhoids). The brochure is illustrated with full color line drawings and is available in English or Spanish. 27 figures.

- **Hemorrhoids**

Source: Fort Worth, TX: Konsyl Pharmaceuticals, Inc. 1998. [2 p.].

Contact: Available from Konsyl Pharmaceuticals, Inc. 4200 South Hulen Street, Suite 513, Fort Worth, TX 76109-4912. (800) 356-6795 or (817) 763-8011. Fax (817) 731-9389. Website: www.konsyl.com. Price: Single copy free.

Summary: This brochure provides basic information about hemorrhoids, vascular tissue pads in and about the anus. The symptoms of hemorrhoids can include rectal pain, protrusion, occasional itching, or bleeding on toilet tissue or in the toilet bowl. The brochure discusses the problems encountered with internal and external hemorrhoids, then outlines the options for the nonsurgical treatment of the condition. This treatment can include an increase in dietary fiber and an increase in water intake, regular exercise, and a decrease in dietary fats. The brochure also briefly outlines surgical treatments for hemorrhoids, including sclerotherapy, infrared coagulation, and banding procedures. The author emphasizes the use of fiber supplements, such as Konsyl (the manufacturer of which is the producer of this brochure). The author also reminds readers that they should have any rectal problems appropriately diagnosed, to rule out a more serious problem, such as polyps, colitis, or cancer. The brochure is illustrated with full color drawings and photographs. 4 figures.

- **Hemorrhoids: A Guide for Patients**

Source: San Ramon, CA: HIN, Inc., The Health Information Network. 1996. 25 p.

Contact: Available from HIN, Inc. 231 Market Place, Number 331, San Ramon, CA 94583. (800) HIN-1121. Fax (925) 358-4377. Website: www.hinbooks.com. Price: $36.25 plus shipping per set of 25 booklets; quantity discounts available. Order Number 0204. ISBN: 1885274262.

Summary: This patient education brochure familiarizes readers with hemorrhoids and their treatment. The brochure is written in nontechnical language and discusses what hemorrhoids are; symptoms; nonhemorrhoid conditions; determining when to consult a health care provider; treatment options, including treatment at home and treatment at the doctor's office, and surgery; recovery after surgery; and preventing recurrence of hemorrhoids. The brochure is illustrated with simple line drawings and figures and includes a glossary.

- **Hemorrhoids: Questions and Answers**

Source: Arlington Heights, IL: American Society of Colon and Rectal Surgeons. 1996. [4 p.].

Contact: Available from American Society for Colon and Rectal Surgeons (ASCRS). 85 West Algonquin Road, Suite 550, Arlington Heights, IL 60005. (800) 791-0001 or (847) 290-9184. Website: www.fascrs.org. Price: Single copy free.

Summary: This brochure describes hemorrhoids, enlarged bulging blood vessels in and about the anus and lower rectum. There are two types of hemorrhoids: external and internal. External (outside) hemorrhoids develop near the anus and are covered by very sensitive skin. Internal (inside) hemorrhoids develop within the anus beneath the lining. Painless bleeding and protrusion during bowel movements are the most common symptom. The exact causes are not known, but contributing factors include the upright posture of human beings, aging, chronic constipation or diarrhea, pregnancy, heredity, faulty bowel function, and spending long periods of time (e.g., reading) on the toilet. There is no relationship between hemorrhoids and cancer; however, the symptoms are similar to those of colorectal cancer and other diseases of the digestive system and therefore call for investigation by a health care provider. Mild symptoms can be relieved frequently by increasing the amount of fiber and fluids in the diet. Eliminating excessive straining reduces the pressure on hemorrhoids and helps prevent them from protruding. Severe hemorrhoids require treatment, much of which can be performed on an outpatient basis. The brochure describes treatment options, including ligation (rubber band treatment), injection and coagulation, hemorrhoidectomy, and other treatments, including cryotherapy (freezing). The brochure concludes with a brief description of the specialty of colon and rectal surgeons. 4 figures.

- **Relief from Hemorrhoids: Recognizing Symptoms, Relieving Discomfort**

Source: Cincinnati, OH: Procter and Gamble. 1994. 12 p.

Contact: Available from Metamucil-Procter and Gamble. P.O. Box 9032, Cincinnati, OH 45209-9970. Price: Single copy free; bulk copies available.

Summary: This brochure provides a general overview of hemorrhoids and gives readers recommendations on how to manage the condition. Topics include symptoms; causes; treatment options; prevention, including the role of a high fiber diet; and the use of fiber supplements, including the product Metamucil. The brochure is produced by the manufacturer of Metamucil. The brochure includes a reply card to obtain more information about Metamucil products. 2 figures. 1 table.

- **Hemorrhoids: Reducing the Pain and Discomfort**

Source: Kansas City, MO: American Academy of Family Physicians. 1994. 4 p.

Contact: Available from American Academy of Family Physicians. 11400 Tomahawk Creek Parkway, Leawood, KS 66211-2672. (800) 274-2237. Website: www.aafp.org. Price: $22.00 for 100 copies for members, $33.00 for 100 copies for nonmembers.

Summary: This patient education brochure helps readers understand hemorrhoids and what to do to reduce the pain and discomfort they may cause. Hemorrhoids are swollen veins in the rectum or anus. Internal hemorrhoids involve the veins inside the rectum; external hemorrhoids involve veins in the skin outside the anus. One of the main things that can lead to hemorrhoids is straining while trying to have a bowel movement. Other risk factors for hemorrhoids include genetics (inherited tendency to have hemorrhoids), pregnancy, obesity, and standing or lifting too much. A health care provider should be consulted for any rectal bleeding, in order to rule out more serious causes and possibly to treat the hemorrhoids. One sidebar provides suggestions for preventing constipation, including increasing dietary fiber, drinking plenty of fluids, and exercising regularly. Strategies for the home care management of hemorrhoids are also outlined. These include: soaking in a warm bath, cleaning the anus carefully after each bowel movement, using ice packs to relieve swelling, using acetaminophen or aspirin to relieve pain, and using a cream or ointment to sooth and numb itching and pain. The brochure concludes with a brief description of the surgical treatments for hemorrhoids and the indications for surgery. 1 figure. 2 tables. (AA-M).

- **Understanding: Hemorrhoids**

  Source: Pittsburgh, PA: SmithKline Beecham Consumer Brands. 1991. 4 p.

  Contact: Available from SmithKline Beecham. Consumer Brands, P.O. Box 1467, Pittsburgh, PA 15230. (800) 245-1040. Price: Single copy free. Bulk orders available to physicians by calling (800) 233-2426.

  Summary: This patient education brochure provides basic information about hemorrhoids. Topics include a definition of hemorrhoids; causes and incidence; the lack of dietary fiber in the typical Western diet; treatments, including a high fiber diet; and prevention. The brochure concludes with a section summarizing facts about fiber. The brochure, produced by the manufacturers of CITRUCEL, a fiber product, describes the use of CITRUCEL as part of a therapeutic program to prevent hemorrhoids. 3 references.

- **Constipation**

  Source: Bethesda, MD: American Gastroenterological Association. 199x. [4 p.].

  Contact: American Gastroenterological Association (AGA). 7910 Woodmont Avenue, Seventh Floor, Bethesda, MD 20814. (800) 668-5237 or (301) 654-2055. Fax (301) 652-3890. Website: www.gastro.org. Price: Single copy free; bulk copies available.

  Summary: Constipation is the infrequent and difficult passage of stool. This brochure from the American Gastroenterological Association (AGA) emphasizes that the frequency of bowel movements among healthy people varies greatly, ranging from three movements a day to three a week. This brochure reviews common misconceptions about constipation, the causes of constipation (including that in children and in older adults), the diagnostic tests used to help determine the causes of constipation, complications arising from constipation, and treatment strategies. The symptoms of constipation are key to helping the physician determine a diagnosis and treatment. Symptoms can include infrequency of bowel movements, straining, pain, or unsatisfied defecation. The causes of constipation include poor diet, irritable bowel syndrome (IBS), poor bowel habits, laxative abuse, travel, hormonal disturbances, pregnancy, fissures and hemorrhoids, specific diseases, loss of body salts, mechanical compression, nerve damage, medications, and colonic motility disorders. Constipation in children may be related to any of these causes, but is usually due to poor bowel habits. In older adults, poor diet, insufficient intake of fluids, lack of exercise, the use of certain drugs to treat other conditions, and poor bowel habits can result in constipation. In addition to routine blood, urine, and stool tests, a sigmoidoscopy may be used to detect problems in the rectum and lower colon. Constipation can lead to complications, such as hemorrhoids or fissures, or fecal impactions. A physician should be consulted when symptoms are severe, last longer than three weeks, are disabling, or when any of the complications occur. For most people, dietary and lifestyle improvements can lessen the chances of constipation. The brochure includes a list of references, a sidebar that reviews steps to prevent constipation, and a diagram of the digestive tract, with organs labeled. 1 figure. 5 references.

- **Hemorrhoids. [Hemorroides]**

Source: Camp Hill, PA: Chek-Med Systems, Inc. 1996. 2 p.

Contact: Available from Chek-Med Systems, Inc. 200 Grandview Avenue, Camp Hill, PA 17011. (800) 451-5797. Fax (717) 761-0216. Price: $22 per pack of 50 pamphlets for order of 3-10 packs; 3 packet minimum. Discounts available for larger quantities and complete kits of gastroenterology pamphlets.

Summary: This patient brochure, available in English and Spanish, provides information about the causes, complications, and treatment of hemorrhoids ('piles'). Hemorrhoids alone are rarely serious. They can, however, mask a more serious disorder, such as colon or rectal cancer, and require proper diagnosis and treatment by a physician. The complications of hemorrhoids include thrombosis and pain, bleeding, and itching and irritation. Practical guidelines are included for treating hemorrhoids, involving both hygienic measures and dietary considerations. Treatment requiring surgical and non-surgical approaches also are discussed. Steps for preventing hemorrhoids are listed. It is noted that hemorrhoids are an especially common disorder, and often reduce by themselves or with minimal treatment.

The National Guideline Clearinghouse™

The National Guideline Clearinghouse™ offers hundreds of evidence-based clinical practice guidelines published in the United States and other countries. You can search their site located at **http://www.guideline.gov** by using the keyword "hemorrhoids" or synonyms. The following was recently posted:

- **Surgical management of hemorrhoids.**

  Source: Society for Surgery of the Alimentary Tract, Inc..; 1998 June 3 (revised 2000 Jan); 3 pages

  http://www.guideline.gov/FRAMESETS/guideline_fs.asp?guideline=00 1397&sSearch_string=hemorrhoids

Healthfinder™

Healthfinder™ is an additional source sponsored by the U.S. Department of Health and Human Services which offers links to hundreds of other sites that contain healthcare information. This Web site is located at **http://www.healthfinder.gov**. Again, keyword searches can be used to find guidelines. The following was recently found in this database:

- **Hemorrhoids**

  Summary: Basic information for consumers about the causes and treatment of hemorrhoids.

  Source: National Institute of Diabetes and Digestive and Kidney Diseases, National Institutes of Health

  http://www.healthfinder.gov/scripts/recordpass.asp?RecordType=0&R ecordID=1449

- **Hemorrhoids: Reducing the Pain and Discomfort**

  Summary: The information presented on this page includes a general description of hemorrhoids along with information about the care and treatment of this disorder.

  Source: American Academy of Family Physicians

  http://www.healthfinder.gov/scripts/recordpass.asp?RecordType=0&RecordID=6130

- **Patient Brochures: Colon and Rectal Disorders**

  Summary: Consumer health education information about colon and rectal disorders, including rectal prolapse, diverticular disease, hemorrhoids, polyps of the colon & rectum, and surgical options for related

  Source: American Society of Colon and Rectal Surgeons

  http://www.healthfinder.gov/scripts/recordpass.asp?RecordType=0&RecordID=4298

- **Practice Parameters for the Treatment of Hemorrhoids**

  Summary: Practice parameters outline principles and provides suggestions to assist physicians in caring for patients with hemorrhoidal symptoms.

  Source: American Society of Colon and Rectal Surgeons

  http://www.healthfinder.gov/scripts/recordpass.asp?RecordType=0&RecordID=2324

- **Questions and Answers About Hemorrhoids**

  Summary: A general overview about hemorrhoids -- includes causes, symptoms, prevention, prognosis and management. From this page users can also link to a search engine to locate colorectal surgeons locally.

  Source: American Society of Colon and Rectal Surgeons

  http://www.healthfinder.gov/scripts/recordpass.asp?RecordType=0&RecordID=6129

The NIH Search Utility

After browsing the references listed at the beginning of this chapter, you may want to explore the NIH Search Utility. This allows you to search for documents on over 100 selected Web sites that comprise the NIH-WEB-SPACE. Each of these servers is "crawled" and indexed on an ongoing basis. Your search will produce a list of various documents, all of which will relate in some way to hemorrhoids. The drawbacks of this approach are that the information is not organized by theme and that the references are often a mix of information for professionals and patients. Nevertheless, a large number of the listed Web sites provide useful background information. We can only recommend this route, therefore, for relatively rare or specific disorders, or when using highly targeted searches. To use the NIH search utility, visit the following Web page: **http://search.nih.gov/index.html**.

Additional Web Sources

A number of Web sites that often link to government sites are available to the public. These can also point you in the direction of essential information. The following is a representative sample:

- AOL: **http://search.aol.com/cat.adp?id=168&layer=&from=subcats**

- drkoop.com®: **http://www.drkoop.com/conditions/ency/index.html**

- Family Village: **http://www.familyvillage.wisc.edu/specific.htm**

- Google:
  http://directory.google.com/Top/Health/Conditions_and_Diseases/

- Med Help International: **http://www.medhelp.org/HealthTopics/A.html**

- Open Directory Project:
  http://dmoz.org/Health/Conditions_and_Diseases/

- Yahoo.com: **http://dir.yahoo.com/Health/Diseases_and_Conditions/**

- WebMD®Health: **http://my.webmd.com/health_topics**

Vocabulary Builder

The material in this chapter may have contained a number of unfamiliar words. The following Vocabulary Builder introduces you to terms used in this chapter that have not been covered in the previous chapter:

Abdomen: That portion of the body that lies between the thorax and the pelvis. [NIH]

Acetaminophen: Analgesic antipyretic derivative of acetanilide. It has weak anti-inflammatory properties and is used as a common analgesic, but may cause liver, blood cell, and kidney damage. [NIH]

Alimentary: Pertaining to food or nutritive material, or to the organs of digestion. [EU]

Anesthesia: A state characterized by loss of feeling or sensation. This depression of nerve function is usually the result of pharmacologic action and is induced to allow performance of surgery or other painful procedures. [NIH]

Anorectal: Pertaining to the anus and rectum or to the junction region between the two. [EU]

Anus: The distal or terminal orifice of the alimentary canal. [EU]

Baths: The immersion or washing of the body or any of its parts in water or other medium for cleansing or medical treatment. It includes bathing for personal hygiene as well as for medical purposes with the addition of therapeutic agents, such as alkalines, antiseptics, oil, etc. [NIH]

Chronic: Persisting over a long period of time. [EU]

Coagulation: 1. the process of clot formation. 2. in colloid chemistry, the solidification of a sol into a gelatinous mass; an alteration of a disperse phase or of a dissolved solid which causes the separation of the system into a liquid phase and an insoluble mass called the clot or curd. Coagulation is usually irreversible. 3. in surgery, the disruption of tissue by physical means to form an amorphous residuum, as in electrocoagulation and photocoagulation. [EU]

Colitis: Inflammation of the colon. [EU]

Colonoscopy: Endoscopic examination, therapy or surgery of the luminal surface of the colon. [NIH]

Colorectal: Pertaining to or affecting the colon and rectum. [EU]

Constipation: Infrequent or difficult evacuation of the faeces. [EU]

Cryosurgery: The use of freezing as a special surgical technique to destroy or excise tissue. [NIH]

Defecation: The normal process of elimination of fecal material from the rectum. [NIH]

Diarrhea: Passage of excessively liquid or excessively frequent stools. [NIH]

Endocrinology: A subspecialty of internal medicine concerned with the metabolism, physiology, and disorders of the endocrine system. [NIH]

Fats: One of the three main classes of foods and a source of energy in the body. Fats help the body use some vitamins and keep the skin healthy. They also serve as energy stores for the body. In food, there are two types of fats: saturated and unsaturated. [NIH]

Fissure: Any cleft or groove, normal or otherwise; especially a deep fold in the cerebral cortex which involves the entire thickness of the brain wall. [EU]

Gastrointestinal: Pertaining to or communicating with the stomach and intestine, as a gastrointestinal fistula. [EU]

Hematology: A subspecialty of internal medicine concerned with morphology, physiology, and pathology of the blood and blood-forming tissues. [NIH]

Hemorrhoids: Varicosities of the hemorrhoidal venous plexuses. [NIH]

Heredity: 1. the genetic transmission of a particular quality or trait from parent to offspring. 2. the genetic constitution of an individual. [EU]

Hormonal: Pertaining to or of the nature of a hormone. [EU]

Hygienic: Pertaining to hygiene, or conducive to health. [EU]

Ligation: Application of a ligature to tie a vessel or strangulate a part. [NIH]

Methylcellulose: Methylester of cellulose. Methylcellulose is used as an emulsifying and suspending agent in cosmetics, pharmaceutics and the chemical industry. It is used therapeutically as a bulk laxative. [NIH]

Molecular: Of, pertaining to, or composed of molecules : a very small mass of matter. [EU]

Motility: The ability to move spontaneously. [EU]

Mucus: The free slime of the mucous membranes, composed of secretion of the glands, along with various inorganic salts, desquamated cells, and leucocytes. [EU]

Prolapse: 1. the falling down, or sinking, of a part or viscus; procidentia. 2. to undergo such displacement. [EU]

Pruritus: Itching skin; may be a symptom of diabetes. [NIH]

Recurrence: The return of a sign, symptom, or disease after a remission. [NIH]

Sclerotherapy: Treatment of varicose veins, hemorrhoids, gastric and esophageal varices, and peptic ulcer hemorrhage by injection or infusion of chemical agents which cause localized thrombosis and eventual fibrosis and obliteration of the vessels. [NIH]

Sedentary: 1. sitting habitually; of inactive habits. 2. pertaining to a sitting posture. [EU]

Sigmoid: 1. shaped like the letter S or the letter C. 2. the sigmoid colon. [EU]

Sigmoidoscopy: Endoscopic examination, therapy or surgery of the sigmoid flexure. [NIH]

Spectrum: A charted band of wavelengths of electromagnetic vibrations obtained by refraction and diffraction. By extension, a measurable range of activity, such as the range of bacteria affected by an antibiotic (antibacterial s.) or the complete range of manifestations of a disease. [EU]

Suppository: A medicated mass adapted for introduction into the rectal, vaginal, or urethral orifice of the body, suppository bases are solid at room temperature but melt or dissolve at body temperature. Commonly used bases are cocoa butter, glycerinated gelatin, hydrogenated vegetable oils, polyethylene glycols of various molecular weights, and fatty acid esters of polyethylene glycol. [EU]

Thrombosis: The formation, development, or presence of a thrombus. [EU]

Toxicology: The science concerned with the detection, chemical composition, and pharmacologic action of toxic substances or poisons and the treatment and prevention of toxic manifestations. [NIH]

Urology: A surgical specialty concerned with the study, diagnosis, and treatment of diseases of the urinary tract in both sexes and the genital tract in the male. It includes the specialty of andrology which addresses both male genital diseases and male infertility. [NIH]

Vascular: Pertaining to blood vessels or indicative of a copious blood supply. [EU]

Veins: The vessels carrying blood toward the heart. [NIH]

CHAPTER 2. SEEKING GUIDANCE

Overview

Some patients are comforted by the knowledge that a number of organizations dedicate their resources to helping people with hemorrhoids. These associations can become invaluable sources of information and advice. Many associations offer aftercare support, financial assistance, and other important services. Furthermore, healthcare research has shown that support groups often help people to better cope with their conditions.[8] In addition to support groups, your physician can be a valuable source of guidance and support. Therefore, finding a physician that can work with your unique situation is a very important aspect of your care.

In this chapter, we direct you to resources that can help you find patient organizations and medical specialists. We begin by describing how to find associations and peer groups that can help you better understand and cope with hemorrhoids. The chapter ends with a discussion on how to find a doctor that is right for you.

Associations and Hemorrhoids

As mentioned by the Agency for Healthcare Research and Quality, sometimes the emotional side of an illness can be as taxing as the physical side.[9] You may have fears or feel overwhelmed by your situation. Everyone has different ways of dealing with disease or physical injury. Your attitude, your expectations, and how well you cope with your condition can all

---

[8] Churches, synagogues, and other houses of worship might also have groups that can offer you the social support you need.
[9] This section has been adapted from **http://www.ahcpr.gov/consumer/diaginf5.htm**.

influence your well-being. This is true for both minor conditions and serious illnesses. For example, a study on female breast cancer survivors revealed that women who participated in support groups lived longer and experienced better quality of life when compared with women who did not participate. In the support group, women learned coping skills and had the opportunity to share their feelings with other women in the same situation.

In addition to associations or groups that your doctor might recommend, we suggest that you consider the following list (if there is a fee for an association, you may want to check with your insurance provider to find out if the cost will be covered):

- **American Society of Colon and Rectal Surgeons**

  Address: American Society of Colon and Rectal Surgeons 85 West Algonquin Road, Suite 550, Arlington Heights, IL 60005

  Telephone: (847) 290-9184

  Fax: (847) 290-9203

  Email: ascrs@fascrs.org

  Web Site: http://www.fascrs.org

  Background: The American Society of Colon and Rectal Surgeons (ASCRS) is a medical professional society representing more than 1,000 board certified colon and rectal surgeons and other surgeons. The Society's membership is dedicated to advancing and promoting the science and practice of the treatment of individuals with diseases and disorders affecting the colon, rectum, and anus. The Society's Standards Task Force is committed to developing practice parameters for the treatment of colon and rectal diseases and disorders including ambulatory anorectal surgery, treatment of hemorrhoids, management of anal fissure, treatment of rectal carcinoma, and detection of colorectal neoplasms. The Society's web site provides links to such practice parameters as well as to core subject updates on such topics as colonic volvulus, ostomies and stomal therapy, familial adenomatous polyposis, and colon and rectal cancer. The Society also publishes the 'Washington Report,' which offers updates on current federal legislative and regulatory actions, and provides professional publications including the 'ASCRS Newsletter' and the Society's official journal entitled 'Diseases of the Colon and Rectum.' The ASCRS also provides an email discussion group (listserv) for the benefit of ASCRS members and fellows in colon and rectal surgery. The primary purpose of the listserv is to provide a forum for the informal discussion of clinical cases and other issues of general interest to the colon and rectal surgeon community. The Society's web site also provides information on the Collaborative Group of the

Americas on Inherited Colorectal Cancer. The Group was established in 1995 to improve understanding of the basic science of inherited colorectal cancer and the clinical management of affected families. Its broad aims are to promote education of physicians, allied health care professionals, patients, and their families; provide linkage to clinical and chemoprevention trials; promote the integration of molecular and clinical research at local and national levels; and serve as a resource for developing similar genetic registers. The American Society of Colon and Rectal Surgeons also provides patient information on a variety of topics including anal abscess/fistula, anal fissure, anal warts, bowel incontinence, colonoscopy, colorectal cancer, constipation, Crohn's disease, diverticular disease, irritable bowel syndrome, ostomy, rectal prolapse, and ulcerative colitis.

Finding More Associations

There are a number of directories that list additional medical associations that you may find useful. While not all of these directories will provide different information than what is listed above, by consulting all of them, you will have nearly exhausted all sources for patient associations.

The National Health Information Center (NHIC)

The National Health Information Center (NHIC) offers a free referral service to help people find organizations that provide information about hemorrhoids. For more information, see the NHIC's Web site at **http://www.health.gov/NHIC/** or contact an information specialist by calling 1-800-336-4797.

DIRLINE

A comprehensive source of information on associations is the DIRLINE database maintained by the National Library of Medicine. The database comprises some 10,000 records of organizations, research centers, and government institutes and associations which primarily focus on health and biomedicine. DIRLINE is available via the Internet at the following Web site: **http://dirline.nlm.nih.gov/**. Simply type in "hemorrhoids" (or a synonym) or the name of a topic, and the site will list information contained in the database on all relevant organizations.

The Combined Health Information Database

Another comprehensive source of information on healthcare associations is the Combined Health Information Database. Using the "Detailed Search" option, you will need to limit your search to "Organizations" and "hemorrhoids". Type the following hyperlink into your Web browser: **http://chid.nih.gov/detail/detail.html**. To find associations, use the drop boxes at the bottom of the search page where "You may refine your search by." For publication date, select "All Years." Then, select your preferred language and the format option "Organization Resource Sheet." By making these selections and typing in "hemorrhoids" (or synonyms) into the "For these words:" box, you will only receive results on organizations dealing with hemorrhoids. You should check back periodically with this database since it is updated every 3 months.

The National Organization for Rare Disorders, Inc.

The National Organization for Rare Disorders, Inc. has prepared a Web site that provides, at no charge, lists of associations organized by specific diseases. You can access this database at the following Web site: **http://www.rarediseases.org/cgi-bin/nord/searchpage**. Select the option called "Organizational Database (ODB)" and type "hemorrhoids" (or a synonym) in the search box.

Online Support Groups

In addition to support groups, commercial Internet service providers offer forums and chat rooms for people with different illnesses and conditions. WebMD®, for example, offers such a service at their Web site: **http://boards.webmd.com/roundtable**. These online self-help communities can help you connect with a network of people whose concerns are similar to yours. Online support groups are places where people can talk informally. If you read about a novel approach, consult with your doctor or other healthcare providers, as the treatments or discoveries you hear about may not be scientifically proven to be safe and effective.

Finding Doctors

One of the most important aspects of your treatment will be the relationship between you and your doctor or specialist. All patients with hemorrhoids must go through the process of selecting a physician. While this process will vary from person to person, the Agency for Healthcare Research and Quality makes a number of suggestions, including the following:[10]

- If you are in a managed care plan, check the plan's list of doctors first.

- Ask doctors or other health professionals who work with doctors, such as hospital nurses, for referrals.

- Call a hospital's doctor referral service, but keep in mind that these services usually refer you to doctors on staff at that particular hospital. The services do not have information on the quality of care that these doctors provide.

- Some local medical societies offer lists of member doctors. Again, these lists do not have information on the quality of care that these doctors provide.

Additional steps you can take to locate doctors include the following:

- Check with the associations listed earlier in this chapter.

- Information on doctors in some states is available on the Internet at **http://www.docboard.org**. This Web site is run by "Administrators in Medicine," a group of state medical board directors.

- The American Board of Medical Specialties can tell you if your doctor is board certified. "Certified" means that the doctor has completed a training program in a specialty and has passed an exam, or "board," to assess his or her knowledge, skills, and experience to provide quality patient care in that specialty. Primary care doctors may also be certified as specialists. The AMBS Web site is located at **http://www.abms.org/newsearch.asp**.[11] You can also contact the ABMS by phone at 1-866-ASK-ABMS.

- You can call the American Medical Association (AMA) at 800-665-2882 for information on training, specialties, and board certification for many licensed doctors in the United States. This information also can be found in "Physician Select" at the AMA's Web site: **http://www.ama-assn.org/aps/amahg.htm**.

If the previous sources did not meet your needs, you may want to log on to the Web site of the National Organization for Rare Disorders (NORD) at **http://www.rarediseases.org/**. NORD maintains a database of doctors with

---

[10] This section is adapted from the AHRQ: **www.ahrq.gov/consumer/qntascii/qntdr.htm**.

[11] While board certification is a good measure of a doctor's knowledge, it is possible to receive quality care from doctors who are not board certified.

expertise in various rare diseases. The Metabolic Information Network (MIN), 800-945-2188, also maintains a database of physicians with expertise in various metabolic diseases.

Selecting Your Doctor[2]

When you have compiled a list of prospective doctors, call each of their offices. First, ask if the doctor accepts your health insurance plan and if he or she is taking new patients. If the doctor is not covered by your plan, ask yourself if you are prepared to pay the extra costs. The next step is to schedule a visit with your chosen physician. During the first visit you will have the opportunity to evaluate your doctor and to find out if you feel comfortable with him or her. Ask yourself, did the doctor:

- Give me a chance to ask questions about hemorrhoids?

- Really listen to my questions?

- Answer in terms I understood?

- Show respect for me?

- Ask me questions?

- Make me feel comfortable?

- Address the health problem(s) I came with?

- Ask me my preferences about different kinds of treatments for hemorrhoids?

- Spend enough time with me?

Trust your instincts when deciding if the doctor is right for you. But remember, it might take time for the relationship to develop. It takes more than one visit for you and your doctor to get to know each other.

---

[2] This section has been adapted from the AHRQ: **www.ahrq.gov/consumer/qntascii/qntdr.htm**.

Working with Your Doctor[13]

Research has shown that patients who have good relationships with their doctors tend to be more satisfied with their care and have better results. Here are some tips to help you and your doctor become partners:

- You know important things about your symptoms and your health history. Tell your doctor what you think he or she needs to know.

- It is important to tell your doctor personal information, even if it makes you feel embarrassed or uncomfortable.

- Bring a "health history" list with you (and keep it up to date).

- Always bring any medications you are currently taking with you to the appointment, or you can bring a list of your medications including dosage and frequency information. Talk about any allergies or reactions you have had to your medications.

- Tell your doctor about any natural or alternative medicines you are taking.

- Bring other medical information, such as x-ray films, test results, and medical records.

- Ask questions. If you don't, your doctor will assume that you understood everything that was said.

- Write down your questions before your visit. List the most important ones first to make sure that they are addressed.

- Consider bringing a friend with you to the appointment to help you ask questions. This person can also help you understand and/or remember the answers.

- Ask your doctor to draw pictures if you think that this would help you understand.

- Take notes. Some doctors do not mind if you bring a tape recorder to help you remember things, but always ask first.

- Let your doctor know if you need more time. If there is not time that day, perhaps you can speak to a nurse or physician assistant on staff or schedule a telephone appointment.

- Take information home. Ask for written instructions. Your doctor may also have brochures and audio and videotapes that can help you.

---

[13] This section has been adapted from the AHRQ:
www.ahrq.gov/consumer/qntascii/qntdr.htm.

- After leaving the doctor's office, take responsibility for your care. If you have questions, call. If your symptoms get worse or if you have problems with your medication, call. If you had tests and do not hear from your doctor, call for your test results. If your doctor recommended that you have certain tests, schedule an appointment to get them done. If your doctor said you should see an additional specialist, make an appointment.

By following these steps, you will enhance the relationship you will have with your physician.

Broader Health-Related Resources

In addition to the references above, the NIH has set up guidance Web sites that can help patients find healthcare professionals. These include:[14]

- Caregivers:
  http://www.nlm.nih.gov/medlineplus/caregivers.html

- Choosing a Doctor or Healthcare Service:
  http://www.nlm.nih.gov/medlineplus/choosingadoctororhealthcareserv ice.html

- Hospitals and Health Facilities:
  http://www.nlm.nih.gov/medlineplus/healthfacilities.html

Vocabulary Builder

Carcinoma: A malignant new growth made up of epithelial cells tending to infiltrate the surrounding tissues and give rise to metastases. [EU]

Neoplasms: New abnormal growth of tissue. Malignant neoplasms show a greater degree of anaplasia and have the properties of invasion and metastasis, compared to benign neoplasms. [NIH]

Warts: Benign epidermal proliferations or tumors; some are viral in origin. [NIH]

---

[14] You can access this information at:
http://www.nlm.nih.gov/medlineplus/healthsystem.html.

PART II: ADDITIONAL RESOURCES AND ADVANCED MATERIAL

ABOUT PART II

In Part II, we introduce you to additional resources and advanced research on hemorrhoids. All too often, patients who conduct their own research are overwhelmed by the difficulty in finding and organizing information. The purpose of the following chapters is to provide you an organized and structured format to help you find additional information resources on hemorrhoids. In Part II, as in Part I, our objective is not to interpret the latest advances on hemorrhoids or render an opinion. Rather, our goal is to give you access to original research and to increase your awareness of sources you may not have already considered. In this way, you will come across the advanced materials often referred to in pamphlets, books, or other general works. Once again, some of this material is technical in nature, so consultation with a professional familiar with hemorrhoids is suggested.

CHAPTER 3. STUDIES ON HEMORRHOIDS

Overview

Every year, academic studies are published on hemorrhoids or related conditions. Broadly speaking, there are two types of studies. The first are peer reviewed. Generally, the content of these studies has been reviewed by scientists or physicians. Peer-reviewed studies are typically published in scientific journals and are usually available at medical libraries. The second type of studies is non-peer reviewed. These works include summary articles that do not use or report scientific results. These often appear in the popular press, newsletters, or similar periodicals.

In this chapter, we will show you how to locate peer-reviewed references and studies on hemorrhoids. We will begin by discussing research that has been summarized and is free to view by the public via the Internet. We then show you how to generate a bibliography on hemorrhoids and teach you how to keep current on new studies as they are published or undertaken by the scientific community.

The Combined Health Information Database

The Combined Health Information Database summarizes studies across numerous federal agencies. To limit your investigation to research studies and hemorrhoids, you will need to use the advanced search options. First, go to **http://chid.nih.gov/index.html**. From there, select the "Detailed Search" option (or go directly to that page with the following hyperlink: **http://chid.nih.gov/detail/detail.html**). The trick in extracting studies is found in the drop boxes at the bottom of the search page where "You may refine your search by." Select the dates and language you prefer, and the format option "Journal Article." At the top of the search form, select the number of records you would like to see (we recommend 100) and check the box to display "whole records." We recommend that you type in "hemorrhoids" (or synonyms) into the "For these words:" box. Consider using the option "anywhere in record" to make your search as broad as possible. If you want to limit the search to only a particular field, such as the title of the journal, then select this option in the "Search in these fields" drop box. The following is a sample of what you can expect from this type of search:

- **Local Injection of Bupivacaine After Rubber Band Ligation of Hemorrhoids: Prospective, Randomized Study**

  Source: Diseases of the Colon and Rectum. 42(2): 174-179. February 1999.

  Contact: Available from Williams and Wilkins. 352 West Camden Street, Baltimore, MD 21201-2436.

  Summary: This article reports on a study to determine if local injection of bupivacaine after hemorrhoidal banding causes a decrease in pain and in the incidence of associated symptoms. After hemorrhoidal banding, patients were randomly assigned to receive a local injection of bupivacaine with 1:200,000 epinephrine, an injection of normal saline, or no injection, just superior to each band. Pain was graded by the patient and by the study nurse within 30 minutes, and any associated symptoms were recorded. At intervals of 6, 24, and 48 hours postbanding, the patient record pain, limitation of activities, and analgesic requirements. Associated symptoms at home were also recorded. Of 115 patients studied, 42 received bupivacaine, 42 received normal saline injection, and 31 received no injection. In patients receiving bupivacaine compared with no injection, within 30 minutes postbanding there was a significant reduction in pain graded by the patient and by the nurse and a significant reduction in incidence of nausea and shaking. However, in the bupivacaine group compared with the other two groups, at the intervals of 6, 24, and 48 hours postbanding there was no sustained reduction in the severity of pain and no reduction in analgesic requirements or limitation of normal activities. In the week after banding, there was no difference between groups in symptoms of nausea, shaking, lightheadedness, urinary retention, or bleeding. The authors conclude that bupivacaine injection may be useful for reducing pain and associated symptoms long enough to tolerate a trip home from the outpatient department, but does not show a sustained effect. 1 figure. 5 tables. 8 references.

- **Is It Hemorrhoids, or Rectal Cancer?**

Source: Primary Care and Cancer. 21(4):23-26, April 2001.

Summary: A physician discusses the diagnosis of patients with anal symptoms, including symptoms and diagnosis of rectal cancer and hemorrhoids. There should be no difficulty with diagnosing people with anal symptoms if the physician does a digital rectal examination and a proctoscopic examination on any patient with anal complaints and on patients undergoing a complete physical examination. Periodic examinations are the best way to identify early cancers and precancerous lesions and offer the best prognosis when the diagnosis is cancer. Symptoms and signs of cancer of the rectum are more likely to be present the lower the cancer is in the rectum and the larger it is in size. Tumors may shed blood onto the stool surface, though the stool will be passed before mixing of blood can occur. Rectal urges or the sensation of the presence of a mass may be felt, depending on the ability of the rectum to recognize a tumor as a luminal mass. If the tumor is large enough, or if it involves a significant length of the rectal wall, there may be bowel habit changes. Symptoms and signs of hemorrhoids may be similar. Symptoms such as weight loss, anorexia, and ill health occur after widespread dissemination, which is unusual for rectal cancer. Hemorrhoids rarely cause general health problems unless anemia occurs. While cancers can often be recognized on sight, biopsy confirmation is necessary before planning treatment. The earlier the stage of the cancer, the fewer symptoms there will be and the more favorable the treatment outcome. Regular examinations and a surveillance program for polyp detection are recommended, since most cancers of the bowel are probably benign polyps for at least 5 years prior to becoming neoplasms. Proctosigmoidoscopic and anoscopic examinations allow for visualization of the entire rectum and anus. If these examinations are done regularly, it is unlikely that cancer will develop in the rectum, since polyps can be seen and destroyed prior to becoming cancer. 2 figures, 11 references.

- **Review of the Causes of Lower Gastrointestinal Tract Bleeding in Children**

Source: Gastroenterology Nursing. 24(2): 77-83. March-April 2001.

Contact: Available from Williams and Wilkins. 351 West Camden Street, Baltimore, MD 21201-2436. (410) 528-8555.

Summary: Bleeding may occur anywhere along the gastrointestinal (GI) tract, which covers a large surface area and is highly vascularized. Pediatric patients who present with blood in their stools (bowel movements) are a special challenge for the health care team. Seeing blood in the child's stools, the caregiver and child may become extremely anxious, fearing a devastating diagnosis. This article reviews the causes of lower GI tract bleeding in children. The differential diagnosis of this symptoms in infants and children includes numerous possibilities ranging from benign disorders, which require little or no treatment at all, to serious diseases that require immediate intervention. A complete history, including progression, duration, frequency, and severity of symptoms, is essential in assessing GI bleeding. Associated symptoms that help define the diagnosis include vomiting, diarrhea, constipation, abdominal pain, anorexia (lack of appetite), rash, joint pain or swelling, weight loss, fever, irritability, history of GI bleeding, or history of hematological or immunological disorders. Constipation with fissure (a tear in the anus) formation is the most common cause for rectal bleeding in toddlers and school age children. Infection is one of the more common causes of bleeding from the lower GI tract; infections can be due to Salmonella, Shigella, Campylobacter jejuni; Yersinia enterocolitica, Escherichia coli, Clostridium difficile, or Entamoeba histolytica. Other causes include swallowed blood, hemorrhoids, inflammatory bowel disease (IBD), intussusception (a portion of the bowel turns in on itself, creating an obstruction), polyps, lymphonodular hyperplasia, Meckel's diverticulum, allergic colitis, Henoch Schonlein purpura, hemolytic uremic syndrome (HUS), enterocolitis, child sexual abuse, and Munchausen syndrome by proxy.

- **Hemorrhoids and More: Common Causes of Blood in the Stool**

Source: Digestive Health and Nutrition. 3(4): 24-26. July-August 2001.

Contact: Available from American Gastroenterological Association. 7910 Woodmont Avenue, 7th Floor, Bethesda, MD 20814. (877) DHN-4YOU or (301) 654-2055, ext. 650. E-mail: DHN@gastro.org.

Summary: Most rectal bleeding is caused by hemorrhoids, which usually can be simply and effectively treated. This article reviews the many other conditions, including some serious disorders, that can cause blood in the stool. The author reminds readers that bleeding from any part of the nearly 40 foot long digestive tract can cause blood in the stool. Accurate and timely diagnostic tests are important to determine the cause of any bleeding. Bleeding higher up in the gut, from the esophagus or stomach, can result in stools with a black, tarry appearance. Bleeding from the lower end, such as the colon, or in large amounts, can appear as pure blood, blood clots, or as blood mixed with or streaking the stool. Another kind of blood, occult or hidden blood, may not be visible at all. A number of prescription and over the counter (OTC) medications can cause bleeding in the stomach and small intestine. The blood thinning drug warfarin also can induce bleeding in the intestine, as can some antibiotics. Other causes of bleeding can include ulcers, gastritis (inflammation of the stomach lining), ulcerative colitis, Crohn's disease, polyps (small growths inside the intestine), diverticular disease, abnormalities in the blood vessels (vascular anomalies), anal fissures (tears) and fistulas (abnormal openings between the anal canal and other organs, such as the bladder), and abscesses (pockets of infection. The author reiterates the importance of timely diagnosis, including a thorough patient history and evaluation of symptoms. Diagnostic tests can include blood tests, digital rectal examination, endoscopy, colonoscopy, sigmoidoscopy, fecal occult blood test, barium x rays, angiography (x rays of blood vessels), and nuclear scanning. Treatment depends on the source and extent of the bleeding.

- **Quest for Painless Surgical Treatment of Hemorrhoids Continues**

Source: Journal of the American College of Surgeons. 193(2): 174-178. August 2001.

Contact: Available from Journal of the American College of Surgeons. P.O. Box 2127, Marion, OH 43306-8227. (800) 214-8489 or (740) 382-3322. Fax (740) 382-5866.

Summary: This editorial discusses the quest for painless surgical treatment of hemorrhoids. The author notes that pain after hemorrhoidectomy (removal of hemorrhoids) is to be expected. The reasons for this pain are related to the anatomy and intended function of the anus. The lining of the anal canal is certainly among the most richly innervated (filled with nerves) tissue in the digestive tract; it has the ability to sense temperature, vibration, stretch, noxious stimuli, and to, importantly, differentiate among gas, liquid, and solid material. The author reviews the historical treatments for hemorrhoidectomy, including the various instruments that have been used. The author notes that, thus far, the various techniques have not resulted in significant reductions in postoperative pain. The techniques described have in common that they excise, destroy, or ablate the hemorrhoidal tissue, removing or ligating (tying off) the arterial and venous supplies. The author then comments on an accompanying article in this Journal issue, in which the researchers (Arnaud et al) use the technique of stapling for hemorrhoids. While this is not a new technique (indeed the research article includes a table summarizing three other studies), it is coming back into interest with a current research project. The commentary author reports on an initial pilot study of 10 patients who underwent a stapling procedure. While early symptom control (including pain management) and functional outcomes appear normal, longterm symptomatic and functional outcomes require further study. Certainly the possibility of an increased rate of recurrence (compared to traditional surgery for hemorrhoids) is a possibility. The author concludes that the stapling technique could finally offer patients suffering from third degree hemorrhoids a painless or relatively painless method of treatment. 37 references.

- **Treatment of Hemorrhoids with Circular Stapler, a New Alternative to Conventional Methods: A Prospective Study of 140 Patients**

Source: Journal of the American College of Surgeons. 193(2): 161-165. August 2001.

Contact: Available from Journal of the American College of Surgeons. P.O. Box 2127, Marion, OH 43306-8227. (800) 214-8489 or (740) 382-3322. Fax (740) 382-5866.

Summary: Surgical hemorrhoidectomy (removal of hemorrhoids) has a reputation for being a painful procedure. This article reports on a study undertaken to determine the efficacy and safety of a new procedure for the surgical treatment of hemorrhoid disease. From April 1998 to August 1998, 140 patients (83 men and 57 women) with an average age of 43.8 years (range 19 to 83 years) underwent hemorrhoidectomy using a circular stapler. Operative times, peri and postoperative complications, mean hospital stay, assessment of the postoperative pain, period of incapacity for work, and functional results were collected. All patients were evaluated at 2 weeks, 2 months, and 18 months after operation. The average length of the operation was 18 minutes (range 8 to 60 minutes). There were no perioperative complications. The postoperative complication rate was 6.4 percent (n = 9). Mean hospital stay was 36 hours (range 8 to 72 hours). Paracetamol was the only analgesic (painkiller) used. Eighty three patients (59.3 percent) required analgesic for less than 2 days, 45 patients (32.1 percent) between 2 and 7 days, and 12 patients (8.6 percent) for more than 7 days. No patients had anal wound care. The period of incapacity for work was less than 3 days for 22 patients (21.2 percent), between 3 and 7 days for 13 patients (12.5 percent), between 7 and 14 days for 62 patients (59.6 percent), and more than 14 days for 7 patients (6.8 percent). At 18 months, 95. 7 percent of the patients were fully satisfied with the results, 3.6 percent were somewhat satisfied (n = 4), and 0.7 percent were unsatisfied. The authors conclude that treatment of hemorrhoids with a circular stapler appears to be safe, effective, and rapid, causing few postoperative complications and minimal postoperative pain. 2 figures. 1 table. 17 references.

- **Hemorrhoids, Genital Warts, and other Perianal Complaints**

  Source: JAAPA. Journal of the American Academy of Physician Assistants. 14(9): 37-39, 43-44, 47. September 2001.

  Contact: Available from Medical Economics. 5 Paragon Drive, Montvale, NJ 07645. (800) 432-4570. Fax (201) 573-4956.

  Summary: Reluctance to discuss a perianal problem may cause a patient to delay seeking medical attention. Although anorectal symptoms account for 10 percent of visits to a medical provider, 80 percent of patients who have symptoms of benign anorectal disease do not seek medical attention. Yet 75 percent of Americans will be given a diagnosis of hemorrhoids during their lifetime. This article helps physician assistants learn about hemorrhoids, genital warts, and other perianal complaints and how to help patients who present with these complaints. The authors describe the components of a thorough rectal examination and the diagnosis and treatment of the five most common causes of perianal discomfort or pain: hemorrhoids, anal fissure, anorectal abscess, pruritus ani (itching), and condylomata acuminata (genital warts). Although most conditions prove benign, the differential diagnosis can include neoplasia (including cancer). Readers can qualify for continuing medical education credit by completing the posttest printed in the journal. 3 figures. 34 references.

- **Coping with the Pain and Annoyance of Hemorrhoids**

  Source: Digestive Health and Nutrition. p. 20-23. January-February 2000.

  Contact: Available from American Gastroenterological Association. 7910 Woodmont Avenue, 7th Floor, Bethesda, MD 20814. (877) DHN-4YOU or (301) 654-2055, ext. 650. E-mail: DHN@gastro.org.

  Summary: This article helps readers understand and cope with hemorrhoids. The author describes how to distinguish between types of hemorrhoids, how to recognize the possible symptoms, and what treatment options are available. Following is a description of typical hemorrhoidal bleeding (bright red blood on the toilet tissue or in the toilet water); readers are encouraged to consult with a health care provider for even relatively minor rectal bleeding. Hemorrhoids are then defined in terms of their location. Internal hemorrhoids arise from blood vessels that lie up to 2 inches inside the anus, and external hemorrhoids form under the anal skin. Internal hemorrhoids, which are not usually seen or felt unless they protrude downward outside the anus, can cause other symptoms, including a feeling of fullness in the rectum (particularly after passing stool) or deep itching (pruritus). The author explores possible reasons why some people develop hemorrhoids, including certain working conditions (such as lots of sitting), weak muscles within the bowels, low fiber diets (which can result in straining with defecation), and pregnancy. Diagnostic tests can rule out other possible causes of rectal bleeding, including anal fissure, Crohn's disease or ulcerative colitis (inflammatory bowel diseases), Meckel's diverticulum, and cancer or noncancerous polyps in the bowel. Treatment options are reviewed, from lifestyle and dietary changes to topical therapy, to surgical treatments (rubber band ligation, laser treatment, and sclerosing injections).

- **Triple Rubber Band Ligation for Hemorrhoids: Prospective, Randomized Trial of Use of Local Anesthetic Injection**

Source: Diseases of the Colon and Rectum. 42(3): 363-366. March 1999.

Contact: Available from Williams and Wilkins. 352 West Camden Street, Baltimore, MD 21201-2436.

Summary: Rubber band ligation is a common office procedure for hemorrhoids. Triple rubber band ligation in a single session has been shown to be a safe, economical way of treating hemorrhoids. However, postligation discomfort after triple rubber band ligation is not uncommon. This article reports on a study undertaken to evaluate the effectiveness of injecting local anesthetic into the banded hemorrhoidal tissue to reduce postligation discomfort. Patients attending an outpatient clinic for symptomatic hemorrhoids suitable for triple rubber band ligation were randomly assigned to two groups. In the treatment group, rubber band ligation was performed on three columns of hemorrhoids, and 1 to 2 mL of 2 percent lignocaine was injected into the banded hemorrhoidal tissue. In the control group, triple rubber band ligation was performed in a similar manner, but local anesthetic was not given. Patients were followed up by telephone in the second week and in the clinic after 6 weeks. In all, 101 patients entered the study; 62 received the injection of local anesthetic and 39 were in the control group. Overall, good to excellent results occurred in 89 percent of patients, and there was no difference between the two groups. Postligation pain occurred in 26 and 20 percent of patients in the treatment and control groups, respectively. Postligation tenesmus (pain on defecation) occurred in 32 and 41 percent of patients in the treatment and control groups, respectively. No patients suffered from septic complications or bleeding that required transfusion. The authors conclude that injecting local anesthetic into the banded hemorrhoidal tissue did not help reduce postligation discomfort. 3 tables. 13 references. (AA-M).

- **Necrotizing Fascitis After Injection Sclerotherapy for Hemorrhoids: Report of a Case**

Source: Diseases of the Colon and Rectum. 42(3): 419-420. March 1999.

Contact: Available from Williams and Wilkins. 352 West Camden Street, Baltimore, MD 21201-2436.

Summary: This article presents a case report of a patient who underwent submucosal injection sclerotherapy for hemorrhoids. The patient subsequently developed necrotizing fascitis of the anorectum, perianal region, and scrotum that necessitated emergency debridement and defunctioning colostomy. Necrotizing fascitis is a term used to describe a rapidly progressive inflammation and necrosis of subcutaneous tissue, superficial fascia, and the superficial part of the deep fascia, with secondary necrosis of the overlying skin. It is caused by the mixed growth of aerobic and anaerobic organisms, and underlying systemic disease (such as diabetes or immune disorders) may predispose people to this disorder. Postoperatively, the patient developed septicemia and renal failure requiring an extended hospital stay. Restoration of bowel continuity was done after 3 months. The authors provide a brief review of known complications of this technique (sclerotherapy) and note that necrotizing fascitis should be added to the list. 5 references.

- **Constipation in the Elderly**

Source: American Family Physician. 58(4): 907-914. September 15, 1998.

Contact: Available from American Academy of Family Physicians. 11400 Tomahawk Creek Parkway, Leawood, KS 66211-2672. (800) 274-2237. Website: www.aafp.org.

Summary: Constipation affects as many as 26 percent of older men and 34 percent of older women and is a problem that has been related to diminished perception of quality of life. This article reviews the problem of constipation in older people and encourages family physicians to learn about and address this problem in their patients. Constipation may be a sign of a serious problem such as a mass lesion, a manifestation of a systemic disorder such as hypothyroidism, or a side effect of medications such as narcotic analgesics. The patient with constipation should be questioned about fluid and food intake, medications, supplements, and homeopathic remedies. The physical examination may reveal local masses or thrombosed hemorrhoids, which may be contributing to the constipation. Visual inspection of the colon is useful when no obvious cause of constipation can be determined. Treatment should address the underlying abnormality. The chronic use of certain treatments, such as laxatives, should be avoided. First-line therapy should include bowel retraining, increased dietary fiber and fluid intake, and exercise when possible. Laxatives, stool softeners, and nonabsorbable solutions may be needed in some patients with chronic constipation. 1 figure. 4 tables. 17 references. (AA-M).

- **Hemorrhoids, Anal Fissure, and Carcinoma of the Colon, Rectum, and Anus During Pregnancy**

Source: Surgical Clinics of North America. 75(1): 77-88. February 1995.

Contact: Available from W.B. Saunders Company, Periodicals Fulfillment, 6277 Sea Harbor Drive, Orlando, FL 32887. (800) 654-2452.

Summary: In this journal article, from a special issue on surgery in the pregnant patient, the authors review the problems of hemorrhoids, anal fissure, and carcinoma of the colon, rectum, and anus during pregnancy. The chapter covers the etiology, symptoms, complications, conservative therapy, and surgery for hemorrhoids; the etiology and treatment of anal fissures; colorectal carcinoma, including presenting symptoms and signs, treatment considerations, and outcome; and anal carcinoma. The authors stress the need for open discussions between patient and physician about the pros and cons of operative and nonoperative approaches. 3 tables. 33 references.

- **Nonsurgical Treatment Options for Internal Hemorrhoids**

Source: American Family Physician. 52(3): 821-834, 839-841. September 1, 1995.

Summary: In this article, the authors summarize the nonsurgical treatment options for internal hemorrhoids. They note that hemorrhoids are the most common etiology for the complaints of rectal pain and/or bleeding, but the family physician should always be alert to other pathologic explanations, such as fissure, abscess, fistula, condyloma, or cancer. Topics include feelings of embarrassment or apprehension about surgery that may make patients reluctant to discuss anorectal symptoms with their physician; the anatomic origin and grade of disease; the etiologies of hemorrhoids; symptoms; patient history and physical examination; indications and contraindications for treatment; preparation for treatment; treatment modalities for internal hemorrhoids, including rubber band ligation, infrared coagulation, bipolar electrocoagulation, low-voltage direct current, sclerotherapy and cryotherapy, and laser therapy; postoperative care; and treatment complications. The author concludes that proper anal hygiene and correction of chronic constipation or diarrhea are essential to prevent recurrence of hemorrhoids. The article concludes with a reproducible patient education handout on the nonsurgical treatment of hemorrhoids. 11 figures. 1 table. 20 references. (AA-M).

- **No Strain No Pain: The Bottom Line in Treating Hemorrhoids**

  Source: FDA Consumer. 26(2): 31-33. March 1992.

  Summary: This article presents an overview of hemorrhoids. Topics covered include the types of hemorrhoids, the importance of a thorough physical examination to rule out non-hemorrhoidal causes of bleeding, and treatment for hemorrhoids. Treatment options discussed include a high-fiber diet, increased fluid intake, over-the counter remedies, and surgical options, including rubber band ligation, infrared photocoagulation, laser coagulation, and sclerotherapy. 2 figures.

Federally-Funded Research on Hemorrhoids

The U.S. Government supports a variety of research studies relating to hemorrhoids and associated conditions. These studies are tracked by the Office of Extramural Research at the National Institutes of Health.[15] CRISP (Computerized Retrieval of Information on Scientific Projects) is a searchable database of federally-funded biomedical research projects conducted at universities, hospitals, and other institutions. Visit the CRISP Web site at **http://commons.cit.nih.gov/crisp3/CRISP.Generate_Ticket**.   You   can perform targeted searches by various criteria including geography, date, as well as topics related to hemorrhoids and related conditions.

For most of the studies, the agencies reporting into CRISP provide summaries or abstracts. As opposed to clinical trial research using patients, many federally-funded studies use animals or simulated models to explore hemorrhoids and related conditions. In some cases, therefore, it may be difficult to understand how some basic or fundamental research could eventually translate into medical practice.

---

[15] Healthcare projects are funded by the National Institutes of Health (NIH), Substance Abuse and Mental Health Services (SAMHSA), Health Resources and Services Administration (HRSA), Food and Drug Administration (FDA), Centers for Disease Control and Prevention (CDCP), Agency for Healthcare Research and Quality (AHRQ), and Office of Assistant Secretary of Health (OASH).

The National Library of Medicine: PubMed

One of the quickest and most comprehensive ways to find academic studies in both English and other languages is to use PubMed, maintained by the National Library of Medicine. The advantage of PubMed over previously mentioned sources is that it covers a greater number of domestic and foreign references. It is also free to the public.[16] If the publisher has a Web site that offers full text of its journals, PubMed will provide links to that site, as well as to sites offering other related data. User registration, a subscription fee, or some other type of fee may be required to access the full text of articles in some journals.

To generate your own bibliography of studies dealing with hemorrhoids, simply go to the PubMed Web site at **www.ncbi.nlm.nih.gov/pubmed**. Type "hemorrhoids" (or synonyms) into the search box, and click "Go." The following is the type of output you can expect from PubMed for "hemorrhoids" (hyperlinks lead to article summaries):

- **Ask the midwife. Prevention and care of hemorrhoids, including homeopathic remedies.**
  Author(s): Goldstein L.
  Source: Birth Gaz. 2000 Spring; 16(2): 13-6. No Abstract Available.

- **Piles. Ideas on how to reduce the pain from hemorrhoids.**
  Author(s): Hartley J.
  Source: Pract Midwife. 1999 April; 2(4): 12-3. No Abstract Available.
  http://www.ncbi.nlm.nih.gov:80/entrez/query.fcgi?cmd=Retrieve&db=PubMed&list_uids=10427282&dopt=Abstract

Vocabulary Builder

Abdominal: Pertaining to the abdomen. [EU]

Aerobic: 1. having molecular oxygen present. 2. growing, living, or occurring in the presence of molecular oxygen. 3. requiring oxygen for respiration. [EU]

Anaerobic: 1. lacking molecular oxygen. 2. growing, living, or occurring in

---

[16] PubMed was developed by the National Center for Biotechnology Information (NCBI) at the National Library of Medicine (NLM) at the National Institutes of Health (NIH). The PubMed database was developed in conjunction with publishers of biomedical literature as a search tool for accessing literature citations and linking to full-text journal articles at Web sites of participating publishers. Publishers that participate in PubMed supply NLM with their citations electronically prior to or at the time of publication.

the absence of molecular oxygen; pertaining to an anaerobe. [EU]

Analgesic: An agent that alleviates pain without causing loss of consciousness. [EU]

Anemia: A reduction in the number of circulating erythrocytes or in the quantity of hemoglobin. [NIH]

Angiography: Radiography of blood vessels after injection of a contrast medium. [NIH]

Angiotensinogen: An alpha-globulin of which a fragment of 14 amino acids is converted by renin to angiotensin I, the inactive precursor of angiotensin II. It is a member of the serpin superfamily. [NIH]

Angiotensins: Oligopeptides ranging in size from angiotensin precursors with 14 amino acids to the active vasoconstrictor angiotensin II with 8 amino acids, or their analogs or derivatives. The amino acid content varies with the species and changes in that content produce antagonistic or inactive compounds. [NIH]

Anomalies: Birth defects; abnormalities. [NIH]

Anorexia: Lack or loss of the appetite for food. [EU]

Antibiotic: A chemical substance produced by a microorganism which has the capacity, in dilute solutions, to inhibit the growth of or to kill other microorganisms. Antibiotics that are sufficiently nontoxic to the host are used as chemotherapeutic agents in the treatment of infectious diseases of man, animals and plants. [EU]

Antibody: An immunoglobulin molecule that has a specific amino acid sequence by virtue of which it interacts only with the antigen that induced its synthesis in cells of the lymphoid series (especially plasma cells), or with antigen closely related to it. Antibodies are classified according to their ode of action as agglutinins, bacteriolysins, haemolysins, opsonins, precipitins, etc. [EU]

Antigens: Substances that cause an immune response in the body. The body "sees" the antigens as harmful or foreign. To fight them, the body produces antibodies, which attack and try to eliminate the antigens. [NIH]

Bacteria: Unicellular prokaryotic microorganisms which generally possess rigid cell walls, multiply by cell division, and exhibit three principal forms: round or coccal, rodlike or bacillary, and spiral or spirochetal. [NIH]

Bacteriophages: Viruses whose host is a bacterial cell. [NIH]

Biochemical: Relating to biochemistry; characterized by, produced by, or involving chemical reactions in living organisms. [EU]

Biopsy: The removal and examination, usually microscopic, of tissue from the living body, performed to establish precise diagnosis. [EU]

Bupivacaine: A widely used local anesthetic agent. [NIH]

Campylobacter: A genus of bacteria found in the reproductive organs, intestinal tract, and oral cavity of animals and man. Some species are pathogenic. [NIH]

Capillary: Any one of the minute vessels that connect the arterioles and venules, forming a network in nearly all parts of the body. Their walls act as semipermeable membranes for the interchange of various substances, including fluids, between the blood and tissue fluid; called also vas capillare. [EU]

Cholera: An acute diarrheal disease endemic in India and Southeast Asia whose causative agent is vibrio cholerae. This condition can lead to severe dehydration in a matter of hours unless quickly treated. [NIH]

Clostridium: A genus of motile or nonmotile gram-positive bacteria of the family bacillaceae. Many species have been identified with some being pathogenic. They occur in water, soil, and in the intestinal tract of humans and lower animals. [NIH]

Concomitant: Accompanying; accessory; joined with another. [EU]

Contamination: The soiling or pollution by inferior material, as by the introduction of organisms into a wound, or sewage into a stream. [EU]

Cytokines: Non-antibody proteins secreted by inflammatory leukocytes and some non-leukocytic cells, that act as intercellular mediators. They differ from classical hormones in that they are produced by a number of tissue or cell types rather than by specialized glands. They generally act locally in a paracrine or autocrine rather than endocrine manner. [NIH]

Cytotoxins: Substances elaborated by microorganisms, plants or animals that are specifically toxic to individual cells; they may be involved in immunity or may be contained in venoms. [NIH]

Diathermy: Heating of the body tissues due to their resistance to the passage of high-frequency electromagnetic radiation, electric currents, or ultrasonic waves. In medical d. (thermopenetration) the tissues are warmed but not damaged; in surgical d. (electrocoagulation) tissue is destroyed. [EU]

Diverticulum: A pathological condition manifested as a pouch or sac opening from a tubular or sacular organ. [NIH]

Dysentery: Any of various disorders marked by inflammation of the intestines, especially of the colon, and attended by pain in the abdomen, tenesmus, and frequent stools containing blood and mucus. Causes include chemical irritants, bacteria, protozoa, or parasitic worms. [EU]

Edema: Excessive amount of watery fluid accumulated in the intercellular spaces, most commonly present in subcutaneous tissue. [NIH]

Endocytosis: Cellular uptake of extracellular materials within membrane-limited vacuoles or microvesicles. Endosomes play a central role in endocytosis. [NIH]

Endoscopy: Visual inspection of any cavity of the body by means of an endoscope. [EU]

Endothelium: The layer of epithelial cells that lines the cavities of the heart and of the blood and lymph vessels, and the serous cavities of the body, originating from the mesoderm. [EU]

Entamoeba: A genus of ameboid protozoa characterized by the presence of beaded chromatin on the inner surface of the nuclear membrane. Its organisms are parasitic in invertebrates and vertebrates, including humans. [NIH]

Enterocolitis: Inflammation involving both the small intestine and the colon; see also enteritis. [EU]

Enzyme: A protein molecule that catalyses chemical reactions of other substances without itself being destroyed or altered upon completion of the reactions. Enzymes are classified according to the recommendations of the Nomenclature Committee of the International Union of Biochemistry. Each enzyme is assigned a recommended name and an Enzyme Commission (EC) number. They are divided into six main groups; oxidoreductases, transferases, hydrolases, lyases, isomerases, and ligases. [EU]

Epinephrine: The active sympathomimetic hormone from the adrenal medulla in most species. It stimulates both the alpha- and beta- adrenergic systems, causes systemic vasoconstriction and gastrointestinal relaxation, stimulates the heart, and dilates bronchi and cerebral vessels. It is used in asthma and cardiac failure and to delay absorption of local anesthetics. [NIH]

Escherichia: A genus of gram-negative, facultatively anaerobic, rod-shaped bacteria whose organisms occur in the lower part of the intestine of warm-blooded animals. The species are either nonpathogenic or opportunistic pathogens. [NIH]

Fibrin: The insoluble protein formed from fibrinogen by the proteolytic action of thrombin during normal clotting of blood. Fibrin forms the essential portion of the blood clot. [EU]

Fibrinolytic: Pertaining to, characterized by, or causing the dissolution of fibrin by enzymatic action [EU]

Filtration: The passage of a liquid through a filter, accomplished by gravity, pressure, or vacuum (suction). [EU]

Gastritis: Inflammation of the stomach. [EU]

Genotype: The genetic constitution of the individual; the characterization of the genes. [NIH]

Glomerular: Pertaining to or of the nature of a glomerulus, especially a renal glomerulus. [EU]

Gynecology: A medical-surgical specialty concerned with the physiology and disorders primarily of the female genital tract, as well as female endocrinology and reproductive physiology. [NIH]

Haemorrhoid: A varicose dilatation of a vein of the superior or inferior haemorrhoidal plexus, resulting from a persistent increase in venous pressure. [EU]

Hyperplasia: The abnormal multiplication or increase in the number of normal cells in normal arrangement in a tissue. [EU]

Hypothyroidism: Deficiency of thyroid activity. In adults, it is most common in women and is characterized by decrease in basal metabolic rate, tiredness and lethargy, sensitivity to cold, and menstrual disturbances. If untreated, it progresses to full-blown myxoedema. In infants, severe hypothyroidism leads to cretinism. In juveniles, the manifestations are intermediate, with less severe mental and developmental retardation and only mild symptoms of the adult form. When due to pituitary deficiency of thyrotropin secretion it is called secondary hypothyroidism. [EU]

Hypoxia: Reduction of oxygen supply to tissue below physiological levels despite adequate perfusion of the tissue by blood. [EU]

Immunoassay: Immunochemical assay or detection of a substance by serologic or immunologic methods. Usually the substance being studied serves as antigen both in antibody production and in measurement of antibody by the test substance. [NIH]

Induction: The act or process of inducing or causing to occur, especially the production of a specific morphogenetic effect in the developing embryo through the influence of evocators or organizers, or the production of anaesthesia or unconsciousness by use of appropriate agents. [EU]

Inflammation: A pathological process characterized by injury or destruction of tissues caused by a variety of cytologic and chemical reactions. It is usually manifested by typical signs of pain, heat, redness, swelling, and loss of function. [NIH]

Ingestion: The act of taking food, medicines, etc., into the body, by mouth. [EU]

Intestines: The section of the alimentary canal from the stomach to the anus. It includes the large intestine and small intestine. [NIH]

Lesion: Any pathological or traumatic discontinuity of tissue or loss of function of a part. [EU]

Lipid: Any of a heterogeneous group of flats and fatlike substances characterized by being water-insoluble and being extractable by nonpolar (or fat) solvents such as alcohol, ether, chloroform, benzene, etc. All contain as a major constituent aliphatic hydrocarbons. The lipids, which are easily stored in the body, serve as a source of fuel, are an important constituent of cell structure, and serve other biological functions. Lipids may be considered to include fatty acids, neutral fats, waxes, and steroids. Compound lipids comprise the glycolipids, lipoproteins, and phospholipids. [EU]

Localization: 1. the determination of the site or place of any process or lesion. 2. restriction to a circumscribed or limited area. 3. prelocalization. [EU]

Mediator: An object or substance by which something is mediated, such as (1) a structure of the nervous system that transmits impulses eliciting a specific response; (2) a chemical substance (transmitter substance) that induces activity in an excitable tissue, such as nerve or muscle; or (3) a substance released from cells as the result of the interaction of antigen with antibody or by the action of antigen with a sensitized lymphocyte. [EU]

Membrane: A thin layer of tissue which covers a surface, lines a cavity or divides a space or organ. [EU]

Metabolite: Any substance produced by metabolism or by a metabolic process. [EU]

Microbiology: The study of microorganisms such as fungi, bacteria, algae, archaea, and viruses. [NIH]

Microcirculation: The flow of blood in the entire system of finer vessels (100 microns or less in diameter) of the body (the microvasculature). [EU]

Microvilli: Minute projections of cell membranes which greatly increase the surface area of the cell. [NIH]

Mobility: Capability of movement, of being moved, or of flowing freely. [EU]

Narcotic: 1. pertaining to or producing narcosis. 2. an agent that produces insensibility or stupor, applied especially to the opioids, i.e. to any natural or synthetic drug that has morphine-like actions. [EU]

Nausea: An unpleasant sensation, vaguely referred to the epigastrium and abdomen, and often culminating in vomiting. [EU]

Necrosis: The sum of the morphological changes indicative of cell death and caused by the progressive degradative action of enzymes; it may affect groups of cells or part of a structure or an organ. [EU]

Neonatal: Pertaining to the first four weeks after birth. [EU]

Obstetrics: A medical-surgical specialty concerned with management and care of women during pregnancy, parturition, and the puerperium. [NIH]

Oral: Pertaining to the mouth, taken through or applied in the mouth, as an oral medication or an oral thermometer. [EU]

Organelles: Specific particles of membrane-bound organized living substances present in eukaryotic cells, such as the mitochondria; the golgi apparatus; endoplasmic reticulum; lysomomes; plastids; and vacuoles. [NIH]

Parenteral: Not through the alimentary canal but rather by injection through some other route, as subcutaneous, intramuscular, intraorbital, intracapsular, intraspinal, intrasternal, intravenous, etc. [EU]

Pathologic: 1. indicative of or caused by a morbid condition. 2. pertaining to pathology (= branch of medicine that treats the essential nature of the disease, especially the structural and functional changes in tissues and organs of the body caused by the disease). [EU]

Pediatrics: A medical specialty concerned with maintaining health and providing medical care to children from birth to adolescence. [NIH]

Perioperative: Pertaining to the period extending from the time of hospitalization for surgery to the time of discharge. [EU]

Phenotype: The outward appearance of the individual. It is the product of interactions between genes and between the genotype and the environment. This includes the killer phenotype, characteristic of yeasts. [NIH]

Photocoagulation: Using a special strong beam of light (laser) to seal off bleeding blood vessels such as in the eye. The laser can also burn away blood vessels that should not have grown in the eye. This is the main treatment for diabetic retinopathy. [NIH]

Placenta: A highly vascular fetal organ through which the fetus absorbs oxygen and other nutrients and excretes carbon dioxide and other wastes. It begins to form about the eighth day of gestation when the blastocyst adheres to the decidua. [NIH]

Plague: An acute infectious disease caused by yersinia pestis that affects humans, wild rodents, and their ectoparasites. This condition persists due to its firm entrenchment in sylvatic rodent-flea ecosystems throughout the world. Bubonic plague is the most common form. [NIH]

Postoperative: Occurring after a surgical operation. [EU]

Preclinical: Before a disease becomes clinically recognizable. [EU]

Preeclampsia: A condition that some women with diabetes have during the late stages of pregnancy. Two signs of this condition are high blood pressure and swelling because the body cells are holding extra water. [NIH]

Proteins: Polymers of amino acids linked by peptide bonds. The specific sequence of amino acids determines the shape and function of the protein. [NIH]

Proximal: Nearest; closer to any point of reference; opposed to distal. [EU]

Proxy: A person authorized to decide or act for another person, for example, a person having durable power of attorney. [NIH]

Purpura: Purplish or brownish red discoloration, easily visible through the epidermis, caused by hemorrhage into the tissues. [NIH]

Reagent: A substance employed to produce a chemical reaction so as to detect, measure, produce, etc., other substances. [EU]

Receptor: 1. a molecular structure within a cell or on the surface characterized by (1) selective binding of a specific substance and (2) a specific physiologic effect that accompanies the binding, e.g., cell-surface receptors for peptide hormones, neurotransmitters, antigens, complement fragments, and immunoglobulins and cytoplasmic receptors for steroid hormones. 2. a sensory nerve terminal that responds to stimuli of various kinds. [EU]

Renin: An enzyme of the hydrolase class that catalyses cleavage of the leucine-leucine bond in angiotensin to generate angiotensin. 1. The enzyme is synthesized as inactive prorenin in the kidney and released into the blood in the active form in response to various metabolic stimuli. Not to be confused with rennin (chymosin). [EU]

Retrograde: 1. moving backward or against the usual direction of flow. 2. degenerating, deteriorating, or catabolic. [EU]

Salmonella: A genus of gram-negative, facultatively anaerobic, rod-shaped bacteria that utilizes citrate as a sole carbon source. It is pathogenic for humans, causing enteric fevers, gastroenteritis, and bacteremia. Food poisoning is the most common clinical manifestation. Organisms within this genus are separated on the basis of antigenic characteristics, sugar fermentation patterns, and bacteriophage susceptibility. [NIH]

Secretion: 1. the process of elaborating a specific product as a result of the activity of a gland; this activity may range from separating a specific substance of the blood to the elaboration of a new chemical substance. 2. any substance produced by secretion. [EU]

Septic: Produced by or due to decomposition by microorganisms; putrefactive. [EU]

Septicemia: Systemic disease associated with the presence and persistence of pathogenic microorganisms or their toxins in the blood. Called also blood poisoning. [EU]

Species: A taxonomic category subordinate to a genus (or subgenus) and superior to a subspecies or variety, composed of individuals possessing common characters distinguishing them from other categories of individuals of the same taxonomic level. In taxonomic nomenclature, species are designated by the genus name followed by a Latin or Latinized adjective or noun. [EU]

Stasis: A word termination indicating the maintenance of (or maintaining) a constant level; preventing increase or multiplication. [EU]

Stomach: An organ of digestion situated in the left upper quadrant of the abdomen between the termination of the esophagus and the beginning of the duodenum. [NIH]

Symptomatic: 1. pertaining to or of the nature of a symptom. 2. indicative (of a particular disease or disorder). 3. exhibiting the symptoms of a particular disease but having a different cause. 4. directed at the allying of symptoms, as symptomatic treatment. [EU]

Systemic: Pertaining to or affecting the body as a whole. [EU]

Tears: The fluid secreted by the lacrimal glands. This fluid moistens the conjunctiva and cornea. [NIH]

Tenesmus: Straining, especially ineffectual and painful straining at stool or in urination. [EU]

Thrombocytopenia: Decrease in the number of blood platelets. [EU]

Topical: Pertaining to a particular surface area, as a topical anti-infective applied to a certain area of the skin and affecting only the area to which it is applied. [EU]

Toxicity: The quality of being poisonous, especially the degree of virulence of a toxic microbe or of a poison. [EU]

Toxin: A poison; frequently used to refer specifically to a protein produced by some higher plants, certain animals, and pathogenic bacteria, which is highly toxic for other living organisms. Such substances are differentiated from the simple chemical poisons and the vegetable alkaloids by their high molecular weight and antigenicity. [EU]

Trophoblast: The outer layer of cells of the blastocyst which works its way into the endometrium during ovum implantation and grows rapidly, later combining with mesoderm. [NIH]

Warfarin: An anticoagulant that acts by inhibiting the synthesis of vitamin K-dependent coagulation factors. Warfarin is indicated for the prophylaxis and/or treatment of venous thrombosis and its extension, pulmonary embolism, and atrial fibrillation with embolization. It is also used as an adjunct in the prophylaxis of systemic embolism after myocardial infarction. Warfarin is also used as a rodenticide. [NIH]

Yersinia: A genus of gram-negative, facultatively anaerobic rod- to coccobacillus-shaped bacteria that occurs in a broad spectrum of habitats. [NIH]

CHAPTER 4. PATENTS ON HEMORRHOIDS

Overview

You can learn about innovations relating to hemorrhoids by reading recent patents and patent applications. Patents can be physical innovations (e.g. chemicals, pharmaceuticals, medical equipment) or processes (e.g. treatments or diagnostic procedures). The United States Patent and Trademark Office defines a patent as a grant of a property right to the inventor, issued by the Patent and Trademark Office.[17] Patents, therefore, are intellectual property. For the United States, the term of a new patent is 20 years from the date when the patent application was filed. If the inventor wishes to receive economic benefits, it is likely that the invention will become commercially available to patients with hemorrhoids within 20 years of the initial filing. It is important to understand, therefore, that an inventor's patent does not indicate that a product or service is or will be commercially available to patients with hemorrhoids. The patent implies only that the inventor has "the right to exclude others from making, using, offering for sale, or selling" the invention in the United States. While this relates to U.S. patents, similar rules govern foreign patents.

In this chapter, we show you how to locate information on patents and their inventors. If you find a patent that is particularly interesting to you, contact the inventor or the assignee for further information.

---

[17] Adapted from The U. S. Patent and Trademark Office:
http://www.uspto.gov/web/offices/pac/doc/general/whatis.htm.

Patents on Hemorrhoids

By performing a patent search focusing on hemorrhoids, you can obtain information such as the title of the invention, the names of the inventor(s), the assignee(s) or the company that owns or controls the patent, a short abstract that summarizes the patent, and a few excerpts from the description of the patent. The abstract of a patent tends to be more technical in nature, while the description is often written for the public. Full patent descriptions contain much more information than is presented here (e.g. claims, references, figures, diagrams, etc.). We will tell you how to obtain this information later in the chapter. The following is an example of the type of information that you can expect to obtain from a patent search on hemorrhoids:

- **Pharmaceutical preparation for the treatment of gastrointestinal ulcers and hemorrhoids**

  Inventor(s): Niazi; Sarfaraz K. (Deerfield, IL)

  Assignee(s): Gulf Pharmaceutical Industries (AE)

  Patent Number: 6,365,198

  Date filed: January 28, 2001

  Abstract: A pharmaceutical preparation for the treatment of gastrointestinal ulcers and hemorrhoids in humans and animals and a method of preparation for this composition are provided here. The preferred composition consists of an alcoholic extract of Huangqin, Huanglian, Huangbo, Opuntia and Pheretima dissolved in vegetable oil from where alcohol is essentially removed by evaporation. The composition is then packaged in a soft gelatin capsule for oral administration or mixed with wax to make an ointment suitable for rectal administration.

  Excerpt(s): This invention relates to a pharmaceutical preparation mainly for treating gastrointestinal wounds, ulcers and rectal inflammation conditions such as hemorrhoids. An alcoholic extract of natural ingredients in dried powdered state consisting of Huangqin (baikal skullcap), Huanglian (rhizome of Chinese goldthread or rhizoma Coptidis), Huangbo (cortex phellodendri), Pheretima (dilong) and Cactus (opuntia ficus indica) is used in an oily medium such that the quantity of each ingredient in its dried form represents less than 2% of the final amount of preparation. In the foregoing assertion, efforts have been made to find a suitable palliative and/or curative agent for the treatment of gastrointestinal ulcer conditions and hemorrhoids from medicinal plants and other natural ingredients. ... Inflammation, itching, and ulcerations characterize various diseases of the anorectic region of the human body. The anorectic region is generally comprised of the anus, rectum, and lower colon. In particular, hemorrhoids or piles are a common ailment of the anorectic region, and may be internally or externally located in the anorectic area. Notwithstanding their location, veins in the anorectic area become inflamed and frequently result in itching. The causes of hemorrhoids include predisposing causes such as erect posture, heredity, occupation and diet, constipation, diarrhea, pregnancy, anal infection, pelvic tumors, rectal carcinoma, cardiac failure, portal hypertension, vomiting and physical exertion. ... Presently, there are millions of people around the world who suffer from hemorrhoids. A common condition, characterized by a mass of dilated tortuous veins in swollen tissue situated at the anal margin, hemorrhoids can be a source of extreme discomfort and pain to both men and women. Depending on the severity of the condition, there are various treatments and medical procedures, which are presently used to alleviate the pain or to remove hemorrhoid veins and swollen tissue. People suffering from minor hemorrhoids are ordinarily advised to use laxatives or stool softeners to reduce pain. Additionally, less severe cases are typically treated with topical ointments, such as petroleum jelly based products, to lubricate and, in some instances, numb the inflamed hemorrhoid mass. In more severe cases, it may be necessary to reduce pain and inflammation by injection of corticosteroid drugs or other medicinal drugs having the effect of reducing swelling and pain. Otherwise, banding may be required in order to push the hemorrhoids back into the rectal cavity. All of these treatment methods are generally useful to reduce the pain and discomfort of hemorrhoids. However, all of these treatment methods set forth above provide only temporary relief and must be repeated during and throughout flare-ups of the hemorrhoid condition.

Web site: http://www.delphion.com/details?pn=US06365198__

- **Dietary supplement composition for the treatment of hemorrhoids**

Inventor(s): Pruthi; Som C. (25675 Meadow View Ct., Salinas, CA 93908), Pruthy; Jasvant Rai (25675 Meadow View Ct., Salinas, CA 93908), Pruthy; Puneet (25675 Meadow View Ct., Salinas, CA 93908)

Assignee(s): none reported

Patent Number: 6,264,982

Date filed: September 23, 2000

Abstract: A composition for a dietary supplement for use in treating hemorrhoids (bleeding and non-bleeding) includes: 30%-80% Indian Barberry extract by weight; 15%-67% Karchi seeds by weight; 2%-9%

Margosa tree leaves by weight; and 1%-10% Soap Nut fruit shells by weight.

Excerpt(s): Presently, there are millions of people around the world who suffer from hemorrhoids. A common condition, characterized by a mass of dilated tortuous veins in swollen tissue situated at the anal margin, hemorrhoids can be a source of extreme discomfort and pain to both men and women. Depending on the severity of the condition, there are various treatments and medical procedures which presently used to alleviate the pain or to remove hemorrhoidal veins and swollen tissue. People suffering from minor hemorrhoids are ordinarily advised to use laxatives or stool softeners to reduce pain. Additionally, less severe cases are typically treated with topical ointments, such as petroleum jelly based products, to lubricate and, in some instances, numb the inflamed hemorrhoidal mass. In more severe cases, it may be necessary to reduce pain and inflammation by injection of cortisteriod drugs or other medicinal drugs having the effect of reducing swelling and pain. Otherwise, banding may be required in order to push the hemorrhoids back into the rectal cavity. All of these treatment methods are generally useful to reduce the pain and discomfort of hemorrhoids. However, all of these treatment methods set forth above provide only temporary relief and must be repeated during and throughout flare-ups of the hemorrhoidal condition. ... The most severe cases of hemorrhoids often require cryosurgery or a hemorrhoidectomy to surgically remove the hemorrhoids. These procedures, while generally effective, are painful and considerably expensive. For this reason, surgical removal of hemorrhoids is a last resort performed only on those patients having severe, chronic hemorrhoidal flare-ups. ... Both the present composition and my previous composition disclosed in U.S. Pat. No. 5,591,436 address the need for a less expensive, yet effective means of treating hemorrhoids without side effects and without toxicity. The present invention, as disclosed and claimed herein, improves upon my previous composition. In particular, the present invention provides a composition of natural ingredients for the long term treatment of hemorrhoids, including severe cases.

Web site: http://www.delphion.com/details?pn=US06264982__

- **Method for treating hemorrhoids**

Inventor(s): Laufer; Michael D. (Menlo Park, CA), Farley; Brian E. (Los Altos, CA)

Assignee(s): Vnus Medical Technologies, Inc. (Sunnyvale, CA)

Patent Number: 6,135,997

Date filed: November 16, 1998

Abstract: A catheter delivers an electrode within a vein for a minimally invasive treatment of hemorrhoids using RF energy. The catheter is introduced into a patient and positioned within the section of the vein to be treated. The electrode radiates high frequency energy towards the vein, and the surrounding venous tissue becomes heated and begins to shrink. The catheter includes a controllable member for limiting the amount of shrinkage of the vein to the diameter of the member. The electrode remains active until there has been sufficient shrinkage of the vein. The extent of shrinkage of the vein can be detected by fluoroscopy. After treating one section of the vein, the catheter and the electrode can be repositioned within the hemorrhoidal venous system to treat different sections until all desired venous sections and valves are repaired and rendered functionally competent. Shrinkage of the vein further thickens and stiffens the vein wall which reduces the potential for the hemorrhoid vein to dilate.

Excerpt(s): This invention relates to the treatment and correction of hemorrhoids, and more particularly to a minimally invasive procedure using a catheter-based system to intravenously deploy one or more electrodes for providing radio frequency (RF) energy, microwave energy, or thermal energy to shrink a dilated vein in order to change the fluid flow dynamics and to restore the competency of the venous valve and the proper function of the vein. ... Hemorrhoids are a common ailment involving dilated veins which can result in bleeding, itching, and pain. Hemorrhoids are dilated veins in and around the anus and lower rectum. Dilation may result from an increased pressure in the hemorrhoidal vein. Constipation, including the frequent straining to pass hard stools increases pressure in hemorrhoidal veins, is a common cause of hemorrhoids. Other contributing factors include pregnancy, a low fiber diet, and obesity. As the hemorrhoidal vein becomes more dilated from the increased pressure, the venous valves of the hemorrhoidal vein may begin to fail and become incompetent. This can exacerbate the dilation of the hemorrhoidal vein as reflux of blood is allowed in the vein by the open incompetent valve. The vein may eventually form a sac-like protrusion if the condition is allowed to persist. Hemorrhoids are generally classified as being either internal or external, depending on their location relative to the dentate line. The dentate line is easily identified as the demarcation between the pink mucosa that form the anoderm. The dentate line separates the internal and external hemorrhoid systems. Internal hemorrhoids are located inside the anus above the dentate line. External hemorrhoids are located below the dentate line. Either can extend out of the anus. ... Straining or irritation caused by passing stool can injure the delicate surface of an internal hemorrhoid and cause bleeding. If the pressure and dilation of the hemorrhoidal vein continues, the internal hemorrhoids may prolapse and be forced through the anal opening. If a hemorrhoid remains prolapsed, considerable discomfort, including itching and bleeding, may result. The blood supply to these prolapsed hemorrhoids may become cut off by the anal sphincter, which gives rise to a strangulated hemorrhoid. Thrombosis may result where the blood within the prolapsed vein becomes clotted. This extremely painful condition can cause edema and inflammation.

Web site: http://www.delphion.com/details?pn=US06135997__

- **Device for reducing symptoms of prolapsed hemorrhoids**

   Inventor(s): Majlessi; Heshmat (233 Purchase St., Rye, NY 10580)

   Assignee(s): Majlessi; Heshmat (Rye, NY)

   Patent Number: 5,924,423

   Date filed: April 22, 1997

   Abstract: The device for reducing the symptoms of prolapsed hemorrhoids has a continuous contour and a bulbous portion between leading and trailing ends of the device. The bulbous portion has a leading inclined surface and a trailing inclined surface which meet at an intermediate point of maximum radial dimensions. A rounded tip is provided at the leading end and a stop plate at the trailing end to control the extent of insertion.

   Excerpt(s): The invention generally relates to medical devices and, more specifically to a device for reducing the symptoms of prolapsed hemorrhoids. ... Forty million Americans suffer from hemorrhoids. Yet there is no effective device to relieve symptoms other than surgery. At this time prolapsed hemorrhoids are pushed back into the rectum manually, patients being instructed to use a glove to accomplish this task. Certain commercial preparations, such as "Anusol" and "Preparation H", improve the symptoms briefly but have no effect on congestion and actual treatment of the condition itself. ... It is an object of the invention to provide a device for relieving the symptoms of hemorrhoids.

   Web site: http://www.delphion.com/details?pn=US05924423__

- **Cooling cylindrical device for therapeutic treatment of hemorrhoids**

Inventor(s): Trop; Moshe (Brooklyn, NY), Kushelvesky; Avraham (Metar, IL), Mazor; Gedalya (Metar, IL), Popov; Sergay (Ofakim, IL), Baybikov; Boris (Mahale Edomim, IL)

Assignee(s): Trop Life Ltd. (Ofakim, IL)

Patent Number: 5,800,485

Date filed: February 22, 1995

Abstract: A cooling cylindrical insert device to aid in the removal of pain and for the therapeutic treatment of hemorrhoids and anal fissures. The device includes a hollow insert, finger or bulb contoured for insertion into the anus. At least one inlet and/or outlet opening is provided in the insert at its base, with one or two tubes connected to the openings. A container of cold liquid is provided connected to the inlet and outlet tubes. Thus, cold liquid is circulated from the container, through the inlet tube and inlet opening, through the cylindrical insert device, through the outlet opening and outlet tubes back into the container. A pump is provided to circulate the liquid.

Excerpt(s): The present invention relates to a cooling cylindrical device for therapeutic treatment of hemorrhoids. More specifically, said invention relates to a cooling cylindrical finger adapted in its contour for insertion into the anus, wherein said cylindrical finger is cooled by cold water or ice or by expansion of gas or by thermoelectric cooler component. ... Commonly known as piles, hemorrhoids are varicose veins in the anal area. They are similar to the twisted and swollen veins that are frequently noticeable on a person's legs, especially in older women who have had several children. When these varicosities occur high in the anal canal they are referred to as internal hemorrhoids. Many people with internal hemorrhoids are unaware of their presence. External hemorrhoids are those near the anal opening; sometimes they prolapse and bulge outside the anus. When a person complains of having hemorrhoids, they are usually referring to the external type. ... The most frequent cause of hemorrhoids is straining at stools, which is most likely to happen when a person is constipated, obese or pregnant. People with liver disease such as cirrhosis may also develop hemorrhoids due to increased pressure in the veins of the intestine.

Web site: http://www.delphion.com/details?pn=US05800485__

- **Elastic band ligation device for treatment of hemorrhoids**

Inventor(s): O'Regan; Patrick J. (912-750 West Broadway, Vancouver, B.C., CA)

Assignee(s): none reported

Patent Number: 5,741,273

Date filed: March 8, 1996

Abstract: An elastic band ligation device for treatment of hemorrhoids permits a doctor to band hemorrhoidal tissue without an assistant and does not have to be attached to an aspirator. The device has the capability of suctioning tissue into a tubular member before banding. A plastic inner tubular member retains a stretched elastic band over a front end of an inner tubular member which extends for a sufficient length for insertion into the rectum of a patient. A plunger in the tubular member may be slid backwards to draw a suction in the tubular member to draw tissue in through the front end. A plastic outer pusher sleeve fits over the tubular member and is adapted to push the elastic band off the front end of the tubular member to capture the hemorrhoidal tissue drawn into the tubular member.

Excerpt(s): The present invention relates to the treatment of hemorrhoids by elastic band ligation, sometimes referred to as rubber band ligation, and more specifically to an elastic band ligation device that may be used by a single operator. ... The treatment of hemorrhoids by elastic band ligation is credited to Blaisdell who described this technique in Diseases of the Colon and Rectum in 1963. The technique involves placing an elastic band on tissue in the rectum above the area of the hemorrhoid where there is little sensation. The tissue trapped in the band being cut off from its blood supply degenerates and is sloughed, and the elastic band along with the sloughed tissue is passed with the bowel motions. More importantly, however, the resulting healing process causes the tissue in the vicinity to become fixed and prolapse of the hemorrhoidal tissue is minimized. Furthermore, the elastic band ligation technique has been found to give relief of hemorrhoidal symptoms. ... Many devices exist on the market today utilizing the elastic band ligation technique. Examples are U.S. Pat. No. 5,203,863 to Bidoia, U.S. Pat. No. 5,122,149 to Broome and U.S. Pat. No. 5,158,563 to Cosman. The devices disclosed in these patents are generally designed to be used in conjunction with an instrument such as a proctoscope or anoscope to directly see the area to be banded. In some cases it is necessary to have an assistant to hold the proctoscope or anoscope and the use of these scopes, which are generally larger in diameter than the banding apparatus, can cause considerable discomfort to a patient and more specifically to one who is suffering symptoms of hemorrhoids.

Web site: http://www.delphion.com/details?pn=US05741273__

- **Analgesic lotion for hemorrhoids and method of making such lotion**

Inventor(s): Ivy; Jeffery Wade (Van Zandt County, TX), Payne; Curtis Emery (Smith County, TX), Burda; Christopher Dominic (Caddo Parish, LA)

Assignee(s): Au Pharmaceuticals, Inc. (Tyler, TX)

Patent Number: 5,720,962

Date filed: October 4, 1995

Abstract: This invention relates to an externally applied lotion that causes irritation or mild inflammation of the skin or mucous membranes for the purpose of relieving pain in hemorrhoids and the method of making such lotion. The formulation of the present invention contains ingredients to perform the five functions of vasoconstrictor, astringent, analgesic, antipruritic, and anesthetic. An alternate embodiment of the invention provides a formulation of the invention having a suitable viscosity to enable the lotion to be applied by a spray applicator directly to the site of application.

Excerpt(s): This invention relates to externally applied lotions that cause irritation or mild inflammation of the skin or mucous membranes for the purpose of relieving pain in hemorrhoids and other anorectal inflammation. ... This invention provides an externally applied lotion for relieving pain in hemorrhoids and other anorectal inflammation and the method of making such lotion. The active ingredients of the invention perform the five functions of vasoconstrictor, astringent, analgesic, antipruritic, and anesthetic. An alternate embodiment of the invention provides a formulation of the invention having a suitable viscosity to enable the lotion to be applied by a spray applicator directly to the site of application. ... It is an object of the present invention to provide an analgesic lotion containing a number of ingredients to relieve pain in hemorrhoids and a method of making such lotion.

Web site: http://www.delphion.com/details?pn=US05720962__

- **Physical therapeutic instrument for prevention and treatment of hemorrhoids**

Inventor(s): Lee; Hyung Jun (29-1 Shinsul-dong, Dongdaemoon-Ku, Seoul, KR)

Assignee(s): none reported

Patent Number: 5,676,637

Date filed: December 8, 1994

Abstract: A physical therapeutic instrument for treatment of hemorrhoids is disclosed. The instrument treats existing hemorrhoids through a nonoperative method and prevents possible anal diseases. The instrument has a rectal insert having a shape agreeable to the anal anatomy of the human body. The rectal insert is carried on a carriage and is movably orthogonally received in a through hole of a seat of the instrument. The rectal insert is lifted and inserted into the rectum by a lifting unit and vibrated vertically and/or horizontally by a vibration unit. The rectal insert also heats the rectum at about 36.degree.-60.degree. C., thus providing a heating effect for the rectum. Insertion of the rectal insert into the rectum also pushes up drooping anal sphincter muscles, thus strengthening the anal muscles. The instrument thus maintains and strengthens active contractible motion of the anal muscles.

Excerpt(s): The present invention relates in general to the prevention and treatment of hemorrhoids and, more particularly, to a physical therapeutic instrument for the prevention and treatment of hemorrhoids by stimulating good circulation of blood in the human anal area by producing a smooth massage and heating effect. ... Hemorrhoids or piles are swollen varicose veins in the mucous membrane inside or just outside the rectum. ... Hemorrhoids can further deteriorate or rupture with additional pressure during constipation and straining at stool, or by external pressure because of long sitting when the piles are external.

Web site: http://www.delphion.com/details?pn=US05676637__

- **Composition for a dietary supplement for the treatment of hemorrhoids**

Inventor(s): Pruthi; Som C. (2001 N. Ocean Blvd., #1602, Boca Raton, FL 33431)

Assignee(s): none reported

Patent Number: 5,591,436

Date filed: March 10, 1995

Abstract: A composition for a dietary supplement for use in treating hemorrhoids includes: 60% to 95% Indian Barberry by weight; 4.8% to 38% Nagkesar by weight; and 0.2% to 2% Margosa Tree Leaves by weight.

Excerpt(s): The present invention relates to a dietary supplement, and more particularly, to a dietary supplement for alleviating the symptoms associated with hemorrhoids. ... Presently, there are millions of people around the world who suffer from hemorrhoids. A common condition, characterized by a mass of dilated tortuous veins in swollen tissue situated at the anal margin, hemorrhoids can be a source of extreme discomfort and pain to both men and women. Depending on the severity of the condition, there are various treatments and medical procedures which are presently used to alleviate the pain or to remove hemorrhoidal veins and swollen tissue. People suffering from minor hemorrhoids are ordinarily advised to use laxatives or stool softeners to reduce pain. Additionally, less severe cases are typically treated with topical ointments, such as petroleum jelly based products, to lubricate and, in some instances, numb the inflamed hemorrhoidal mass. In more severe cases, it may be necessary to reduce pain and inflammation by injection of cortisteroid drugs or other medicinal drugs having the effect of reducing swelling and pain. Otherwise, banding may be required in order to push the hemorrhoids back into the rectal cavity. All of these treatment methods are generally useful to reduce the pain and discomfort of hemorrhoids. However, all of these treatment methods set forth above provide only temporary relief and must be repeated during and throughout flare-ups of the hemorrhoidal condition. ... The most severe cases of hemorrhoids often require cryosurgery or a hemorrhoidectomy to surgically remove the hemorrhoids. These procedures, while generally effective, are painful and considerably expensive. For this reason, surgical removal of hemorrhoids is a last resort performed only on those patients having severe, chronic hemorrhoidal flare-ups.

Web site: http://www.delphion.com/details?pn=US05591436__

- **Treatment of hemorrhoids with 5-HT.sub.2 antagonists**

Inventor(s): Amer; Moh. Samir (3177 Padaro La., Carpinteria, CA 93013)

Assignee(s): none reported

Patent Number: 5,266,571

Date filed: January 9, 1992

Abstract: This invention relates to a method for treating or preventing hemorrhoids, comprising administering to a susceptible animal a 5-

hydroxytryptamine.sub.2 (5-HT.sub.2) receptor antagonist at an anti-hemorrhoidally effective therapeutic dose.

Excerpt(s): This invention relates to a method and a class of pharmaceutical agents for treating hemorrhoids. The method comprises administering to a susceptible animal a 5-hydroxytryptamine-.sub.2 receptor antagonist (5-HT.sub.2) at an anti-hemorrhoidally effective therapeutic dose. ... Hemorrhoids are a varicose dilatation of veins in the superior or inferior hemorrhoidal plexus. More commonly, hemorrhoids refer to a mass of dilated veins in swollen tissue situated near the anal sphincter. They are believed to result from a persistent increase in venous pressure, which may be due, in part, to a constriction of the large downstream colonic veins. Occlusion due to platelet aggregation and thrombus formation may also contribute to the symptoms of hemorrhoids by interrupting blood flow and increasing blood stasis and tissue congestion. ... It is an object of this invention to provide a novel method to treat or prevent hemorrhoids.

Web site: http://www.delphion.com/details?pn=US05266571__

- **Methods of treating hemorrhoids and anorecial disease**

  Inventor(s): Gallina; Damian J. (Erie, PA)

  Assignee(s): Patent Biopharmaceutics, Inc. (Erie, PA)

  Patent Number: 5,234,914

  Date filed: November 27, 1991

  Abstract: A method of treating hemorrhoids and anorectal disease which includes applying to the hemorrhoids and anorectal tissues an effective amount of a composition including a pharmaceutically acceptable carrier and hyaluronic acid or pharmaceutically acceptable salts thereof.

  Excerpt(s): The present invention relates to methods of treating hemorrhoids and diseases of the anorectum employing novel pharmaceutical compositions. In particular, the present invention relates to topical applications of hyaluronate preparations as rectal bonding and adhesion agents, anti-inflammatory agents and bio-repair materials. The use of hyaluronate preparations employs their properties to reduce the inflammation, pain, swelling, and sequelae of injured, irritated, diseased, strained, or traumatized anorectal tissues while adhering to and protecting sensitive tissues of the anorectum. The source of the hyaluronate used in the treatment compositions may be a hyaluronic acid or any acceptable salt form of hyaluronic acid. The term "hyaluronate" is often used to mean "hyaluronic acid equivalent" which equates to hyaluronic acid of varying molecular weights and any of their salt forms. ... The present invention relates to a method of treating hemorrhoids and other anorectal diseases by topically applying to hemorrhoidal and anorectal tissues a pharmaceutical preparation comprising a hyaluronate acid moiety such as hyaluronic acid or an acceptable salt form of hyaluronic acid, in an effective amount for the treatment of anorectal disease. The disease states of the anorectum include but are not limited to hemorrhoids, rectal fissures, inflamed anorectal tissues, pruritis ani and proctitis. ... It is a related object of the present invention to provide an improved method of treating hemorrhoids and other anorectal problems by utilizing the advantageous bonding and adhering properties as well as the anti-inflammatory and healing properties of hyaluronic acid and its various salt forms.

Web site: http://www.delphion.com/details?pn=US05234914__

- **Treatment of viral tumors and hemorrhoids with artemisinin and derivatives**

Inventor(s): Thornfeldt; Carl R. (Ontario, OR)

Assignee(s): Dermatologic Research Corporation (Novato, CA)

Patent Number: 5,219,880

Date filed: March 29, 1991

Abstract: Hemorrhoids and viral-induced skin tumors such as warts and molluscum contagiosum are successfully treated with topical administration of artemisinin, dihydroartemisinin, its semisynthetic derivatives and its synthetic analogs.

Excerpt(s): This invention relates to the topical and/or systemic treatment of viral-induced skin tumors and hemorrhoids with a class of compounds having sesquiterpene structures, including artemisinin, dihydroartemisinin, and derivatives and analogs of these compounds. ... Hemorrhoids are the end result of swelling and inflammation of anorectal veins. Current treatments consist of topical analgesics and antiinflammatory agents as well as cathartics. Surgery often is curative but is extremely painful and requires prolonged convalescence. ... Artemisinin or Qinghaosu is a proven systemic antimalarial agent purified from the herb Artemisia Annua. Artemisinin is a sesquiterpene lactone with a peroxide grouping that is water insoluble but is extremely safe. There are reports from China that artemisinin 1) is virustatic against influenza virus in chick embryo, 2) suppresses humoral immunity, 3) stimulates cell mediated immunity, and 4) inhibits protein and DNA synthesis thus halting hypertrophy and hyperproliferation of cells. A tea made from the herb Artemisia Annua was used for centuries to treat hemorrhoids, malaria and other maladies.

Web site: http://www.delphion.com/details?pn=US05219880__

- **Instrument for the ligation of hemorrhoids or the like**

  Inventor(s): Bidoia; Gianfranco (Via Bressanone, 3/A, 35100 Padova, IT)

  Assignee(s): none reported

  Patent Number: 5,203,863

  Date filed: March 2, 1992

  Abstract: The instrument for the ligation of hemorrhoids or the like includes a substantially cylindrical container with a coupling for the connection of an air aspiration apparatus and a grip handle for the operator. The container is suitable for internally accommodating a hemorrhoid or the like aspirated through its open end, on which a dilated ring-like elastic ligature, to be transferred so as to throttle the "neck" of the hemorrhoid or the like, is arrangeable externally and circumferentially. The instrument is characterized in that the container is provided with a thumb-actuated hole for adjusting the pressure inside it while the aspiration apparatus is operating.

  Excerpt(s): The present invention relates to an instrument for the ligation of hemorrhoids or the like. ... Various methods for the therapy of hemorrhoids are currently used when said hemorrhoids no longer respond to strictly medical cures or when their size becomes such that any non-surgical therapy would produce no result or even negative results. ... A second method is constituted by cryosurgery, which in practice consists in "freezing" the hemorrhoids at temperatures which can vary between -59 degrees Celsius and -89 degrees Celsius for cycles lasting a few minutes.

  Web site: http://www.delphion.com/details?pn=US05203863__

- **Compositions and methods of treating hemorrhoids and wounds**

  Inventor(s): Packman; Elias W. (Merion, PA)

  Assignee(s): Oskman; Norman H. (Baltimore, MD)

  Patent Number: 5,196,405

  Date filed: February 27, 1990

Abstract: Hemorrhoidal compositions containing disaccharide polysulfate-aluminum compounds such as sucralfate, above or in combination with other hemorrhoidal products, as an agent effective for alleviating the symptoms of anorectal disease when topically applied to the human skin. Method for alleviating the symptoms of hemorrhoids in humans. Compositions containing disaccharide polysulfate-aluminum compounds such as sucralfate, alone or in combination with antibiotics, antifungal agents, anti-acne agents, or local anesthetics as an active agent effective in promoting the healing of wounds which are not anorectal when topically applied to the surface of a wound. Method for promoting healing at the surface of a wound in humans.

Excerpt(s): This invention relates to a method and medication for the treatment of wounds and lesions. It further relates to a method and medication for the treatment of the symptoms of anorectal disease or irritation and in particular relates to a method and medication for the treatment of hemorrhoids. ... Anorectal disease is an annoying and uncomfortable disorder. Hemorrhoids is a common ailment of the anorectal area and may be either or both internal and external. Anorectal disorders are characterized by the signs and symptoms of itching, burning, pain, bleeding, seepage, protrusion, inflammation, irritation, swelling general discomfort and changes in bowel pattern or any combination thereof. Many remedies have been suggested and tried for the alleviation of these ailments with varying degrees of success. Anorectal disease, though rare in other animals, is very common in . humans. No human is immune. The vast majority of adults suffer from one or more anorectal symptoms at some time in their life. Anorectal disease has caused an unaccountable number of man-hours to be lost annually in the work place. ... Some of the compositions disclosed to be useful in the treatment of hemorrhoids include a powdered mixture of alum, quinine sulfate and aspirin mixed with petroleum jelly (U.S. Pat. No. 4,613,498); a mixture of oxidase enzymes (U.S. Patent RE 28,011); a mixture of the powdered or chipped limbs or roots of the shrub Celastrus scandens (U.S. Pat. No. 3,935,310); a mixture of polyglycerides and ripe berry products of the plant Solanum carolinese to which sublimed sulfur, ammonium alum and turpentine are added (U.S. Pat. No. 4,192,866). Other compositions, which are well known, include those marketed over-the-counter. Non-limiting examples of these numerous products of varying compositions include Anusol, Balneol, Lanacane, Nupercainal, Preparation H and Vaseline.

Web site: http://www.delphion.com/details?pn=US05196405__

Patent Applications on Hemorrhoids

As of December 2000, U.S. patent applications are open to public viewing.[18] Applications are patent requests which have yet to be granted (the process to achieve a patent can take several years). The following patent applications have been filed since December 2000 relating to hemorrhoids:

- **Method and device for treating hemorrhoids**

  Inventor(s): Eveland, Winsor ; (Englewood, FL)

  Correspondence: Laura G. Barrow ESQ.; P. O. BOX 215; Estero; FL; 33928-0215; US

  Patent Application Number: 20020071879

  Date filed: December 7, 2000

  Abstract: A method and device for treating hemorrhoids is described and illustrated herein comprising, in part, the application of external heat to the affected rectal area of a person suffering from hemorrhoids.

  Excerpt(s): Hemorrhoids are caused by the swelling and thrombosis of a large plexus of veins in the anal canal followed by edema. Conditions that frequently cause the formation of hemorrhoids include chronic constipation, irregularity in bowel movements, poor diet, and pregnancy-induced interference with the venous return flow due to fetal pressures against the pelvic area. Hemorrhoids can be quite painful and on occasion may be accompanied by cracks in the anal cavity, resulting in bleeding and infection. ... Current treatments for hemorrhoids include sitz baths three to four times daily in water as hot as the patient can tolerate comfortably. Patients often consume bulk stool formers to aid in bowel movements while acute hemorrhoids often require surgical intervention. ... The present invention is directed to a method of treating external hemorrhoids by applying externally to the rectal area a stream of hot air at least once a day until shrinkage of the hemorrhoids results. Certain aspects of the present invention include a hot air blower specifically designed for applying a stream hot air to the rectal area with greater ease.

  Web site: http://appft1.uspto.gov/netahtml/PTO/search-bool.html

---

[18] This has been a common practice outside the United States prior to December 2000.

Keeping Current

In order to stay informed about patents and patent applications dealing with hemorrhoids, you can access the U.S. Patent Office archive via the Internet at no cost to you. This archive is available at the following Web address: **http://www.uspto.gov/main/patents.htm**. Under "Services," click on "Search Patents." You will see two broad options: (1) Patent Grants, and (2) Patent Applications. To see a list of granted patents, perform the following steps: Under "Patent Grants," click "Quick Search." Then, type "hemorrhoids" (or synonyms) into the "Term 1" box. After clicking on the search button, scroll down to see the various patents which have been granted to date on hemorrhoids. You can also use this procedure to view pending patent applications concerning hemorrhoids. Simply go back to the following Web address: **http://www.uspto.gov/main/patents.htm**. Under "Services," click on "Search Patents." Select "Quick Search" under "Patent Applications." Then proceed with the steps listed above.

Vocabulary Builder

Acne: An inflammatory disease of the pilosebaceous unit, the specific type usually being indicated by a modifying term; frequently used alone to designate common acne, or acne vulgaris. [EU]

Aluminum: A metallic element that has the atomic number 13, atomic symbol Al, and atomic weight 26.98. [NIH]

Anesthetics: Agents that are capable of inducing a total or partial loss of sensation, especially tactile sensation and pain. They may act to induce general anesthesia, in which an unconscious state is achieved, or may act locally to induce numbness or lack of sensation at a targeted site. [NIH]

Antifungal: Destructive to fungi, or suppressing their reproduction or growth; effective against fungal infections. [EU]

Antipruritic: Relieving or preventing itching. [EU]

Astringent: Causing contraction, usually locally after topical application. [EU]

Biopharmaceutics: The study of the physical and chemical properties of a drug and its dosage form as related to the onset, duration, and intensity of its action. [NIH]

Catheter: A tubular, flexible, surgical instrument for withdrawing fluids from (or introducing fluids into) a cavity of the body, especially one for introduction into the bladder through the urethra for the withdraw of urine. [EU]

Cirrhosis: Liver disease characterized pathologically by loss of the normal microscopic lobular architecture, with fibrosis and nodular regeneration. The term is sometimes used to refer to chronic interstitial inflammation of any organ. [EU]

Cortex: The outer layer of an organ or other body structure, as distinguished from the internal substance. [EU]

Curative: Tending to overcome disease and promote recovery. [EU]

Dilatation: The condition, as of an orifice or tubular structure, of being dilated or stretched beyond the normal dimensions. [EU]

Elastic: Susceptible of resisting and recovering from stretching, compression or distortion applied by a force. [EU]

Embryo: In animals, those derivatives of the fertilized ovum that eventually become the offspring, during their period of most rapid development, i.e., after the long axis appears until all major structures are represented. In man, the developing organism is an embryo from about two weeks after fertilization to the end of seventh or eighth week. [EU]

Fluoroscopy: Production of an image when x-rays strike a fluorescent screen. [NIH]

Gelatin: A product formed from skin, white connective tissue, or bone collagen. It is used as a protein food adjuvant, plasma substitute, hemostatic, suspending agent in pharmaceutical preparations, and in the manufacturing of capsules and suppositories. [NIH]

Humoral: Of, relating to, proceeding from, or involving a bodily humour - now often used of endocrine factors as opposed to neural or somatic. [EU]

Hypertension: Persistently high arterial blood pressure. Various criteria for its threshold have been suggested, ranging from 140 mm. Hg systolic and 90 mm. Hg diastolic to as high as 200 mm. Hg systolic and 110 mm. Hg diastolic. Hypertension may have no known cause (essential or idiopathic h.) or be associated with other primary diseases (secondary h.). [EU]

Hypertrophy: Nutrition) the enlargement or overgrowth of an organ or part due to an increase in size of its constituent cells. [EU]

Immunity: The condition of being immune; the protection against infectious disease conferred either by the immune response generated by immunization or previous infection or by other nonimmunologic factors (innate i.). [EU]

Influenza: An acute viral infection involving the respiratory tract. It is marked by inflammation of the nasal mucosa, the pharynx, and conjunctiva, and by headache and severe, often generalized, myalgia. [NIH]

Membranes: Thin layers of tissue which cover parts of the body, separate adjacent cavities, or connect adjacent structures. [NIH]

Ointments: Semisolid preparations used topically for protective emollient effects or as a vehicle for local administration of medications. Ointment bases are various mixtures of fats, waxes, animal and plant oils and solid and liquid hydrocarbons. [NIH]

Palliative: 1. affording relief, but not cure. 2. an alleviating medicine. [EU]

Petroleum: Naturally occurring complex liquid hydrocarbons which, after distillation, yield combustible fuels, petrochemicals, and lubricants. [NIH]

Plexus: A network or tangle; a general term for a network of lymphatic vessels, nerves, or veins. [EU]

Semisynthetic: Produced by chemical manipulation of naturally occurring substances. [EU]

Sphincter: A ringlike band of muscle fibres that constricts a passage or closes a natural orifice; called also musculus sphincter. [EU]

Sucralfate: A basic aluminum complex of sulfated sucrose. It is advocated in the therapy of peptic, duodenal, and prepyloric ulcers, gastritis, reflux esophagitis, and other gastrointestinal irritations. It acts primarily at the ulcer site, where it has cytoprotective, pepsinostatic, antacid, and bile acid-binding properties. The drug is only slightly absorbed by the digestive mucosa, which explains the absence of systemic effects and toxicity. [NIH]

Sulfur: An element that is a member of the chalcogen family. It has an atomic symbol S, atomic number 16, and atomic weight 32.066. It is found in the amino acids cysteine and methionine. [NIH]

Thrombus: An aggregation of blood factors, primarily platelets and fibrin with entrapment of cellular elements, frequently causing vascular obstruction at the point of its formation. Some authorities thus differentiate thrombus formation from simple coagulation or clot formation. [EU]

Ulceration: 1. the formation or development of an ulcer. 2. an ulcer. [EU]

Viscosity: A physical property of fluids that determines the internal resistance to shear forces. [EU]

CHAPTER 5. BOOKS ON HEMORRHOIDS

Overview

This chapter provides bibliographic book references relating to hemorrhoids. You have many options to locate books on hemorrhoids. The simplest method is to go to your local bookseller and inquire about titles that they have in stock or can special order for you. Some patients, however, feel uncomfortable approaching their local booksellers and prefer online sources (e.g. **www.amazon.com** and **www.bn.com**). In addition to online booksellers, excellent sources for book titles on hemorrhoids include the Combined Health Information Database and the National Library of Medicine. Once you have found a title that interests you, visit your local public or medical library to see if it is available for loan.

Book Summaries: Federal Agencies

The Combined Health Information Database collects various book abstracts from a variety of healthcare institutions and federal agencies. To access these summaries, go to **http://chid.nih.gov/detail/detail.html**. You will need to use the "Detailed Search" option. To find book summaries, use the drop boxes at the bottom of the search page where "You may refine your search by." Select the dates and language you prefer. For the format option, select "Monograph/Book." Now type "hemorrhoids" (or synonyms) into the "For these words:" box. You will only receive results on books. You should check back periodically with this database which is updated every 3 months. The following is a typical result when searching for books on hemorrhoids:

- **Digestive Diseases and Disorders Sourcebook**

    Source: Detroit, MI: Omnigraphics. 2000. 300 p.

Contact: Available from Omnigraphics, Inc. 615 Griswold, Detroit, MI 48226. (800) 234-1340. Fax (800) 875-1340. Price: $48.00 plus shipping and handling. ISBN: 0780803272.

Summary: This sourcebook provides basic information for the layperson about common disorders of the upper and lower digestive tract. The sourcebook also includes information about medications and recommendations for maintaining a healthy digestive tract. The book's 40 chapters are arranged in three major parts. The first section, Maintaining a Healthy Digestive Tract, offers basic information about the digestive system and digestive diseases, information about tests and treatments, and recommendations for maintaining a healthy digestive system. The second section, Digestive Diseases and Functional Disorders, describes nearly 40 different diseases and disorders affecting the digestive system. These include appendicitis, bleeding in the digestive tract, celiac disease, colostomy, constipation, constipation in children, Crohn's disease, cyclic vomiting syndrome, diarrhea, diverticulosis and diverticulitis, gallstones, gas in the digestive tract, heartburn (gastroesophageal reflux disease), hemorrhoids, hernias, Hirschsprung's disease, ileostomy, indigestion (dyspepsia), intestinal pseudo-obstruction, irritable bowel syndrome (IBS), IBS in children, lactose intolerance, Menetrier's disease, rapid gastric emptying, short bowel syndrome, ulcerative colitis, ulcers, Whipple's disease, and Zollinger Ellison syndrome. The final section offers a glossary of terms, a subject index and a directory of digestive diseases organizations (which includes website and email addresses as available). Material in the book was collected from a wide range of government agencies, nonprofit organizations, and periodicals.

- **ABC of Colorectal Diseases. 2nd ed**

Source: London, UK: BMJ Publishing Group. 1999. 120 p.

Contact: Available from BMJ Publishing Group. BMA Books, BMA House, Tavistock Square, London WCIH 9JR. Fax 44 (0)20 7383 6402. E-mail: orders@bmjbooks.com. Website: www.bmjbooks.com. Price: Contact publisher for price. ISBN: 0727911058.

Summary: Colorectal diseases are common and patients may present to doctors in almost any sphere of medical practice. This atlas is a reference to all the major colorectal diseases, covering signs and symptoms, initial diagnoses, and patient care management, as well as advice on when to refer for specialist treatment. The editor notes that minor anorectal problems, such as hemorrhoids, may be regarded by doctor and patient as being of little consequence, but they can cause considerable distress and may indicate serious underlying pathology. Fortunately, most anorectal conditions are easily diagnosed and can be effectively treated.

The atlas includes 26 chapters, covering anatomy and physiology, investigation of colorectal disorders, constipation, diarrhea, lower gastrointestinal hemorrhage, irritable bowel syndrome (IBS), hemorrhoids, anal fissures and fistulas, pilonidal sinus, pruritis (itching) ani, rectal prolapse, fecal incontinence, appendicitis, diverticular disease, inflammatory bowel disease (IBD), colorectal neoplasia (benign tumors and bowel cancer), anal cancer, intestinal stomas, large bowel volvulus, colorectal trauma, sexually transmitted diseases and papillomas, tropical colonic diseases, pediatric problems, and drugs in the management of colorectal diseases. Each chapter includes full color photographs and illustrations, sidebars that summarize the information presented, and patient care management algorithms. A subject index concludes the text.

- **PDR for Herbal Medicines. 1st ed**

Source: Montvale, NJ: Medical Economics Company. 1998. 1244 p.

Contact: Available from Medical Economics Publishing Inc. P.O. Box 10689, Des Moines, IA 50336. (800) 922-0937. Fax (515) 284-6714. Website: www.medecbookstore.com. Price: $59.99. ISBN: 1563632926.

Summary: Most of today's herbal remedies exhibit varying degrees of therapeutic value. Some, such as ginkgo, valerian, and saw palmetto, seem genuinely useful, while others, such as ephedra, tansy, and nightshade, can actually be dangerous. As the use of unfamiliar botanicals spreads, the need to steer patients toward the few truly useful preparations and warn them away from ineffective, dangerous alternatives is becoming an increasingly significant priority. This volume, from the publishers of Physicians Desk Reference, brings together the findings of the German Regulatory Authority's herbal watchdog agency (commonly caused Commission E). This agency conducted an intensive assessment of the peer-reviewed literature on some 300 common botanicals, weighing the quality of the clinical evidence and identifying the uses for which the herb can reasonably be considered effective. This reference book contains profiles of over 600 medicinal herbs. Each entry contains up to 9 standard sections: name(s), description, actions and pharmacology, indications and usage, contraindications, precautions and adverse reactions, overdosage, dosage, and literature. The entries have also been indexed by scientific and common name, indications, therapeutic category, and side effects. To assist in identification, the reference book includes a section of full-color plates of the plants included. The book concludes with a glossary of the specialized botanical nomenclature and other unfamiliar terminology, a list of poison control centers, and a list of drug information centers. Some of the herbs are listed for use for abdominal cramps or distress, acid indigestion, appetite stimulation, rectal bleeding, various bowel disorders, stomach cancer, cholelithiasis (gallstones), colic, colitis, constipation, dehydration, diarrhea, digestive disorders, dysentery, enteritis, anal fissure, flatulence (intestinal gas), gastritis, gastroenteritis, gastrointestinal disorders, gout, helminthiasis, hemorrhage, hemorrhoids, hepatitis, hypercholesterolemia, jaundice, liver and gall bladder complaints, liver disorders, malaria, nausea, abdominal pain, and vomiting.

- **Healthwise Handbook: A Self-Care Manual for You. 13th ed. [La Salud en Casa: Guia Practica de Healthwise]**

  Source: Boise, ID: Healthwise, Incorporated. 1997. 354 p.

  Contact: Available from Healthwise, Incorporated. 2601 North Bogus Basin Road, P.O. Box 1989, Boise, ID 83702-1989. (800) 706-9646 or (208) 345-1161. Fax (208) 345-1897. Website: www.healthwise.org. Price: $9.95 per copy plus shipping and handling; bulk copies available. ISBN: 1877930296 for English version; 1877930474 for Spanish version.

  Summary: This self-care handbook includes basic guidelines on how to recognize and cope with more than 180 of the most common health problems. These guidelines are based on medical information from leading medical and consumer publications, with review and input from doctors, nurses, pharmacists, and other health professionals. The book is divided into five sections: Self-Care Basics, which covers what a wise medical consumer should know and how to deal with first aid and emergencies; Health Problems, which discusses the prevention, treatment, and decisions on when to call a doctor for more than 180 common illnesses and injuries; Men's and Women's Health; Staying Healthy, which offers tips and techniques for fitness, nutrition, stress management, and mental health; and Self-Care Resources, including how to manage medications and what should be kept in the home to cope with health problems. Other topics include how to make the most of doctor's visits, how to improve quality and lower the cost of necessary health care, what immunizations and screening tests are important, and which medications, supplies, equipment, and resources to have on hand. Sections related to digestive system diseases include abdominal wounds, choking, poisoning, appendicitis, constipation, dehydration, diarrhea, heartburn, hemorrhoids, hernia, irritable bowel syndrome, nausea and vomiting, stomach flu and food poisoning, ulcers, mouth and dental problems, eating disorders, and nutrition. A subject index concludes the volume.

- **Power of Your Plate: A Plan for Better Living**

  Source: Summertown, TN: Book Publishing Company. 1995. 255 p.

Contact: Available from Book Publishing Company. Mail Order Catalog, P.O. Box 180, Summertown, TN 38483. (800) 695-2241. Wholesale orders available from Book Publishing Company. P.O. Box 99, Summertown, TN 38483. (615) 964-3571. Price: $12.95 plus $2.50 shipping. ISBN: 157067003X.

Summary: This book provides detailed information on how food choices can improve health, emphasizing the benefits of a vegetarian diet. Eleven chapters cover topics including cholesterol, food, and the heart; tackling cancer; new strategies for weight control; foodborne illness; common health problems that are related to diet; food and the mind; the evolution of the human diet; lessons from Asia; recommendations; will power; and food ideas and recipes. The book also includes an interview with Dr. Michael DeBakey, a cardiovascular surgeon and pioneer in heart transplants. The chapter on common health problems covers constipation, hemorrhoids, hiatus hernia, diabetes, osteoporosis and kidney disease as problems related to food. A brief discussion of Dr. Denis Burkitt's work with dietary fiber is included. 83 references.

- **Digestive Diseases in the United States: Epidemiology and Impact**

Source: Bethesda, MD: National Institute of Diabetes and Digestive and Kidney Diseases (NIDDK). 1994. 799 p.

Contact: Available from National Digestive Diseases Information Clearinghouse. 2 Information Way, Bethesda, MD 20892-3570. (800) 891-5389 or (301) 654-3810. E-mail: nddic@info.niddk.nih.gov. Price: $15.00.

Summary: This monograph is a compendium of descriptive statistics about the scope and impact of digestive diseases in the United States. Each chapter provides national and population data based on the prevalence, incidence, medical care, disability, mortality, and research needs. Twenty chapters cover the following conditions: infectious diarrheas, viral hepatitis, esophageal cancer, gastric cancer, colorectal cancer, liver cancer, pancreatic cancer, hemorrhoids, esophageal diseases, peptic ulcer, gastritis and nonulcer dyspepsia, acute appendicitis, abdominal wall hernia, inflammatory bowel diseases, diverticular disease of the colon, constipation, irritable bowel syndrome, chronic liver disease and cirrhosis, gallstones, and pancreatitis. These chapters compare the impact and costs of the disease to other diseases. The book also includes an overview chapter, a chapter about the cost of digestive diseases in the United States, and a listing of all digestive diseases diagnostic codes for the ninth and tenth editions of the International Classification of Diseases. Extensive figures are used throughout the volume. 3 appendices.

- **Instructions for Patients. 5th ed**

  Source: Philadelphia, PA: W.B. Saunders Company. 1994. 598 p.

  Contact: Available from W.B. Saunders Company. Book Order Fulfillment, 6277 Sea Harbor Drive, Orlando, FL 32887-4430. (800) 545-2522. Fax (800) 874-6418. Price: $49.95. ISBN: 0721649300 (English); 0721669972 (Spanish).

  Summary: This paper-bound book presents a number of patient instruction fact sheets. Each fact sheet includes three sections: basic information on signs and symptoms, causes, risk factors, etc.; treatment; and when to contact one's health care provider. Digestive system topics include food allergy, anal fissure, celiac disease, appendicitis, Crohn's disease, constipation, ulcerative colitis, cirrhosis of the liver, cholecystitis or cholangitis, diarrhea, diverticular disease, gallstones, gastritis, hiatal hernia, hemorrhoids, heartburn, irritable bowel syndrome, and lactose intolerance, among others. The fact sheets are designed to be photocopied and distributed to patients as a reinforcement of oral instructions and as a teaching tool. The book is available in English or Spanish.

- **Current Therapy in Colon and Rectal Surgery**

  Source: Philadelphia, PA: B.C. Decker, Inc. 1990. 440 p.

  Contact: Available from C.V. Mosby Company. 11830 Westline Industrial Drive, St. Louis, MO 63146. (800) 426-4545. Price: $99; plus shipping and handling (as of 1994). ISBN: 1556640439.

  Summary: This book, comprised of 81 papers by surgeons, provides specific information and guidelines concerning current surgical practices in the treatment of colorectal diseases. The papers cover disease processes occurring proximal to or outside the large intestine, but within the domain of the abdominal or colorectal surgeon. Medical management of certain conditions commonly encountered by surgeons, such as inflammatory bowel disease, also is covered. In certain cases, information which is not readily available is provided on complications of common specific procedures and methods of management. In some sections, such as those dealing with ulcerative colitis and rectal cancer, surgical options are discussed. The 81 papers are grouped among five general categories: anal and perianal region (anatomy and physiology of the anorectum; hemorrhoids; anal fissure and fistula; pruritus ani; Bowen's, Paget's and Hirschsprung's disease; and anal carcinoma); rectal and pararectal region (rectal stricture, prolapse, and trauma; tumors; and rectal cancer); the colon (medical and surgical alternatives for and complications of ulcerative colitis; Crohn's disease; diverticulitis of the colon; vascular ectasia; large bowel obstruction; volvulus of the colon; colorectal cancer, tumors, and polyps; and constipation); the small bowel (small bowel obstruction, short bowel syndrome, Crohn's disease, and small bowel and carcinoid tumors); and other complications (stapling techniques in rectal surgery, nutritional support, urologic complications of colorectal surgery, stoma complications, and enterostomal therapy). Selected tabular data and numerous illustrations are presented throughout the text.

- **Advanced Therapeutic Endoscopy**

Source: New York, NY: Raven Press, Ltd. 1990. 379 p.

Contact: Available from Raven Press. 1185 Avenue of the Americas, Dept. 5B, New York, NY 10036. (800) 777-2836 or (212) 930-9500. Fax (212) 869-3495. Price: $139 plus shipping (as of 1995). ISBN: 0881676810.

Summary: This medical textbook is designed to provide the experienced endoscopist with information about the newest and most innovative techniques in the therapeutic use of endoscopy. Thirty chapters, each authored by specialists in the field, are organized into sections considering the esophagus, the stomach, the colon, the small bowel and liver, the biliary system, general considerations, and pediatric endoscopy. Specific topics include dilation of benign esophageal strictures; foreign bodies and bezoars of the upper gastrointestinal tract; sclerotherapy of esophageal varices; therapy for upper gastrointestinal hemorrhage; hemorrhoids; dilatation of colonic strictures; anorectal manometry; enteroscopy; endoscopic sphincterotomy; endoscopic retrograde cholangiopancreatography; biliary and pancreatic manometry; the use of antibiotic prophylaxis; and gastroscopy and colonoscopy in children. Each chapter includes diagrams and charts, black-and-white photographs, and numerous references. A subject index concludes the volume.

Book Summaries: Online Booksellers

Commercial Internet-based booksellers, such as Amazon.com and Barnes & Noble.com, offer summaries which have been supplied by each title's publisher. Some summaries also include customer reviews. Your local bookseller may have access to in-house and commercial databases that index all published books (e.g. Books in Print®). The following have been recently listed with online booksellers as relating to hemorrhoids (sorted alphabetically by title; follow the hyperlink to view more details at Amazon.com):

- **A Cure for Hemorrhoids** by Joseph Bartanus (1996); ISBN: 0806254181; http://www.amazon.com/exec/obidos/ASIN/0806254181/icongroupin terna

- **Bottom Line: About Hemorrhoids, Fissures and Fistulas** by John Egerton (1985); ISBN: 0939838184; http://www.amazon.com/exec/obidos/ASIN/0939838184/icongroupin terna

- **Constipation, piles, and other bowel disorders** by Richard Heatley; ISBN: 0443029156; http://www.amazon.com/exec/obidos/ASIN/0443029156/icongroupin terna

- **Crohn'S, Colitis, Hemorrhoids, and Me: Kathy's Journal** by Kathlene J. O'Leary (1995); ISBN: 0964757133; http://www.amazon.com/exec/obidos/ASIN/0964757133/icongroupin terna

- **Hemorrhoids : a cure & preventative : the problem, personal treatment, medical treatment** by Robert Lawrence Holt; ISBN: 0930926013; http://www.amazon.com/exec/obidos/ASIN/0930926013/icongroupin terna

- **Hemorrhoids : a cure and preventive** by Robert Lawrence Holt; ISBN: 0688085849; http://www.amazon.com/exec/obidos/ASIN/0688085849/icongroupin terna

- **Hemorrhoids : A Guide for Patients** by Larry C. Carey (Editor), et al; ISBN: 1885274262; http://www.amazon.com/exec/obidos/ASIN/1885274262/icongroupin terna

- **Hemorrhoids a Cure and Preventive** by Michael Mitchell (1997); ISBN: 0930926250; http://www.amazon.com/exec/obidos/ASIN/0930926250/icongroupin terna

- **Hemorrhoids: A Book for Silent Suffers** by Jagar Rama, et al (1990); ISBN: 0962529508; http://www.amazon.com/exec/obidos/ASIN/0962529508/icongroupin terna

- **Hemorrhoids: An Evaluation of Methods of Treatment** by C.G.M.I. Baeten (1985); ISBN: 9023221281; http://www.amazon.com/exec/obidos/ASIN/9023221281/icongroupin terna

- **Hemorrhoids: Current Concepts on Causation and Management** by Olive Wood (Editor) (1979); ISBN: 0127949186; http://www.amazon.com/exec/obidos/ASIN/0127949186/icongroupin terna

- **How I Prevented Hemorrhoids** by Mike Tecton (1999); ISBN: 0922070369; http://www.amazon.com/exec/obidos/ASIN/0922070369/icongroupin terna

- **Human hemorrhoids : guidebook for medicine, reference & research** by H. D. El-Aman; ISBN: 0881641359; http://www.amazon.com/exec/obidos/ASIN/0881641359/icongroupin terna

- **Human Hemorrhoids: Guidebook for Medicine, Reference and Research** by Hasu Deway El-Aman (1985); ISBN: 0881641340; http://www.amazon.com/exec/obidos/ASIN/0881641340/icongroupin terna

- **Outpatient hemorrhoidectomy: ligation technique** by Peter F. Eastman; ISBN: 0874887526; http://www.amazon.com/exec/obidos/ASIN/0874887526/icongroupin terna

- **Put Hemorrhoids and Constipation Behind You: New Treatment and Technology for 2 of Today's Most Common Yet Least Talked-About Problems** by Kenneth Yasny, Kenneth Yasney; ISBN: 1884820220; http://www.amazon.com/exec/obidos/ASIN/1884820220/icongroupin terna

- **Relief from Chronic Hemorrhoids** by Barbara Becker, Steven Z. Brandeis (Contributor); ISBN: 0440210747; http://www.amazon.com/exec/obidos/ASIN/0440210747/icongroupin terna

- **The Book of Hemorrhoids and Other Pains in the Ass** (1981); ISBN: 0880090057; http://www.amazon.com/exec/obidos/ASIN/0880090057/icongroupin terna

- **The Doctor's Guide to You and Your Colon/a Candid, Helpful Guide to Our Number One Hidden Health Complaint** by Martin E. Plaut (1986); ISBN: 006091324X; http://www.amazon.com/exec/obidos/ASIN/006091324X/icongroupi nterna

- **The Doctor's Guide to You and Your Colon: A Candid, Helpful Guide to Our #1 Hidden Health Complaint** by M. Plaut, Paul Marttin (1982);

ISBN: 0060149485;
http://www.amazon.com/exec/obidos/ASIN/0060149485/icongroupin
terna

- **The Hemorrhoid Book** by Sidney Wanderman (1981); ISBN: 0448155117;
http://www.amazon.com/exec/obidos/ASIN/0448155117/icongroupin
terna

- **The Hemorrhoids** by Sidney E. Wanderman, Betty Rothbart (1991); ISBN:
0890434468;
http://www.amazon.com/exec/obidos/ASIN/0890434468/icongroupin
terna

- **The Lowdown on Hemorrhoids, Piles & Other Lowdown Disorders** by
Stanley Berkowitz (1975); ISBN: 0917746015;
http://www.amazon.com/exec/obidos/ASIN/0917746015/icongroupin
terna

The National Library of Medicine Book Index

The National Library of Medicine at the National Institutes of Health has a
massive database of books published on healthcare and biomedicine. Go to
the following Internet site, **http://locatorplus.gov/**, and then select "Search
LOCATORplus." Once you are in the search area, simply type
"hemorrhoids" (or synonyms) into the search box, and select "books only."
From there, results can be sorted by publication date, author, or relevance.
The following was recently catalogued by the National Library of Medicine:[19]

- **Ayurvedic management of Arsa (Haemorrhoids).** Author: B.N. Sharma;
Year: 1999; New Delhi: Central Council for Research in Ayurveda &
Siddha, Dept. of ISM&H, Ministry of Health & Family Welfare,
Govt. of India, 1999

---

[19] In addition to LOCATORPlus, in collaboration with authors and publishers, the National
Center for Biotechnology Information (NCBI) is adapting biomedical books for the Web. The
books may be accessed in two ways: (1) by searching directly using any search term or
phrase (in the same way as the bibliographic database PubMed), or (2) by following the
links to PubMed abstracts. Each PubMed abstract has a "Books" button that displays a
facsimile of the abstract in which some phrases are hypertext links. These phrases are also
found in the books available at NCBI. Click on hyperlinked results in the list of books in
which the phrase is found. Currently, the majority of the links are between the books and
PubMed. In the future, more links will be created between the books and other types of
information, such as gene and protein sequences and macromolecular structures. See
http://www.ncbi.nlm.nih.gov/entrez/query.fcgi?db=Books.

- **Bottom line about hemorrhoids, fissures, and fistulas.** Author: by John Egerton in consultation with Oscar M. Grablowsky; Year: 1985; Atlanta, GA: Pritchett & Hull Associates, 1985; ISBN: 0939838184 http://www.amazon.com/exec/obidos/ASIN/0939838184/icongroupin terna

- **Doctor's guide to you and your colon.** Author: by Martin E. Plaut; Year: 1982; New York: Harper & Row, c1982; ISBN: 0060149485 http://www.amazon.com/exec/obidos/ASIN/0060149485/icongroupin terna

- **Haemorrhoid syndrome.** Author: edited by H.D. Kaufman; Year: 1981; Turnbridge Wells, Kent: Abacus Press, 1981; ISBN: 0856263060 http://www.amazon.com/exec/obidos/ASIN/0856263060/icongroupin terna

- **Haemorrhoids: evaluation of methods of treatment.** Author: C.G.M.I. Baeten; Year: 1985; Assen: Van Gorcum, 1985; ISBN: 9023221281 (pbk.) http://www.amazon.com/exec/obidos/ASIN/9023221281/icongroupin terna

- **Haemorrhoids cured by homoeopathic medicines.** Author: by P. Sivaraman; Year: 1979; New Delhi: Jain, 1979

- **Haemorrhoids.** Author: V.L. Rivkin, L.L. Kapuller; Year: 1987; Moscow: Mir Publishers, 1987

- **Haemorrhoids; their aetiology, prophylaxis and treatment by means of injections, by Arthur S. Morley ...** Author: Morley, Arthur Solomon, 1877-; Year: 1929; London, New York [etc.] H. Milford, Oxford university press, 1929

- **Hemorrhoids: a cure and preventive.** Author: by Robert Lawrence Holt; Year: 1980; New York: Morrow, 1980; ISBN: 0688035841 http://www.amazon.com/exec/obidos/ASIN/0688035841/icongroupin terna

- **Hemorrhoids and prolapsus of the rectum; their treatment by the application of nitric acid.** Author: Smith, Henry, 1823-1894; Year: 1859; London, Churchill, 1859

- **Hemorrhoids, by Marion C. Pruitt ... with 73 illustrations, including 7 in color.** Author: Pruitt, Marion Columbus, 1885-; Year: 1938; St. Louis, The C. V. Mosby company, 1938

- **Hemorrhoids, the injection treatment, and pruritus ani, by Lawrence Goldbacher ... illustrated with 31 half-tones and line engravings, some in colors.** Author: Goldbacher, Lawrence, 1891-; Year: 1931; Philadelphia, F. A. Davis company, 1931

- **Homoeopathic therapeutics of haemorrhoids.** Author: by Wm. Jefferson Guernsey; Year: 1892; New Delhi: B. Jain, 1996; ISBN: 8170217393
- **Human hemorrhoids: guidebook for medicine, reference, and research.** Author: Hasu Deway El-Aman; Year: 1985; Washington, D.C.: Abbe Publishers Association, c1985; ISBN: 0881641340 (alk. paper) http://www.amazon.com/exec/obidos/ASIN/0881641340/icongroupin terna
- **Living with your colitis and hemorrhoids, and related disorders.** Author: Theodore Berland, Leslie Jordan Sandlow, Richard Alan Shapiro; Year: 1975; New York: St. Martin's Press, c1975
- **Modern treatment of hemorrhoids, by Joseph Franklin Montague ... foreword by Harlow Brooks ... 116 illustrations.** Author: Montague, Joseph Franklin, 1893-; Year: 1934; Philadelphia and London, J. B. Lippincott company [c1934]
- **Natural treatment of piles, fistula & varicose veins.** Author: by S.J. Singh; editor, Prakriti-Vani; Year: 1985; Lucknow: Nature Cure Council of Medical Research, 1985
- **Office treatment of hemorrhoids, fistula, etc. without operation; together with remarks on the relation of diseases of the rectum to other diseases in both sexes, but especially in women, and the abuse of the operation of colostomy.** Author: Kelsey, Charles Boyd, 1850-; Year: 1898; New York, Pelton, 1898
- **On hemorrhoids [electronic resource].** Author: by Hippocrates; translated by Francis Adams; Year: 2000; [United States]: D.C. Stevenson, Web Atomics, c2000
- **Outpatient hemorrhoidectomy: ligation technique.** Author: Eastman, Peter F., 1914-; Year: 1970; New York, Medical Examination Pub. Co., 1970; ISBN: 874887526
- **Pathological and clinical consideration of hemorrhoidal disease.** Author: Malmgren, George Erland, 1902-; Year: 1930; [Minneapolis] 1930
- **Piles care and treatment in ayurveda.** Author: M. Bhaskar Rao; Year: 2002; Delhi, India: Sri Satguru Publications, 2002; ISBN: 8170307384 http://www.amazon.com/exec/obidos/ASIN/8170307384/icongroupin terna
- **Piles, hemorrhoids, and prolapsus. Practical observations, illustrated with plates from nature, and a variety of additional interesting cases, on the mode of curing these diseases, by means safe and effectual, founded on many years of extensive experience.** Author: Mackenzie, S; Year: 1836; London, Churchill, 1836
- **Proctoscopic examination and the treatment of hemorrhoids and anal pruritus, by Louis A. Buie ... with 72 illustrations.** Author: Buie, Louis

Arthur, 1890-; Year: 1931; Philadelphia and London, W. B. Saunders company, 1931

- **Surgical conditions.** Author: Randi S. Rubenstein ... [et al.]; Year: 1983; Santa Monica, CA: Rand, 1983; ISBN: 0833004301 (pbk.)
http://www.amazon.com/exec/obidos/ASIN/0833004301/icongroupin terna

- **Surgical treatment of haemorrhoids.** Author: Charles Mann (ed.); Year: 2002; London; New York: Springer, c2002; ISBN: 1852334967 (alk. paper)
http://www.amazon.com/exec/obidos/ASIN/1852334967/icongroupin terna

- **Treatises on poisons, hemorrhoids, cohabitation.** Author: translated and annotated by Fred Rosner; Year: 1984; Haifa, Israel: Maimonides Research Institute, c1984

- **Treatment of hemorrhoids by injections of carbolic acid and other substances; by Silas T. Yount ...** Author: Yount, Silas T; Year: 1887; Lafayette, Ind. The Echo music co., printers, 1887

Chapters on Hemorrhoids

Frequently, hemorrhoids will be discussed within a book, perhaps within a specific chapter. In order to find chapters that are specifically dealing with hemorrhoids, an excellent source of abstracts is the Combined Health Information Database. You will need to limit your search to book chapters and hemorrhoids using the "Detailed Search" option. Go directly to the following hyperlink: **http://chid.nih.gov/detail/detail.html**. To find book chapters, use the drop boxes at the bottom of the search page where "You may refine your search by." Select the dates and language you prefer, and the format option "Book Chapter." By making these selections and typing in "hemorrhoids" (or synonyms) into the "For these words:" box, you will only receive results on chapters in books. The following is a typical result when searching for book chapters on hemorrhoids:

- **Gastrointestinal Function and Diseases**

Source: in Byyny, R.L. and Speroff, L. Clinical Guide for the Care of Older Women: Primary and Preventive Care. 2nd ed. Baltimore, MD: Williams and Wilkins. 1996. p. 353-363.

Contact: Available from Williams and Wilkins. 351 West Camden Street, Baltimore, MD 21201-2436. (800) 638-6423 or (410) 528-8555. Fax (800) 447-8438. Price: $69.00. ISBN: 0683011510.

Summary: This chapter on gastrointestinal function and diseases is from a clinical guidebook for the primary and preventive care of older women.

Topics include gastrointestinal changes with aging; esophageal disease, including presbyesophagus, cricopharyngeal achalasia, hiatal hernia and esophageal reflux, achalasia, and esophageal infection; peptic ulcers; nonulcer dyspepsia; diseases of the colon, including diverticular disease, colorectal neoplasms, functional bowel disease, constipation, diarrhea, hemorrhoids and anal fissures; and diseases of the liver, including viral hepatitis, hepatotoxicity from medication, cirrhosis, and cholelithiasis. 33 references.

- **Gastrointestinal System**

Source: in Kelly, R.B., ed. Family Health and Medical Guide. Dallas, TX: Word Publishing. 1996. p. 169-200.

Contact: Available from American Academy of Family Physicians. 11400 Tomahawk Creek Parkway, Leawood, KS 66211-2672. (800) 274-2237. Website: www.aafp.org. Price: $30.00 for members; $35.00 for non-members; plus shipping and handling. ISBN: 0849908396.

Summary: This chapter on the gastrointestinal system is from a family health and medical guide. The chapter first describes the anatomy and function of the gastrointestinal tract, including the mouth, esophagus, stomach, small intestine, pancreas, gallbladder, liver, and large intestine. The chapter then covers problems of the gastrointestinal system, such as anal abscesses, fissures, and itching; appendicitis; bowel blockage; carcinoid tumors; colon polyps; colorectal cancer; constipation; Crohn's disease; dehydration; diarrhea; diverticulosis and diverticulitis; esophageal cancer and varices; gas; gastroenteritis; heartburn; hemorrhoids; hernias (hiatal and inguinal); ileus; irritable bowel syndrome (IBS); malabsorption (including celiac disease, lactose intolerance, pernicious anemia, postsurgical malabsorption, and Whipple's disease); peritonitis; proctitis; stomach cancer; ulcers; ulcerative colitis; and vomiting. For each topic, the authors discuss symptoms, diagnostic tests, treatment options, and prevention. Numerous sidebars cover home remedies for constipation; symptoms of a serious bowel problem; ways to prevent dehydration in adults; the BRAT (bananas, rice, apples, toast) diet; ways to prevent esophageal cancer, gas, and heartburn; hiccups; and home remedies for irritable bowel, as well as when to call the doctor about nausea or vomiting. 10 figures.

- **Gastrointestinal Disorders**

Source: in Norris, J., et al., eds. Professional Guide to Diseases. 5th edition. Springhouse, PA: Springhouse Corporation. 1995. p. 653-719.

Contact: Available from Springhouse Corporation. 1111 Bethlehem Pike, P.O. Box 908, Springhouse, PA 19477-0908. (800) 346-7844 or (215) 646-8700. Fax (215) 646-4508. Price: $34.95 (as of 1995). ISBN: 0874347696.

Summary: This chapter on gastrointestinal disorders is from an extensive reference guide to diseases. The chapter covers diseases of the mouth and esophagus, including stomatitis and other oral infections, gastroesophageal reflux, tracheoesophageal fistula, esophageal atresia, corrosive esophagitis and stricture, Mallory-Weiss syndrome, esophageal diverticula, and hiatal hernia; diseases of the stomach, intestine and pancreas, including gastritis, gastroenteritis, peptic ulcers, ulcerative colitis, necrotizing enterocolitis, Crohn's disease, pseudomembranous enterocolitis, irritable bowel syndrome, celiac disease, diverticular disease, appendicitis, peritonitis, intestinal obstruction, inguinal hernia, intussusception, volvulus, Hirschsprung's disease, inactive colon, and pancreatitis; and diseases of the anorectum, including hemorrhoids, anorectal abscess and fistula, rectal polyps, anorectal stricture, stenosis, or contracture, pilonidal disease, rectal prolapse, anal fissure, pruritus ani, and proctitis. The book defines each disorder and provides information about causes, signs and symptoms, diagnosis, treatment options, and special considerations. 6 references.

- **Gastrointestinal Disease: Bowel Training/Management Program**

Source: in Lawrence, K.E.; Roe, S.N., ed. Geriatric Patient Education Resource Manual, Volume 1. Frederick, MD: Aspen Publishers, Inc. p. 130-145, 210-211.

Contact: Available from Aspen Publishers, Inc. 7201 McKinney Circle, Frederick, MD 21701-9782. (800) 638-8437 or (301) 417-7500. Price: $185; plus $4 handling. ISBN: 0834202255.

Summary: This chapter, from a patient education resource manual for health care providers working in geriatrics, discusses gastrointestinal disease. Topics include care of the digestive system, a caregiver's guide for management of digestion problems with medications, the high-fiber diet, hints to increase fiber intake, care of the patient with a colostomy, teaching guide for bowel obstruction, constipation, diverticular disease, hemorrhoids, and peptic ulcers. A separate section discusses bowel training and management. Each section presents material in chart and diagram form, many of which are easily adaptable for distribution to patients. Nursing objectives and interventions are included for most topics.

General Home References

In addition to references for hemorrhoids, you may want a general home medical guide that spans all aspects of home healthcare. The following list is a recent sample of such guides (sorted alphabetically by title; hyperlinks provide rankings, information, and reviews at Amazon.com):

- **The Digestive System (21st Century Health and Wellness)** by Regina Avraham; Library Binding (February 2000), Chelsea House Publishing (Library); ISBN: 0791055264; http://www.amazon.com/exec/obidos/ASIN/0791055264/icongroupinterna

- **American College of Physicians Complete Home Medical Guide (with Interactive Human Anatomy CD-ROM)** by David R. Goldmann (Editor), American College of Physicians; Hardcover - 1104 pages, Book & CD-Rom edition (1999), DK Publishing; ISBN: 0789444127; http://www.amazon.com/exec/obidos/ASIN/0789444127/icongroupinterna

- **The American Medical Association Guide to Home Caregiving** by the American Medical Association (Editor); Paperback - 256 pages 1 edition (2001), John Wiley & Sons; ISBN: 0471414093; http://www.amazon.com/exec/obidos/ASIN/0471414093/icongroupinterna

- **Anatomica : The Complete Home Medical Reference** by Peter Forrestal (Editor); Hardcover (2000), Book Sales; ISBN: 1740480309; http://www.amazon.com/exec/obidos/ASIN/1740480309/icongroupinterna

- **The HarperCollins Illustrated Medical Dictionary : The Complete Home Medical Dictionary** by Ida G. Dox, et al; Paperback - 656 pages 4th edition (2001), Harper Resource; ISBN: 0062736469; http://www.amazon.com/exec/obidos/ASIN/0062736469/icongroupinterna

- **Mayo Clinic Guide to Self-Care: Answers for Everyday Health Problems** by Philip Hagen, M.D. (Editor), et al; Paperback - 279 pages, 2nd edition (December 15, 1999), Kensington Publishing Corp.; ISBN: 0962786578; http://www.amazon.com/exec/obidos/ASIN/0962786578/icongroupinterna

- **The Merck Manual of Medical Information : Home Edition (Merck Manual of Medical Information Home Edition (Trade Paper)** by Robert Berkow (Editor), Mark H. Beers, M.D. (Editor); Paperback - 1536 pages (2000), Pocket Books; ISBN: 0671027263; http://www.amazon.com/exec/obidos/ASIN/0671027263/icongroupinterna

Vocabulary Builder

Algorithms: A procedure consisting of a sequence of algebraic formulas and/or logical steps to calculate or determine a given task. [NIH]

Bezoars: Concretions of swallowed hair, fruit or vegetable fibers, or similar substances found in the alimentary canal. [NIH]

Cardiovascular: Pertaining to the heart and blood vessels. [EU]

Cholangitis: Inflammation of a bile duct. [EU]

Cholecystitis: Inflammation of the gallbladder. [EU]

Cholelithiasis: The presence or formation of gallstones. [EU]

Colic: Paroxysms of pain. This condition usually occurs in the abdominal region but may occur in other body regions as well. [NIH]

Contracture: A condition of fixed high resistance to passive stretch of a muscle, resulting from fibrosis of the tissues supporting the muscles or the joints, or from disorders of the muscle fibres. [EU]

Cyclic: Pertaining to or occurring in a cycle or cycles; the term is applied to chemical compounds that contain a ring of atoms in the nucleus. [EU]

Dehydration: The condition that results from excessive loss of body water. Called also anhydration, deaquation and hypohydration. [EU]

Diverticulitis: Inflammation of a diverticulum, especially inflammation related to colonic diverticula, which may undergo perforation with abscess formation. Sometimes called left-sided or L-sides appendicitis. [EU]

Dyspepsia: Impairment of the power of function of digestion; usually applied to epigastric discomfort following meals. [EU]

Enteritis: Inflammation of the intestine, applied chiefly to inflammation of the small intestine; see also enterocolitis. [EU]

Esophagitis: Inflammation, acute or chronic, of the esophagus caused by bacteria, chemicals, or trauma. [NIH]

Flatulence: The presence of excessive amounts of air or gases in the stomach or intestine, leading to distention of the organs. [EU]

Gastroenteritis: An acute inflammation of the lining of the stomach and intestines, characterized by anorexia, nausea, diarrhoea, abdominal pain, and weakness, which has various causes, including food poisoning due to infection with such organisms as Escherichia coli, Staphylococcus aureus, and Salmonella species; consumption of irritating food or drink; or psychological factors such as anger, stress, and fear. Called also enterogastritis. [EU]

Gastroscopy: Endoscopic examination, therapy or surgery of the interior of the stomach. [NIH]

Gout: Hereditary metabolic disorder characterized by recurrent acute arthritis, hyperuricemia and deposition of sodium urate in and around the joints, sometimes with formation of uric acid calculi. [NIH]

Heartburn: Substernal pain or burning sensation, usually associated with regurgitation of gastric juice into the esophagus. [NIH]

Helminthiasis: Infestation with parasitic worms of the helminth class. [NIH]

Hemorrhage: Bleeding or escape of blood from a vessel. [NIH]

Hepatitis: Inflammation of the liver. [EU]

Hernia: (he protrusion of a loop or knuckle of an organ or tissue through an abnormal opening. [EU]

Hiccup: A spasm of the diaphragm that causes a sudden inhalation followed by rapid closure of the glottis which produces a sound. [NIH]

Hypercholesterolemia: Abnormally high levels of cholesterol in the blood. [NIH]

Ileostomy: Surgical creation of an external opening into the ileum for fecal diversion or drainage. Loop or tube procedures are most often employed. [NIH]

Ileus: Obstruction of the intestines. [EU]

Inguinal: Pertaining to the inguen, or groin. [EU]

Jaundice: A clinical manifestation of hyperbilirubinemia, consisting of deposition of bile pigments in the skin, resulting in a yellowish staining of the skin and mucous membranes. [NIH]

Malabsorption: Impaired intestinal absorption of nutrients. [EU]

Osteoporosis: Reduction in the amount of bone mass, leading to fractures after minimal trauma. [EU]

Overdosage: 1. the administration of an excessive dose. 2. the condition resulting from an excessive dose. [EU]

Pancreas: An organ behind the lower part of the stomach that is about the size of a hand. It makes insulin so that the body can use glucose (sugar) for energy. It also makes enzymes that help the body digest food. Spread all over the pancreas are areas called the islets of Langerhans. The cells in these areas each have a special purpose. The alpha cells make glucagon, which raises the level of glucose in the blood; the beta cells make insulin; the delta cells make somatostatin. There are also the PP cells and the D1 cells, about which little is known. [NIH]

Pancreatitis: Inflammation (pain, tenderness) of the pancreas; it can make the pancreas stop working. It is caused by drinking too much alcohol, by disease in the gallbladder, or by a virus. [NIH]

Peptic: Pertaining to pepsin or to digestion; related to the action of gastric juices. [EU]

Peritonitis: Inflammation of the peritoneum; a condition marked by exudations in the peritoneum of serum, fibrin, cells, and pus. It is attended by abdominal pain and tenderness, constipation, vomiting, and moderate fever. [EU]

Pernicious: Tending to a fatal issue. [EU]

Poisoning: A condition or physical state produced by the ingestion, injection or inhalation of, or exposure to a deleterious agent. [NIH]

Prophylaxis: The prevention of disease; preventive treatment. [EU]

Stenosis: Narrowing or stricture of a duct or canal. [EU]

Stomatitis: Inflammation of the oral mucosa, due to local or systemic factors which may involve the buccal and labial mucosa, palate, tongue, floor of the mouth, and the gingivae. [EU]

Valerian: Valeriana officinale, an ancient, sedative herb of the large family Valerianaceae. The roots were formerly used to treat hysterias and other neurotic states and are presently used to treat sleep disorders. [NIH]

CHAPTER 6. MULTIMEDIA ON HEMORRHOIDS

Overview

Information on hemorrhoids can come in a variety of formats. Among multimedia sources, video productions, slides, audiotapes, and computer databases are often available. In this chapter, we show you how to keep current on multimedia sources of information on hemorrhoids. We start with sources that have been summarized by federal agencies, and then show you how to find bibliographic information catalogued by the National Library of Medicine. If you see an interesting item, visit your local medical library to check on the availability of the title.

Video Recordings

Most diseases do not have a video dedicated to them. If they do, they are often rather technical in nature. An excellent source of multimedia information on hemorrhoids is the Combined Health Information Database. You will need to limit your search to "video recording" and "hemorrhoids" using the "Detailed Search" option. Go directly to the following hyperlink: **http://chid.nih.gov/detail/detail.html**. To find video productions, use the drop boxes at the bottom of the search page where "You may refine your search by." Select the dates and language you prefer, and the format option "Videorecording (videotape, videocassette, etc.)." By making these selections and typing "hemorrhoids" (or synonyms) into the "For these words:" box, you will only receive results on video productions. The following is a typical result when searching for video recordings on hemorrhoids:

- **Your Digestive System**

    Source: Los Angeles, CA: National Health Video, Inc. 1999. (videocassette).

    Contact: Available from National Health Video, Inc. 12021 Wilshire Blvd., Suite 550, Los Angeles, CA 90025. (800) 543-6803. Fax (310) 477-8198. E-mail: Healthvid@aol.com. Price: $89.00 plus shipping and handling.

    Summary: This health education videotape program reviews the digestive system and basic digestive problems. Narrated by a registered dietitian, the program defines digestion as the process by which food is changed to nourishment for the body. The program first reviews the anatomy of the digestive system, including the mucosa of the mouth, stomach and small intestine; the role of the muscle movements of swallowing and peristalsis; and the lower esophageal sphincter. Swallowing disorders are mentioned briefly. The program then discusses the causes of and therapy for heartburn (gastroesophageal reflux disease, or GERD), gas (belching and flatulence), constipation, hemorrhoids, and peptic ulcers. Lifestyle changes are emphasized as the least invasive, most effective treatment for most digestive problems; the role of exercise is also noted. Drug therapy is discussed as a useful option, but caution is advised when using long term drug therapy for digestive concerns. The videotape includes footage of everyday people, interviews between physicians and patients, and graphics to help explain the physiology and anatomy covered in the discussion.

- **Bottom Line on Hemorrhoids**

    Source: Madison, WI: University of Wisconsin Hospitals and Clinics, Department of Outreach Education. 1996. (videocassette).

    Contact: Available from University of Wisconsin Hospital and Clinics. Picture of Health, 702 North Blackhawk Avenue, Suite 215, Madison, WI 53705-3357. (800) 757-4354 or (608) 263-6510. Fax (608) 262-7172. Price: $19.95 plus shipping and handling; bulk copies available. Order number 051997A.

    Summary: Straining when going to the bathroom, constipation, prolonged sitting, and infection can all contribute to hemorrhoids, defined as enlarged veins around the anus. This videotape is one in a series of health promotion programs called 'Picture of Health,' produced by the University of Wisconsin. In this program, moderated by Mary Lee and featuring gastroenterologist John Wyman, the common symptoms, diagnosis, and management of hemorrhoids are covered. Dr. Wyman explains the difference between internal and external hemorrhoids (merely an anatomical distinction), and prolapsed hemorrhoids, which are enlarged internal hemorrhoids that drop (prolapse) outside the anus. Symptoms include pain and bleeding; pain because of blood clots and bleeding due to trauma to the thin walled veins in that area. The causes of hemorrhoids include straining during defecation, pregnancy, prolonged sitting, constipation, childbirth, and obesity. Dr. Wyman recommends that anyone over the age of 40 who experiences rectal bleeding should consult a physician; younger people who experience recurrent bleeding should **also** see their physician (to rule out inflammatory bowel disease). Treatment options for hemorrhoids include changes in habits, such as not straining, not wiping vigorously, softening the stool with dietary changes (usually the addition of dietary fiber), and not prolonging sitting on the toilet. Surgery is used for external hemorrhoids, to remove the veins and tributaries; for internal hemorrhoids, rubber band ligation is very effective. The program also explores the problem of perianal dermatitis, including its risk factors and treatment options (which focus on keeping the area clean and dry, and not using over the counter creams that are petroleum based). The program reiterates the importance of having any rectal bleeding investigated by one's health care provider. The program concludes by referring viewers to the National Institute of Diabetes and Digestive and Kidney Diseases (NIDDK).

- **Colonic and Anorectal Disorders**

Source: in Schwartz, R.S., ed. Aging and the Elderly: A Review Course of Geriatric Medicine. Seattle, WA: University of Washington School of Medicine. 1992. Tape Number 9, Section 33.

Contact: Available from CME Conference Video, Inc. 2000 Crawford Place, Suite 100, Mount Laurel, NJ 08054. (800) 284-8433. Price: $549; plus $18.25 shipping and handling; Group Practice Package $150 plus $5.25 shipping and handling. Program Number 053.

Summary: This videotape is part of the 16th Annual Symposium on Aging and the Elderly, a continuing medical education (CME) program offered through the University of Washington School of Medicine. This program covers colonic and anorectal disorders, including colorectal neoplasms and benign polyps; diverticular disease; vascular extasia, angiodysplasia, and arteriovenous malformations; infectious colitis; antibiotic-associated diarrhea or colitis; ischemic colitis; idiopathic inflammatory bowel disease; drug-induced colitis; radiation-induced colitis; diversion colitis; appendicitis; adhesions; megacolon; volvulus; abdominal; functional bowel syndrome; anorectal disorders, including anal neoplasms, hemorrhoids; anorectal abscess and fistula; and rectal prolapse; and systemic disorders, including diabetes mellitus,

Parkinson's disease, myxedema, and amyloidosis. The proceedings include the author's outline of his presentation. The videotape includes the question-and-answer period conducted after the section.

- **Electrical Stimulation as a Treatment Option for Incontinence**

Source: Costa Mesa, CA: Wound Ostomy and Continence Nurses Society. 199x. (videocassette).

Contact: Available from Wound Ostomy and Continence Nurses Society. 2755 Bristol Street, Suite 110, Costa Mesa, CA 92626. (888) 224-9629 or (714) 476-0268. Fax (714) 545-3643. Website: www.wocn.org. Price: $15.00 for members; $20.00 for nonmembers.

Summary: Electrical stimulation is a useful adjunctive treatment for selected patients with stress urinary incontinence, urge incontinence (detrusor instability), fecal incontinence, and other pelvic floor dysfunctions, including dyspareunia (painful sexual intercourse). Little systematic research evaluating the optimum parameters or concomitant therapies has been conducted, however. Consequently, there is no single recommended electrical stimulation method. This videotape program presents the method of electrical stimulation as used by Katherine N. Moore for the treatment of stress and urge incontinence. Practical tips concerning patient position, therapist position, sensor position, and closure technique are provided. Electrical stimulation features the application of electrical current to the pelvic viscera or nerve supplies. The program discusses the importance of individual pre-treatment assessment and the contraindications to electrical stimulation, including the presence of metal implants, IUD, or pacemaker; pregnancy; hemorrhoids; or urinary tract infection. The program also emphasizes the need for evaluation of the efficacy of the treatment through such measures as a voiding diary, pad test, quality of life assessment, and assessment of muscle strength. The video then walks the viewer through the procedure itself, noting that the stimulation should be felt by the patient but should not be uncomfortable. A medical model is used to show the positioning for vaginal electrical stimulation; a live patient is used to demonstrate the muscle contractions that can be seen and felt during the electrical stimulation. The narrator then outlines some typical programs of muscle stimulation for each type of urinary incontinence, stressing the importance of the work-rest cycle and the need to adjust intensity to patient tolerance. The best results are obtained with this method when the patient has mild incontinence, the patient can inhibit detrusor contractions voluntarily, and the electrical stimulation is combined with other behavior modification techniques. The program concludes by cautioning viewers that the therapist can be at risk for back and wrist strain; methods to avoid these problems are depicted. The program encourages therapists to employ gentleness and tact while performing this low risk, minimally invasive technique.

Bibliography: Multimedia on Hemorrhoids

The National Library of Medicine is a rich source of information on healthcare-related multimedia productions including slides, computer software, and databases. To access the multimedia database, go to the following Web site: **http://locatorplus.gov/**. Select "Search LOCATORplus." Once in the search area, simply type in hemorrhoids (or synonyms). Then, in the option box provided below the search box, select "Audiovisuals and Computer Files." From there, you can choose to sort results by publication date, author, or relevance. The following multimedia has been indexed on hemorrhoids. For more information, follow the hyperlink indicated:

- **[motion picture].** Source: [M.R. Hill]; Year: 1969; Format: Anorectal and sigmoidoscopic examination with differential diagnosis; [Los Angeles: Hill; [New York: for loan by Ayerst Laboratories, 196-?]

- **Alternatives in the treatment of hemorrhoids.** Source: American College of Surgeons; Year: 1976; Format: Sound recording; Chicago, Ill.: The College, c1976

- **Anorectal anatomy, proctectomy, intestinal stomas and management of hemorrhoids, fistulas, fissures, and pruritis ani [sound recording].** Source: American College of Surgeons; Year: 1977; Format: I.e. pruritus; [Chicago]: The College, 1977

- **Applied anatomy of the ano-rectal area.** Source: Malcom R. Hill, Elton L. Morel; Year: 1969; Format: Motion picture; Los Angeles: Hill; [New York: for loan by Ayerst Laboratories, 196-?]

- **Common anal diseases.** Source: an educational service provided by DG, Davis+Geck; produced by Ciné-Med; Year: 1993; Format: Videorecording; Woodbury, CT: American Cyanamid Co., c1993

- **Diseases of the anus, rectum and colon.** Source: Marvin L. Corman ... [et al.]; Year: 1976; Format: Slide; [New York]: Medcom, c1976

- **Drug abuse emergencies.** Source: with Edward Bernstein; Year: 1985; Format: Videorecording; Secaucus, N.J.: Network for Continuing Medical Education, 1985

- **Hemmorhoid treatment by infrared coagulation [videorecording].** Source: produced by Ciné-Med; Year: 1990; Format: I.e. hemorrhoid; [United States]: Redfield Corp., c1990

- **Hemorrhoidectomy.** Source: sponsored by University of Miami, School of Medicine, Department of Surgery; through an educational grant from Glaxo Pharmaceuticals; Year: 1990; Format: Videorecording; Research Triangle Park, NC: Glaxo Pharmaceuticals, c1990

- **Improved technique for the operative treatment of anorectal lesions.** Source: [Wm. S. Merrell Company]; by Louis E. Moon and J.B. Christensen, with the assistance of Wm. N. Hardman; Year: 1947; Format: Motion picture; [Cincinnati, Ohio]: [The Company], 1947

- **Local anesthesia for anorectal surgery.** Source: video production by Center for Biomedical Communications, College of Physicians & Surgeons, Columbia University; Year: 1991; Format: Videorecording; Danbury, Conn.: Davis & Geck Surgical Film & Videocassette Library, [1991]

- **Medical terminology: gastroenterological disorders and surgery.** Source: Au-Vid, inc; Year: 1975; Format: Sound recording; [Garden Grove, Calif.]: Au-Vid, [1975]

- **Office management of anorectal lesions.** Source: Mayo Clinic; Year: 1966; Format: Motion picture; [Rochester, Minn.: The Clinic; Atlanta: for loan by National Medical Audiovisual Center, 1966?]

- **Outpatient hemorrhoidectomy : ligation technique.** Source: a Billy Burke production; by Peter F. Eastman; presented by Southern California Permanente Medical Group and Kaiser Foundation Hospital, Harbor City, California; Year: 1969; Format: Motion picture; United States: Southern California Medical Group: Kaiser Foundation Hospital, [1969]

- **Routine ano-rectal and sigmoidoscopic examination with differential diagnosis.** Source: Malcolm R. Hill; Year: 1959; Format: Motion picture; Los Angeles: Hill; [Atlanta: for loan by National Medical Audiovisual Center; St. Petersburg, Fla.: for loan by Modern Talking Picture Service, inc., 1959]

- **Treatment of hemorrhoids with laser.** Source: with Howard J. Eddy; Year: 1985; Format: Videorecording; Secaucus, N.J.: Network for Continuing Medical Education, 1985

- **Use of local anesthesia in common surgical disorders of the anorectum.** Source: authors, Robert Klingman, Martin Rothberg, Denitsu Hirai; produced by Medical Media Section, Lincoln VAMC; Year: 1988; Format: Videorecording; Danbury, Conn.: American College of Surgeons, Davis & Geck Surgical Film-Video Library, 1988

Vocabulary Builder

Adhesions: Pathological processes consisting of the union of the opposing surfaces of a wound. [NIH]

Angiodysplasia: Degenerative, acquired lesions consisting of distorted, dilated, thin-walled vessels lined by vascular endothelium. This pathological state is seen especially in the gastrointestinal tract and is frequently a cause of upper and lower gastrointestinal hemorrhage in the elderly. [NIH]

Arteriovenous: Both arterial and venous; pertaining to or affecting an artery and a vein. [EU]

Dermatitis: Inflammation of the skin. [EU]

Dyspareunia: Difficult or painful coitus. [EU]

Idiopathic: Of the nature of an idiopathy; self-originated; of unknown causation. [EU]

Malformation: A morphologic defect resulting from an intrinsically abnormal developmental process. [EU]

Megacolon: An abnormally large or dilated colon; the condition may be congenital or acquired, acute or chronic. [EU]

Myxedema: A condition characterized by a dry, waxy type of swelling with abnormal deposits of mucin in the skin and other tissues. It is produced by a functional insufficiency of the thyroid gland, resulting in deficiency of thyroid hormone. The skin becomes puffy around the eyes and on the cheeks and the face is dull and expressionless with thickened nose and lips. The congenital form of the disease is cretinism. [NIH]

Pacemaker: An object or substance that influences the rate at which a certain phenomenon occurs; often used alone to indicate the natural cardiac pacemaker or an artificial cardiac pacemaker. In biochemistry, a substance whose rate of reaction sets the pace for a series of interrelated reactions. [EU]

Peristalsis: The wormlike movement by which the alimentary canal or other tubular organs provided with both longitudinal and circular muscle fibres propel their contents. It consists of a wave of contraction passing along the tube for variable distances. [EU]

Vaginal: 1. of the nature of a sheath; ensheathing. 2. pertaining to the vagina. 3. pertaining to the tunica vaginalis testis. [EU]

Viscera: Any of the large interior organs in any one of the three great cavities of the body, especially in the abdomen. [NIH]

CHAPTER 7. PERIODICALS AND NEWS ON HEMORRHOIDS

Overview

Keeping up on the news relating to hemorrhoids can be challenging. Subscribing to targeted periodicals can be an effective way to stay abreast of recent developments on hemorrhoids. Periodicals include newsletters, magazines, and academic journals.

In this chapter, we suggest a number of news sources and present various periodicals that cover hemorrhoids beyond and including those which are published by patient associations mentioned earlier. We will first focus on news services, and then on periodicals. News services, press releases, and newsletters generally use more accessible language, so if you do chose to subscribe to one of the more technical periodicals, make sure that it uses language you can easily follow.

News Services & Press Releases

Well before articles show up in newsletters or the popular press, they may appear in the form of a press release or a public relations announcement. One of the simplest ways of tracking press releases on hemorrhoids is to search the news wires. News wires are used by professional journalists, and have existed since the invention of the telegraph. Today, there are several major "wires" that are used by companies, universities, and other organizations to announce new medical breakthroughs. In the following sample of sources, we will briefly describe how to access each service. These services only post recent news intended for public viewing.

PR Newswire

Perhaps the broadest of the wires is PR Newswire Association, Inc. To access this archive, simply go to **http://www.prnewswire.com**. Below the search box, select the option "The last 30 days." In the search box, type "hemorrhoids" or synonyms. The search results are shown by order of relevance. When reading these press releases, do not forget that the sponsor of the release may be a company or organization that is trying to sell a particular product or therapy. Their views, therefore, may be biased. The following is typical of press releases that can be found on PR Newswire:

- **Cellegy Issued U.S. Patent Covering Use of Potassium Channel Openers For Treatment of Anorectal Disorders**

  Summary: South San Francisco, Calif., June 25 /PRNewswire-FirstCall/ -- Cellegy Pharmaceuticals, Inc. (Nasdaq: CLGY) announced today that the United States Patent and Trademark Office (USPTO) has issued a patent (US 6,395,736) that covers methods of treating anorectal disorders by administering certain concentrations of topical potassium channel openers to the anorectal region in order to decrease abnormally high pressure of the anal sphincter muscle. The disorders disclosed in the patent include anal fissures, hemorrhoids and constipation.

  Potassium channel openers help smooth muscle relaxation and, therefore, are anticipated to provide useful medical options in treating anorectal disorders. Data obtained from in vivo experiments demonstrated effective internal anal sphincter relaxation with administration of various potassium channel openers. These agents are expected to compliment Cellegesic's(R) (nitroglycerin ointment) effect on smooth muscle relaxation.

  Dr. Vivien Mak, Vice President of Research at Cellegy, commented, "Over the past two weeks, Cellegy has been issued two important United States patents (covering the use of PDE inhibitors and potassium channel openers) that result from our ongoing efforts to develop products for the treatment of fissures and hemorrhoids. Such products are expected to deepen our Cellegesic product line through the development of new dosage forms, line extensions and product improvements in order to maximize the commercial potential of Cellegy's investment in this greatly underserved therapeutic area. Our patent portfolio in this field has been significantly strengthened by the two recently issued patents."
  Cellegy Pharmaceuticals is a specialty biopharmaceutical company focused on the areas of gastroenterology, sexual dysfunction in males and females, and various women's health conditions.

Cellegy has a significant pipeline of late stage products. Apart from Cellegesic, which is the subject of ongoing discussions with the FDA regarding requirements for marketing approval in the United States, the company recently announced that it has filed an NDA (New Drug Application) on its patented product Tostrex(TM) (testosterone gel), for the treatment of male hypogonadism. Another product in Cellegy's pipeline, Tostrelle(TM), a transdermal testosterone gel for the treatment of female sexual dysfunction entered into Phase II/III clinical testing during the first quarter of 2002.

Additional pipeline products include nitric oxide donors for the treatment of dyspareunia (a form of sexual dysfunction) in females, Raynaud's Disease, Restless Leg Syndrome, and prostate cancer, as well as products for the treatment of male erectile dysfunction. Cellegy is currently exploring various partnering opportunities for these patent protected product candidates in the United States and international markets.

This press release contains forward-looking statements that are made pursuant to the safe harbor provisions of the Securities Litigation Reform Act of 1995. Investors should be aware that these forward-looking statements are subject to risks and uncertainties, known and unknown, which could cause actual results and developments to differ materially from those expressed or implied in such statements. You are cautioned not to place undue reliance on forward-looking statements and we undertake no obligation to update or revise statements made herein. For more information regarding the above, and other risk factors that may affect Cellegy's future results and may cause actual results to vary from results anticipated in forward-looking statements, investors should refer to the company's Annual Report on Form 10-K for the year ended December 31, 2001 and other documents that the company files with the Securities and Exchange Commission, which are available online at http://www.sec.gov or by contacting the company.

Reuters

The Reuters' Medical News database can be very useful in exploring news archives relating to hemorrhoids. While some of the listed articles are free to view, others can be purchased for a nominal fee. To access this archive, go to **http://www.reutershealth.com/frame2/arch.html** and search by "hemorrhoids" (or synonyms). The following was recently listed in this archive for hemorrhoids:

- **Stapling hemorrhoids less painful than removal**
  Source: Reuters Health eLine
  Date: April 11, 2002
  http://www.reuters.gov/archive/2002/04/11/eline/links/20020411elin035.html

- **Nitro for Hemorrhoids**
  Source: Reuters Health eLine
  Date: June 24, 1997
  http://www.reuters.gov/archive/1997/06/24/eline/links/19970624elin002.html

The NIH

Within MEDLINEplus, the NIH has made an agreement with the New York Times Syndicate, the AP News Service, and Reuters to deliver news that can be browsed by the public. Search news releases at **http://www.nlm.nih.gov/medlineplus/alphanews_a.html.** MEDLINEplus allows you to browse across an alphabetical index. Or you can search by date at **http://www.nlm.nih.gov/medlineplus/newsbydate.html**. Often, news items are indexed by MEDLINEplus within their search engine.

Business Wire

Business Wire is similar to PR Newswire. To access this archive, simply go to **http://www.businesswire.com**. You can scan the news by industry category or company name.

Internet Wire

Internet Wire is more focused on technology than the other wires. To access this site, go to **http://www.internetwire.com** and use the "Search Archive" option. Type in "hemorrhoids" (or synonyms). As this service is oriented to technology, you may wish to search for press releases covering diagnostic procedures or tests that you may have read about.

Search Engines

Free-to-view news can also be found in the news section of your favorite search engines (see the health news page at Yahoo: **http://dir.yahoo.com/Health/News_and_Media/,** or use this Web site's general news search page **http://news.yahoo.com/.** Type in "hemorrhoids" (or synonyms). If you know the name of a company that is relevant to hemorrhoids, you can go to any stock trading Web site (such as **www.etrade.com**) and search for the company name there. News items across various news sources are reported on indicated hyperlinks.

BBC

Covering news from a more European perspective, the British Broadcasting Corporation (BBC) allows the public free access to their news archive located at **http://www.bbc.co.uk/.** Search by "hemorrhoids" (or synonyms).

Newsletter Articles

If you choose not to subscribe to a newsletter, you can nevertheless find references to newsletter articles. We recommend that you use the Combined Health Information Database, while limiting your search criteria to "newsletter articles." Again, you will need to use the "Detailed Search" option. Go directly to the following hyperlink: **http://chid.nih.gov/detail/detail.html.** Go to the bottom of the search page where "You may refine your search by." Select the dates and language that you prefer. For the format option, select "Newsletter Article."

By making these selections, and typing in "hemorrhoids" (or synonyms) into the "For these words:" box, you will only receive results on newsletter articles. You should check back periodically with this database as it is updated every 3 months. The following is a typical result when searching for newsletter articles on hemorrhoids:

- **Hemorrhoids: Managing This Harmless but Bothersome Problem**

  Source: Mayo Clinic Health Letter. 14(2): 1-3. February 1996.

Contact: Available from Mayo Clinic Health Letter. Subscription Services, P.O. Box 53889, Boulder, CO 80322-3889. (800) 333-9037.

Summary: This newsletter article presents information on managing hemorrhoids. Topics include how hemorrhoids develop, constipation as a common cause of hemorrhoids, symptoms of different types of hemorrhoids (internal, prolapsed, external), self-care steps to manage hemorrhoidal flareups, medical treatments (rubber band ligation, infrared coagulation, bipolar electrocoagulation, and laser therapy), surgery, and suggestions to avoid hemorrhoids. 2 figures.

- **Facts and Fiction of Rectal Bleeding: What It Is and What It Isn't**

Source: Intestinal Fortitude. 4(4): 1-3. Spring 1994.

Contact: Available from Intestinal Disease Foundation. 1323 Forbes Avenue, Pittsburgh, PA 15219. (412) 261-5888.

Summary: This newsletter article provides basic information on rectal bleeding. The author emphasizes that rectal bleeding is a common occurrence. Since it can be a sign of a serious problem in the gastrointestinal (GI) tract, it should always be evaluated by a health care provider. However, rectal bleeding can be caused by hemorrhoids and other less serious illnesses. The author reviews some typical sources of blood in the stool, including hemorrhoids, fissures, benign growths or polyps of the colon, and tumors or cancer. The appearance of GI bleeding varies based on where the blood is originating from and how severe it is. If bleeding is coming from the anus, rectum, or distal colon, there will be bright red blood coating the stool or mixed with the stool. The stool may be mixed with dark red blood if the bleeding is higher up in the colon or at the far end of the small intestine. The author differentiates between acute massive bleeding (which requires immediate medical attention) and chronic slow bleeding (which may result in anemia). The article concludes with a discussion of the various diagnostic tests used to determine the cause of rectal bleeding. Examinations that should be done for rectal bleeding are digital examination anoscopy, sigmoidoscopy, and possible colonoscopy for the lower GI tract. A barium enema may also be needed. For possible causes in the upper GI tract, esophagogastroduodenoscopy, upper GI barium studies, and small bowel barium studies may be indicated. Testing of the stool may be the first step to determine the presence of blood. (AA-M).

Academic Periodicals covering Hemorrhoids

Academic periodicals can be a highly technical yet valuable source of information on hemorrhoids. We have compiled the following list of periodicals known to publish articles relating to hemorrhoids and which are currently indexed within the National Library of Medicine's PubMed database (follow hyperlinks to view more information, summaries, etc., for each). In addition to these sources, to keep current on articles written on hemorrhoids published by any of the periodicals listed below, you can simply follow the hyperlink indicated or go to the following Web site: **www.ncbi.nlm.nih.gov/pubmed**. Type the periodical's name into the search box to find the latest studies published.

If you want complete details about the historical contents of a periodical, you can also visit **http://www.ncbi.nlm.nih.gov/entrez/jrbrowser.cgi**. Here, type in the name of the journal or its abbreviation, and you will receive an index of published articles. At **http://locatorplus.gov/** you can retrieve more indexing information on medical periodicals (e.g. the name of the publisher). Select the button "Search LOCATORplus." Then type in the name of the journal and select the advanced search option "Journal Title Search." The following is a sample of periodicals which publish articles on hemorrhoids:

- **Alternative Medicine Review : a Journal of Clinical Therapeutic. (Altern Med Rev)**
  http://www.ncbi.nlm.nih.gov/entrez/jrbrowser.cgi?field=0&regexp=Alternative+Medicine+Review+:+a+Journal+of+Clinical+Therapeutic&dispmax=20&dispstart=0

- **Canadian Journal of Surgery. Journal Canadien De Chirurgie. (Can J Surg)**
  http://www.ncbi.nlm.nih.gov/entrez/jrbrowser.cgi?field=0&regexp=Canadian+Journal+of+Surgery.+Journal+Canadien+De+Chirurgie&dispmax=20&dispstart=0

- **Diseases of the Colon and Rectum. (Dis Colon Rectum)**
  http://www.ncbi.nlm.nih.gov/entrez/jrbrowser.cgi?field=0&regexp=Diseases+of+the+Colon+and+Rectum&dispmax=20&dispstart=0

- **The American Journal of Dermatopathology. (Am J Dermatopathol)**
  http://www.ncbi.nlm.nih.gov/entrez/jrbrowser.cgi?field=0&regexp=The+American+Journal+of+Dermatopathology&dispmax=20&dispstart=0

- **The American Journal of Gastroenterology. (Am J Gastroenterol)**
  http://www.ncbi.nlm.nih.gov/entrez/jrbrowser.cgi?field=0&regexp=The+American+Journal+of+Gastroenterology&dispmax=20&dispstart=0

Vocabulary Builder

Distal: Remote; farther from any point of reference; opposed to proximal. In dentistry, used to designate a position on the dental arch farther from the median line of the jaw. [EU]

Enema: A clyster or injection; a liquid injected or to be injected into the rectum. [EU]

Hypogonadism: A condition resulting from or characterized by abnormally decreased functional activity of the gonads, with retardation of growth and sexual development. [EU]

Nitroglycerin: A highly volatile organic nitrate that acts as a dilator of arterial and venous smooth muscle and is used in the treatment of angina. It provides relief through improvement of the balance between myocardial oxygen supply and demand. Although total coronary blood flow is not increased, there is redistribution of blood flow in the heart when partial occlusion of coronary circulation is effected. [NIH]

Potassium: An element that is in the alkali group of metals. It has an atomic symbol K, atomic number 19, and atomic weight 39.10. It is the chief cation in the intracellular fluid of muscle and other cells. Potassium ion is a strong electrolyte and it plays a significant role in the regulation of fluid volume and maintenance of the water-electrolyte balance. [NIH]

Prostate: A gland in males that surrounds the neck of the bladder and the urethra. It secretes a substance that liquifies coagulated semen. It is situated in the pelvic cavity behind the lower part of the pubic symphysis, above the deep layer of the triangular ligament, and rests upon the rectum. [NIH]

Transdermal: Entering through the dermis, or skin, as in administration of a drug applied to the skin in ointment or patch form. [EU]

CHAPTER 8. PHYSICIAN GUIDELINES AND DATABASES

Overview

Doctors and medical researchers rely on a number of information sources to help patients with their conditions. Many will subscribe to journals or newsletters published by their professional associations or refer to specialized textbooks or clinical guides published for the medical profession. In this chapter, we focus on databases and Internet-based guidelines created or written for this professional audience.

NIH Guidelines

For the more common diseases, The National Institutes of Health publish guidelines that are frequently consulted by physicians. Publications are typically written by one or more of the various NIH Institutes. For physician guidelines, commonly referred to as "clinical" or "professional" guidelines, you can visit the following Institutes:

- Office of the Director (OD); guidelines consolidated across agencies available at **http://www.nih.gov/health/consumer/conkey.htm**

- National Institute of General Medical Sciences (NIGMS); fact sheets available at **http://www.nigms.nih.gov/news/facts/**

- National Library of Medicine (NLM); extensive encyclopedia (A.D.A.M., Inc.) with guidelines:
  http://www.nlm.nih.gov/medlineplus/healthtopics.html

- National Institute of Diabetes and Digestive and Kidney Diseases (NIDDK); guidelines available at
  http://www.niddk.nih.gov/health/health.htm

NIH Databases

In addition to the various Institutes of Health that publish professional guidelines, the NIH has designed a number of databases for professionals.[20] Physician-oriented resources provide a wide variety of information related to the biomedical and health sciences, both past and present. The format of these resources varies. Searchable databases, bibliographic citations, full text articles (when available), archival collections, and images are all available. The following are referenced by the National Library of Medicine:[21]

- **Bioethics:** Access to published literature on the ethical, legal and public policy issues surrounding healthcare and biomedical research. This information is provided in conjunction with the Kennedy Institute of Ethics located at Georgetown University, Washington, D.C.: **http://www.nlm.nih.gov/databases/databases_bioethics.html**

- **HIV/AIDS Resources:** Describes various links and databases dedicated to HIV/AIDS research: **http://www.nlm.nih.gov/pubs/factsheets/aidsinfs.html**

- **NLM Online Exhibitions:** Describes "Exhibitions in the History of Medicine": **http://www.nlm.nih.gov/exhibition/exhibition.html**. Additional resources for historical scholarship in medicine: **http://www.nlm.nih.gov/hmd/hmd.html**

- **Biotechnology Information:** Access to public databases. The National Center for Biotechnology Information conducts research in computational biology, develops software tools for analyzing genome data, and disseminates biomedical information for the better understanding of molecular processes affecting human health and disease: **http://www.ncbi.nlm.nih.gov/**

- **Population Information:** The National Library of Medicine provides access to worldwide coverage of population, family planning, and related health issues, including family planning technology and programs, fertility, and population law and policy: **http://www.nlm.nih.gov/databases/databases_population.html**

- **Cancer Information:** Access to caner-oriented databases: **http://www.nlm.nih.gov/databases/databases_cancer.html**

---

[20] Remember, for the general public, the National Library of Medicine recommends the databases referenced in MEDLINE*plus* (**http://medlineplus.gov/** or **http://www.nlm.nih.gov/medlineplus/databases.html**).
[21] See **http://www.nlm.nih.gov/databases/databases.html**.

- **Profiles in Science:** Offering the archival collections of prominent twentieth-century biomedical scientists to the public through modern digital technology: **http://www.profiles.nlm.nih.gov/**

- **Chemical Information:** Provides links to various chemical databases and references: **http://sis.nlm.nih.gov/Chem/ChemMain.html**

- **Clinical Alerts:** Reports the release of findings from the NIH-funded clinical trials where such release could significantly affect morbidity and mortality: **http://www.nlm.nih.gov/databases/alerts/clinical_alerts.html**

- **Space Life Sciences:** Provides links and information to space-based research (including NASA): **http://www.nlm.nih.gov/databases/databases_space.html**

- **MEDLINE:** Bibliographic database covering the fields of medicine, nursing, dentistry, veterinary medicine, the healthcare system, and the pre-clinical sciences: **http://www.nlm.nih.gov/databases/databases_medline.html**

- **Toxicology and Environmental Health Information (TOXNET):** Databases covering toxicology and environmental health: **http://sis.nlm.nih.gov/Tox/ToxMain.html**

- **Visible Human Interface:** Anatomically detailed, three-dimensional representations of normal male and female human bodies: **http://www.nlm.nih.gov/research/visible/visible_human.html**

While all of the above references may be of interest to physicians who study and treat hemorrhoids, the following are particularly noteworthy.

The Combined Health Information Database

A comprehensive source of information on clinical guidelines written for professionals is the Combined Health Information Database. You will need to limit your search to "Brochure/Pamphlet," "Fact Sheet," or "Information Package" and hemorrhoids using the "Detailed Search" option. Go directly to the following hyperlink: **http://chid.nih.gov/detail/detail.html**. To find associations, use the drop boxes at the bottom of the search page where "You may refine your search by." For the publication date, select "All Years," select your preferred language, and the format option "Fact Sheet." By making these selections and typing "hemorrhoids" (or synonyms) into the "For these words:" box above, you will only receive results on fact sheets dealing with hemorrhoids. The following is a sample result:

- **Prevalence of Major Digestive Disorders and Bowel Symptoms, 1989**

  Source: NCHS Advance Data. Number 212. March 24, 1992. p. 1-13, 15.

Summary: This report is based on data from the 1989 National Health Interview Survey (NHIS), a continuous cross-sectional survey of the resident household population of the United States. The NHIS is particularly useful for several reasons: questions regarding digestive conditions have been asked annually for more than 30 years, allowing for an analysis of long-term trends; less common conditions and small subpopulations also can be examined by combining multiple years; data are gathered on common conditions, such as constipation and hemorrhoids, that may not require frequent medical attention; and NHIS is the only continuing source of information regarding disability and activity restriction due to digestive diseases. The authors of this report detail the data and methods of the NHIS, and the results, in the categories of prevalence and onset, sociodemographic differences, and medical diagnosis. 7 tables. 22 references.

- **Understanding GI Bleeding: A Consumer Education Brochure**

  Source: Arlington, VA: American College of Gastroenterology. 200x. 13 p.

  Contact: Available from American College of Gastroenterology. 4900 B South 31st Street, Arlington, VA 22206-1656. (703) 820-7400. Fax (703) 931-4520. Price: Single copy free. Also available for free at http://www.acg.gi.org/acg-dev/patientinfo/frame_gibleeding.html.

Summary: This consumer education brochure outlines the symptoms, causes and treatment of gastrointestinal (GI) bleeding. Bleeding in the gastrointestinal tract means that some part of the GI tract (esophagus, stomach, small intestine, large intestine, and rectum) is bleeding internally, either slightly (which may or may not be very serious) or heavily (which may have serious health consequences). The symptoms of GI bleeding vary, depending on which part of the digestive tract is involved. Symptoms can include vomiting blood, vomiting dark material that looks like coffee grounds, passing black tarry stools, or passing pure blood or blood mixed in stool. Cause of GI bleeding include ulcers, varices, liver disease, gastritis, tumors, colon cancer, polyps, colitis, diverticular disease, and hemorrhoids. The brochure focuses on ulcers and their causes (usually Helicobacter pylori infection) and treatment. The brochure also explores the use of nonsteroidal antiinflammatory drugs (NSAIDs) and the need to balance pain relief and concerns with side effects of these drugs (including GI bleeding). Conventional treatments for ulcers (H2 blockers and proton pump inhibitors) have been found to have a beneficial effect in treating NSAID induced ulcers and in preventing GI bleeding. The brochure concludes by encouraging ongoing monitoring of the patient taking NSAIDs, since problems with GI bleeding can arise with few, if any, symptoms. 2 figures. 2 tables.

- **Fiber Facts**

Source: Fort Worth, TX: Konsyl Pharmaceuticals, Inc. 1999. [2 p.].

Contact: Available from Konsyl Pharmaceuticals, Inc. 4200 South Hulen Street, Suite 513, Fort Worth, TX 76109-4912. (800) 356-6795 or (817) 763-8011. Fax (817) 731-9389. Website: www.konsyl.com. Price: Single copy free.

Summary: This brochure provides basic information about dietary fiber, defined as the part of the plant that cannot be digested by humans. Fiber is found in grains, cereals, fruits, vegetables, nuts, seeds, and legumes (dried beans, peas, and lentils). There are two kinds of fiber and most sources of fiber contain a mixture of both types. Soluble fiber absorbs water and promotes good intestinal health by increasing bowel motility which enhances transit through the intestinal tract. Insoluble fiber absorbs little water but is still important because it improves the transit time necessary to move fecal material through the colon. The National Cancer Institute has recommended eating 25 to 35 grams of fiber a day as a step toward preventing colon cancer. Most Americans consume only 10 to 15 grams of fiber per day. The brochure reviews strategies that readers can implement to increase their fiber intake, but notes that it is important to increase the level slowly. A chart is provided for readers to determine their present level of dietary fiber intake. The author discusses the use of fiber supplements, such as Konsyl (the manufacturer of which is the producer of this brochure). The brochure summarizes how increased fiber will benefit each of six disease areas: constipation, hemorrhoids, diverticular disease, irritable bowel syndrome (IBS), colon cancer, and cardiovascular disease. The brochure is illustrated with full color drawings and photographs. 1 table. 4 figures.

- **Colorectal Health: The Wellness Way. [Salud Colorrectal: Conservacion de la Salud]**

Source: San Bruno, CA: StayWell Company. 1999. [2 p.].

Contact: Available from StayWell Company. Order Department, 1100 Grundy Lane, San Bruno, CA 94066-9821. (800) 333-3032. Fax (650) 244-4512. E-mail: email@staywell.com. Website: www.staywell.com. Price: $20.00 for pack of 50; plus shipping and handling.

Summary: There are three basic ingredients in promoting colorectal health: eating right, exercising regularly, and getting regular screening exams. This patient education brochure describes these strategies. Written in nontechnical language, the brochure first illustrates the colorectal anatomy and defines common problems, including polyps, colitis, cancer, and hemorrhoids. The brochure then focuses on colorectal cancer, including risk factors (age and family history) and symptoms, such as blood in the stool, constipation or diarrhea, increase in intestinal gas, and pain in the abdomen. The brochure stresses that early colorectal cancer is often without symptoms, which is why annual screenings are so important. The brochure then describes two rectal examinations that help doctors diagnose colorectal cancers: the digital rectal examination and the proctosigmoidoscopy (the procto). Each examination is described and illustrated (with a male figure in the illustrations). The brochure also includes a colorectal checklist for readers to see whether they are following recommendations to prevent colorectal cancer and detect problems early. A brief list of health resources, including the toll free telephone number for a cancer information line (1-800-4CANCER) is provided. The brochure is illustrated with full color line drawings and is available in English or Spanish. 12 figures.

- **Medication for Inflammatory Bowel Disease**

Source: Toronto, Canada: Crohn's and Colitis Foundation of Canada. 1997. 12 p.

Contact: Available from Crohn's and Colitis Foundation of Canada. 21 St. Clair Avenue East, Suite 30, Toronto, Ontario, Canada M4T 1L9. (800) 387-1479 or (416) 920-5035. Fax (416) 929-0364. E-mail: ccfc@cycor.ca. Price: Single copy free.

Summary: This booklet describes the role of medications in the management of inflammatory bowel disease (IBD), a term used to describe two similar, but distinct conditions: Crohn's disease and ulcerative colitis (UC). These diseases affect the digestive system and cause the intestines to become inflamed, form sores (ulcers), bleed easily, and scar. People with Crohn's disease or UC may take prescription or over-the-counter medications to reduce inflammation in the gastrointestinal tract, to control diarrhea and cramps, and to treat complications. This booklet describes the most commonly prescribed medications: how they work, and common (or especially serious) side effects. The brochure also discusses the role of nicotine in UC and briefly mentions medications used to treat other symptoms and problems, including hemorrhoids and anal fissures, anal itching, vitamins and minerals, and pain killers. 1 figure.

- **About Fiber in Your Diet**

  Source: South Deerfield, MA: Channing L. Bete Co., Inc. 1997. 15 p.

  Contact: Available from Channing L. Bete, Co., Inc. 200 State Road, South Deerfield, MA 01373-0200. (800) 628-7733. Price: $1.25 each for 1-24 copies; $0.89 each for 25-99 copies; $0.64 each for 100-499 copies.

  Summary: This illustrated brochure outlines the role and importance of two types of dietary fiber: waterinsoluble and watersoluble fiber. Waterinsoluble fiber is the structural part of plants that does not dissolve in water; it is found mainly in whole-grain products, wheat bran, vegetables, and nuts. Watersoluble fiber, a plant substance that forms a gel in water, is found mainly in oats, beans, fruits, and some vegetables. The brochure then outlines the importance of fiber in a healthy diet. Fiber helps the body's digestive system work well and can help prevent or treat constipation, diverticulosis, irritable bowel syndrome, and hemorrhoids. Fiber may also help lower cholesterol levels, prevent colon cancer, control weight, and prevent or treat diabetes. The brochure discusses how much fiber should be in the diet and the importance of increasing the level gradually. Other topics are how to read a nutrition label; foods high in dietary fiber; specific suggestions for adding fiber to meals and snacks; and other dietary components such as fat and cholesterol, simple carbohydrates, salt, alcohol, and vitamins and minerals. Also discussed are weight maintenance and exercise. The brochure concludes with the answers to some basic questions about fiber.

- **About Intestinal Disorders**

  Source: South Deerfield, MA: Channing L. Bete Company, Inc. 1993. 15 p.

  Contact: Available from Channing L. Bete Company, Inc. 200 State Road, South Deerfield, MA 01373. (800) 628-7733. Price: $1.25 (bulk prices available) plus shipping and handling.

  Summary: This booklet, written in easy-to-understand language with numerous illustrations, describes a variety of intestinal disorders. After a brief review of the function and processes of the intestinal tract, the brochure discusses the following common intestinal disorders: irritable bowel syndrome, diverticulitis, inflammatory bowel diseases, intestinal tumors, polyps, appendicitis, and hemorrhoids. Diagnostic tests used for intestinal disorders and the role of diet in managing intestinal disorders also are discussed.

- **Digestive Do's and Don'ts**

  Source: Bethesda, MD: National Institute on Aging. 1992. 4 p.

Contact: Available from National Institute on Aging (NIA) Information Center. P.O. Box 8057, Gaithersburg, MD 20898-8057. (800) 222-2225 or (301) 495-3450. Fax (301) 589-3014. TTY (800) 222-4225. E-mail: niainfo@access.digex.net. Price: Single copy free; bulk copies available.

Summary: This Age Page explains the digestive system, how it works and how to take care of the system in order to help avoid future difficulties. Information is provided on the types of symptoms requiring a doctor's attention. Following the symptomatic conditions, several digestive diseases are listed and described, along with their possible treatment plans. The digestive disorders discussed are constipation, diarrhea, diverticulosis and diverticulitis, functional disorders, gallbladder disease, gas, gastritis, heartburn, peptic ulcer, indigestion, hemorrhoids, hiatal hernia, milk intolerance, and ulcerative colitis.

- **Facts About Fiber**

Source: Waco, TX: Health Edco. 1992. 2 p.

Contact: Available from Health Edco. P.O. Box 21207, Waco, TX 76702-1207. (800) 299-3366, ext. 295. Fax (817) 751-0221. Price: $2.00 each for 1-99 copies, $0.44 each for 100 or more copies.

Summary: This brochure offers a question and answer format to provide information on dietary fiber. The questions are posed on the outside of the brochure, with the answers on a sliding tab answer card. Topics include definitions of the different types of fiber and where it can be found, recommendations on the amount of fiber that should be included in the diet, the role of fiber in lowering cholesterol, how fiber prevents cancer (particularly cancer of the colon or rectum), and the role of fiber in reducing the incidence of hemorrhoids. There are two kinds of fiber: soluble and insoluble. Only soluble fiber produces significant reductions in blood cholesterol and blood sugar. However, insoluble fiber seems to protect against intestinal cancers. Fiber is thought to prevent cancer by weakening or deactivating cancer-causing substances in the bowel. Fiber also speeds the passage of food through the bowel, reducing the time that the bowel is exposed to potential cancer-causing agents. Fiber has been proven to reduce the chance of developing cancer of the colon or rectum and may prevent diverticulitis as well.

- **Same Day Surgery: Rectal Conditions**

Source: Waco, TX: Health Edco. 1991. 2 p.

Contact: Available from Health Edco. P.O. Box 21207, Waco, TX 76702-1207. (800) 299-3366, ext. 295. Fax (817) 751-0221. Price: $2.00 each for 1-99 copies, $0.43 each for 100-199 copies.

Summary: This brochure describes three rectal conditions that can be corrected by same day surgery: hemorrhoids, fissures, and fistulas. Hemorrhoids are varicose veins in the anus. Swollen hemorrhoids cause pain and itching and may clot or bleed. A fissure is a crack in the lining of the rectum or anus, resulting from infection, bruising by straining, or other injury. A fistula is a tunnel-like abnormal connection between two areas. An anorectal fissure extends from an infected area in the rectum or anus to the skin around the anus, and discharges pus. The brochure outlines recommended preoperative care strategies, what to expect the day of the surgery, the types of surgical techniques used to treat each of the three conditions, and postoperative healing at home. The brochure notes that complications from same day surgery are rare, but patients should contact their physician if they experience excessive bleeding, difficulty when urinating or having a bowel movement, or infection around the site of the incision. Full color line drawings illustrate the three conditions covered and the surgery used to treat each one. 9 figures.

- **Rectal Bleeding. [Sangrado Rectal]**

  Source: Camp Hill, PA: Chek-Med Systems, Inc. 199x. 2 p.

  Contact: Available from Chek-Med Systems, Inc. 200 Grandview Avenue, Camp Hill, PA 17011. (800) 451-5797. Fax (717) 761-0216. Price: $22 per packet of 50 pamphlets for order of 3 to 10 packets; minimum order 3 packets. Discounts available for larger quantities and complete kits of gastroenterology pamphlets.

  Summary: This patient education brochure, available in English and Spanish, provides basic information about rectal bleeding. Topics covered include a definition of the problem; the causes of rectal bleeding, including hemorrhoids, fistula, fissure, diverticulosis, proctitis and colitis, polyps and cancer, and protrusion of the rectum; and diagnostic tests used to confirm the cause of rectal bleeding, including the patient history, the visual and digital exam, the use of various types of endoscopic procedures, and the barium enema x-ray. The brochure includes a blank space for the physician to provide individualized patient instructions. One simple line drawing illustrates the nine problems discussed. 1 figure.

- **Understanding Fiber**

  Source: Pittsburgh, PA: SmithKline Beecham. 199x. 6 p.

  Contact: Available from SmithKline Beecham. Consumer Brands, P.O. Box 1467, Pittsburgh, PA 15230. (800) 245-1040. Price: Single copy free. Bulk orders available to physicians, (800) 233-2426.

Summary: This brochure familiarizes readers with the role of fiber in treating irritable bowel syndrome (IBS), diverticular disease, constipation, and other digestive disorders. Topics include the role of fiber in the physiology of digestion and nutrient absorption; how to determine the right amount of fiber for a particular individual; the role of fiber supplements, including Citrucel; sources of dietary fiber; and facts about fiber. A chart summarizes common digestive ailments, who tends to be affected by them, treatment options, and how fiber can help. Ailments covered are hemorrhoids, anal fissures, IBS, diverticular disease, and constipation. The brochure is produced by the manufacturer of Citrucel; a coupon for the product is included.

The NLM Gateway[22]

The NLM (National Library of Medicine) Gateway is a Web-based system that lets users search simultaneously in multiple retrieval systems at the U.S. National Library of Medicine (NLM). It allows users of NLM services to initiate searches from one Web interface, providing "one-stop searching" for many of NLM's information resources or databases.[23] One target audience for the Gateway is the Internet user who is new to NLM's online resources and does not know what information is available or how best to search for it. This audience may include physicians and other healthcare providers, researchers, librarians, students, and, increasingly, patients, their families, and the public.[24] To use the NLM Gateway, simply go to the search site at **http://gateway.nlm.nih.gov/gw/Cmd**. Type "hemorrhoids" (or synonyms) into the search box and click "Search." The results will be presented in a tabular form, indicating the number of references in each database category.

---

22 Adapted from NLM: **http://gateway.nlm.nih.gov/gw/Cmd?Overview.x**.

23 The NLM Gateway is currently being developed by the Lister Hill National Center for Biomedical Communications (LHNCBC) at the National Library of Medicine (NLM) of the National Institutes of Health (NIH).

24 Other users may find the Gateway useful for an overall search of NLM's information resources. Some searchers may locate what they need immediately, while others will utilize the Gateway as an adjunct tool to other NLM search services such as PubMed® and MEDLINEplus®. The Gateway connects users with multiple NLM retrieval systems while also providing a search interface for its own collections. These collections include various types of information that do not logically belong in PubMed, LOCATORplus, or other established NLM retrieval systems (e.g., meeting announcements and pre-1966 journal citations). The Gateway will provide access to the information found in an increasing number of NLM retrieval systems in several phases.

Results Summary

Category	Items Found
Journal Articles	343187
Books / Periodicals / Audio Visual	2561
Consumer Health	292
Meeting Abstracts	3093
Other Collections	100
Total	349233

HSTAT[25]

HSTAT is a free, Web-based resource that provides access to full-text documents used in healthcare decision-making.[26] HSTAT's audience includes healthcare providers, health service researchers, policy makers, insurance companies, consumers, and the information professionals who serve these groups. HSTAT provides access to a wide variety of publications, including clinical practice guidelines, quick-reference guides for clinicians, consumer health brochures, evidence reports and technology assessments from the Agency for Healthcare Research and Quality (AHRQ), as well as AHRQ's Put Prevention Into Practice.[27] Simply search by "hemorrhoids" (or synonyms) at the following Web site: **http://text.nlm.nih.gov**.

Coffee Break: Tutorials for Biologists[28]

Some patients may wish to have access to a general healthcare site that takes a scientific view of the news and covers recent breakthroughs in biology that may one day assist physicians in developing treatments. To this end, we recommend "Coffee Break," a collection of short reports on recent biological

---

[25] Adapted from HSTAT: **http://www.nlm.nih.gov/pubs/factsheets/hstat.html**
[26] The HSTAT URL is **http://hstat.nlm.nih.gov/**.
[27] Other important documents in HSTAT include: the National Institutes of Health (NIH) Consensus Conference Reports and Technology Assessment Reports; the HIV/AIDS Treatment Information Service (ATIS) resource documents; the Substance Abuse and Mental Health Services Administration's Center for Substance Abuse Treatment (SAMHSA/CSAT) Treatment Improvement Protocols (TIP) and Center for Substance Abuse Prevention (SAMHSA/CSAP) Prevention Enhancement Protocols System (PEPS); the Public Health Service (PHS) Preventive Services Task Force's *Guide to Clinical Preventive Services*; the independent, nonfederal Task Force on Community Services *Guide to Community Preventive Services*; and the Health Technology Advisory Committee (HTAC) of the Minnesota Health Care Commission (MHCC) health technology evaluations.
[28] Adapted from **http://www.ncbi.nlm.nih.gov/Coffeebreak/Archive/FAQ.html**

discoveries. Each report incorporates interactive tutorials that demonstrate how bioinformatics tools are used as a part of the research process. Currently, all Coffee Breaks are written by NCBI staff.[29] Each report is about 400 words and is usually based on a discovery reported in one or more articles from recently published, peer-reviewed literature.[30] This site has new articles every few weeks, so it can be considered an online magazine of sorts, and intended for general background information. You can access the Coffee Break Web site at **http://www.ncbi.nlm.nih.gov/Coffeebreak/**.

Other Commercial Databases

In addition to resources maintained by official agencies, other databases exist that are commercial ventures addressing medical professionals. Here are a few examples that may interest you:

- **CliniWeb International:** Index and table of contents to selected clinical information on the Internet; see **http://www.ohsu.edu/cliniweb/**.

- **Image Engine:** Multimedia electronic medical record system that integrates a wide range of digitized clinical images with textual data stored in the University of Pittsburgh Medical Center's MARS electronic medical record system; see the following Web site: **http://www.cml.upmc.edu/cml/imageengine/imageEngine.html**.

- **Medical World Search:** Searches full text from thousands of selected medical sites on the Internet; see **http://www.mwsearch.com/**.

- **MedWeaver:** Prototype system that allows users to search differential diagnoses for any list of signs and symptoms, to search medical literature, and to explore relevant Web sites; see **http://www.med.virginia.edu/~wmd4n/medweaver.html**.

- **Metaphrase:** Middleware component intended for use by both caregivers and medical records personnel. It converts the informal language generally used by caregivers into terms from formal, controlled vocabularies; see the following Web site: **http://www.lexical.com/Metaphrase.html**.

---

[29] The figure that accompanies each article is frequently supplied by an expert external to NCBI, in which case the source of the figure is cited. The result is an interactive tutorial that tells a biological story.

[30] After a brief introduction that sets the work described into a broader context, the report focuses on how a molecular understanding can provide explanations of observed biology and lead to therapies for diseases. Each vignette is accompanied by a figure and hypertext links that lead to a series of pages that interactively show how NCBI tools and resources are used in the research process.

Specialized References

The following books are specialized references written for professionals interested in hemorrhoids (sorted alphabetically by title, hyperlinks provide rankings, information, and reviews at Amazon.com):

- **Blackwell's Primary Care Essentials: Gastointestinal Disease** by David W. Hay; Paperback, 1st edition (December 15, 2001), Blackwell Science Inc; ISBN: 0632045035;
  http://www.amazon.com/exec/obidos/ASIN/0632045035/icongroupinterna

- **Gastrointestinal Problems** by Martin S. Lipsky, M.D. (Editor), Richard Sadovsky, M.D. (Editor); Paperback - 194 pages, 1st edition (August 15, 2000), Lippincott, Williams & Wilkins Publishers; ISBN: 0781720540;
  http://www.amazon.com/exec/obidos/ASIN/0781720540/icongroupinterna

- **Rome II: The Functional Gastrointestinal Disorders** by Douglas A. Drossman (Editor); Paperback - 800 pages, 2nd edition (March 1, 2000), Degnon Associates Inc.; ISBN: 0965683729;
  http://www.amazon.com/exec/obidos/ASIN/0965683729/icongroupinterna

Vocabulary Builder

Carbohydrate: An aldehyde or ketone derivative of a polyhydric alcohol, particularly of the pentahydric and hexahydric alcohols. They are so named because the hydrogen and oxygen are usually in the proportion to form water, $(CH_2O)n$. The most important carbohydrates are the starches, sugars, celluloses, and gums. They are classified into mono-, di-, tri-, poly- and heterosaccharides. [EU]

Helicobacter: A genus of gram-negative, spiral-shaped bacteria that is pathogenic and has been isolated from the intestinal tract of mammals, including humans. [NIH]

Nicotine: Nicotine is highly toxic alkaloid. It is the prototypical agonist at nicotinic cholinergic receptors where it dramatically stimulates neurons and ultimately blocks synaptic transmission. Nicotine is also important medically because of its presence in tobacco smoke. [NIH]

PART III. APPENDICES

ABOUT PART III

Part III is a collection of appendices on general medical topics which may be of interest to patients with hemorrhoids and related conditions.

APPENDIX A. RESEARCHING YOUR MEDICATIONS

Overview

There are a number of sources available on new or existing medications which could be prescribed to patients with hemorrhoids. While a number of hard copy or CD-Rom resources are available to patients and physicians for research purposes, a more flexible method is to use Internet-based databases. In this chapter, we will begin with a general overview of medications. We will then proceed to outline official recommendations on how you should view your medications. You may also want to research medications that you are currently taking for other conditions as they may interact with medications for hemorrhoids. Research can give you information on the side effects, interactions, and limitations of prescription drugs used in the treatment of hemorrhoids. Broadly speaking, there are two sources of information on approved medications: public sources and private sources. We will emphasize free-to-use public sources.

Your Medications: The Basics[31]

The Agency for Health Care Research and Quality has published extremely useful guidelines on how you can best participate in the medication aspects of hemorrhoids. Taking medicines is not always as simple as swallowing a pill. It can involve many steps and decisions each day. The AHCRQ recommends that patients with hemorrhoids take part in treatment decisions. Do not be afraid to ask questions and talk about your concerns. By taking a moment to ask questions early, you may avoid problems later. Here are some points to cover each time a new medicine is prescribed:

- Ask about all parts of your treatment, including diet changes, exercise, and medicines.

- Ask about the risks and benefits of each medicine or other treatment you might receive.

- Ask how often you or your doctor will check for side effects from a given medication.

Do not hesitate to ask what is important to you about your medicines. You may want a medicine with the fewest side effects, or the fewest doses to take each day. You may care most about cost, or how the medicine might affect how you live or work. Or, you may want the medicine your doctor believes will work the best. Telling your doctor will help him or her select the best treatment for you.

Do not be afraid to "bother" your doctor with your concerns and questions about medications for hemorrhoids. You can also talk to a nurse or a pharmacist. They can help you better understand your treatment plan. Feel free to bring a friend or family member with you when you visit your doctor. Talking over your options with someone you trust can help you make better choices, especially if you are not feeling well. Specifically, ask your doctor the following:

- The name of the medicine and what it is supposed to do.

- How and when to take the medicine, how much to take, and for how long.

- What food, drinks, other medicines, or activities you should avoid while taking the medicine.

- What side effects the medicine may have, and what to do if they occur.

- If you can get a refill, and how often.

---

[31] This section is adapted from AHCRQ: **http://www.ahcpr.gov/consumer/ncpiebro.htm**.

- About any terms or directions you do not understand.

- What to do if you miss a dose.

- If there is written information you can take home (most pharmacies have information sheets on your prescription medicines; some even offer large-print or Spanish versions).

Do not forget to tell your doctor about all the medicines you are currently taking (not just those for hemorrhoids). This includes prescription medicines and the medicines that you buy over the counter. Then your doctor can avoid giving you a new medicine that may not work well with the medications you take now. When talking to your doctor, you may wish to prepare a list of medicines you currently take, the reason you take them, and how you take them. Be sure to include the following information for each:

- Name of medicine

- Reason taken

- Dosage

- Time(s) of day

Also include any over-the-counter medicines, such as:

- Laxatives

- Diet pills

- Vitamins

- Cold medicine

- Aspirin or other pain, headache, or fever medicine

- Cough medicine

- Allergy relief medicine

- Antacids

- Sleeping pills

- Others (include names)

Learning More about Your Medications

Because of historical investments by various organizations and the emergence of the Internet, it has become rather simple to learn about the medications your doctor has recommended for hemorrhoids. One such source is the United States Pharmacopeia. In 1820, eleven physicians met in Washington, D.C. to establish the first compendium of standard drugs for the United States. They called this compendium the "U.S. Pharmacopeia (USP)." Today, the USP is a non-profit organization consisting of 800 volunteer scientists, eleven elected officials, and 400 representatives of state associations and colleges of medicine and pharmacy. The USP is located in Rockville, Maryland, and its home page is located at **www.usp.org**. The USP currently provides standards for over 3,700 medications. The resulting USP DI® Advice for the Patient® can be accessed through the National Library of Medicine of the National Institutes of Health. The database is partially derived from lists of federally approved medications in the Food and Drug Administration's (FDA) Drug Approvals database.[32]

While the FDA database is rather large and difficult to navigate, the Phamacopeia is both user-friendly and free to use. It covers more than 9,000 prescription and over-the-counter medications. To access this database, simply type the following hyperlink into your Web browser: **http://www.nlm.nih.gov/medlineplus/druginformation.html**. To view examples of a given medication (brand names, category, description, preparation, proper use, precautions, side effects, etc.), simply follow the hyperlinks indicated within the United States Pharmacopoeia (USP). It is important to read the disclaimer by the USP (**http://www.nlm.nih.gov/medlineplus/drugdisclaimer.html**) before using the information provided.

Of course, we as editors cannot be certain as to what medications you are taking. Therefore, we have compiled a list of medications associated with the treatment of hemorrhoids. Once again, due to space limitations, we only list a sample of medications and provide hyperlinks to ample documentation (e.g. typical dosage, side effects, drug-interaction risks, etc.). The following drugs have been mentioned in the Pharmacopeia and other sources as being potentially applicable to hemorrhoids:

Anesthetics
- **Rectal - U.S. Brands:** Americaine Hemorrhoidal; Fleet Relief; Nupercainal; Pontocaine Cream+; Pontocaine Ointment; ProctoFoam/non-steroid; Tronolane; Tronothane
  http://www.nlm.nih.gov/medlineplus/druginfo/anestheticsrectal 202041.html

---

[32] Though cumbersome, the FDA database can be freely browsed at the following site: **www.fda.gov/cder/da/da.htm**.

Corticosteroids

- **Dental - U.S. Brands:** Kenalog in Orabase; Orabase-HCA; Oracort; Oralone
  http://www.nlm.nih.gov/medlineplus/druginfo/corticosteroidsdental202010.html

- **Inhalation - U.S. Brands:** AeroBid; AeroBid-M; Azmacort; Beclovent; Decadron Respihaler; Pulmicort Respules; Pulmicort Turbuhaler; Vanceril; Vanceril 84 mcg Double Strength
  http://www.nlm.nih.gov/medlineplus/druginfo/corticosteroidsinhalation202011.html

- **Nasal - U.S. Brands:** Beconase; Beconase AQ; Dexacort Turbinaire; Flonase; Nasacort; Nasacort AQ; Nasalide; Nasarel; Nasonex; Rhinocort; Vancenase; Vancenase AQ 84 mcg; Vancenase pockethaler
  http://www.nlm.nih.gov/medlineplus/druginfo/corticosteroidsnasal202012.html

- **Ophthalmic - U.S. Brands:** AK-Dex; AK-Pred; AK-Tate; Baldex; Decadron; Dexair; Dexotic; Econopred; Econopred Plus; Eflone; Flarex; Fluor-Op; FML Forte; FML Liquifilm; FML S.O.P.; HMS Liquifilm; Inflamase Forte; Inflamase Mild; I-Pred; Lite Pred; Maxidex; Ocu-Dex; Ocu-Pred; Ocu-Pr
  http://www.nlm.nih.gov/medlineplus/druginfo/corticosteroidsophthalmic202013.html

- **Otic - U.S. Brands:** Decadron
  http://www.nlm.nih.gov/medlineplus/druginfo/corticosteroidsotic202014.html

- **Rectal - U.S. Brands:** Anucort-HC; Anu-Med HC; Anuprep HC; Anusol-HC; Anutone-HC; Anuzone-HC; Cort-Dome; Cortenema; Cortifoam; Hemorrhoidal HC; Hemril-HC Uniserts; Proctocort; Proctosol-HC; Rectosol-HC
  http://www.nlm.nih.gov/medlineplus/druginfo/corticosteroidsrectal203366.html

Glycerin

- **Systemic - U.S. Brands:** Glyrol; Osmoglyn
  http://www.nlm.nih.gov/medlineplus/druginfo/glycerinsystemic202263.html

Laxatives

- **Oral - U.S. Brands:** Afko-Lube; Afko-Lube Lax 40; Agoral Marshmallow; Agoral Raspberry; Alaxin; Alophen; Alphamul; Alramucil Orange; Alramucil Regular; Bilagog; Bilax; Bisac-Evac; Black-Draught; Black-Draught Lax-Senna; Carter's Little Pills; Cholac; Chronulac; Cillium; Cit
  http://www.nlm.nih.gov/medlineplus/druginfo/laxativesoral202319.html

Pyridoxine (Vitamin B 6)

- **Systemic - U.S. Brands:** Beesix; Doxine; Nestrex; Pyri; Rodex
  http://www.nlm.nih.gov/medlineplus/druginfo/pyridoxinevitaminb6systemic202493.html

Commercial Databases

In addition to the medications listed in the USP above, a number of commercial sites are available by subscription to physicians and their institutions. You may be able to access these sources from your local medical library or your doctor's office.

Reuters Health Drug Database

The Reuters Health Drug Database can be searched by keyword at the hyperlink: **http://www.reutershealth.com/frame2/drug.html**. The following medications are listed in the Reuters' database as associated with hemorrhoids (including those with contraindications):[33]

- **Bisacodyl**
  http://www.reutershealth.com/atoz/html/Bisacodyl.htm

- **Cetirizine**
  http://www.reutershealth.com/atoz/html/Cetirizine.htm

- **Cholestyramine**
  http://www.reutershealth.com/atoz/html/Cholestyramine.htm

- **Colestipol Hydrochloride**
  http://www.reutershealth.com/atoz/html/Colestipol_Hydrochloride.htm

- **Dipyridamole Aspirin**
  http://www.reutershealth.com/atoz/html/Dipyridamole_Aspirin.htm

---

[33] Adapted from *A to Z Drug Facts* by Facts and Comparisons.

- **Estradiol**
  http://www.reutershealth.com/atoz/html/Estradiol.htm

- **Estrogens Conjugated**
  http://www.reutershealth.com/atoz/html/Estrogens_Conjugated.htm

- **Estropipate**
  http://www.reutershealth.com/atoz/html/Estropipate.htm

- **Estropipate (Piperazine Estrone Sulfate)**
  http://www.reutershealth.com/atoz/html/Estropipate_(Piperazine_Estrone_Sulfate).htm

- **Hydrocortisone (Cortisol)**
  http://www.reutershealth.com/atoz/html/Hydrocortisone_(Cortisol).htm

- **Interferon Alfacon-I**
  http://www.reutershealth.com/atoz/html/Interferon_Alfacon-I.htm

- **Rivastigmine Tartrate**
  http://www.reutershealth.com/atoz/html/Rivastigmine_Tartrate.htm

- **Rofecoxib**
  http://www.reutershealth.com/atoz/html/Rofecoxib.htm

Mosby's GenRx

Mosby's GenRx database (also available on CD-Rom and book format) covers 45,000 drug products including generics and international brands. It provides prescribing information, drug interactions, and patient information. Information in Mosby's GenRx database can be obtained at the following hyperlink: **http://www.genrx.com/Mosby/PhyGenRx/group.html**.

Physicians Desk Reference

The Physicians Desk Reference database (also available in CD-Rom and book format) is a full-text drug database. The database is searchable by brand name, generic name or by indication. It features multiple drug interactions reports. Information can be obtained at the following hyperlink: **http://physician.pdr.net/physician/templates/en/acl/psuser_t.htm**.

Other Web Sites

A number of additional Web sites discuss drug information. As an example, you may like to look at **www.drugs.com** which reproduces the information in the Pharmacopeia as well as commercial information. You may also want to consider the Web site of the Medical Letter, Inc. which allows users to download articles on various drugs and therapeutics for a nominal fee: **http://www.medletter.com/**.

Contraindications and Interactions (Hidden Dangers)

Some of the medications mentioned in the previous discussions can be problematic for patients with hemorrhoids--not because they are used in the treatment process, but because of contraindications, or side effects. Medications with contraindications are those that could react with drugs used to treat hemorrhoids or potentially create deleterious side effects in patients with hemorrhoids. You should ask your physician about any contraindications, especially as these might apply to other medications that you may be taking for common ailments.

Drug-drug interactions occur when two or more drugs react with each other. This drug-drug interaction may cause you to experience an unexpected side effect. Drug interactions may make your medications less effective, cause unexpected side effects, or increase the action of a particular drug. Some drug interactions can even be harmful to you.

Be sure to read the label every time you use a nonprescription or prescription drug, and take the time to learn about drug interactions. These precautions may be critical to your health. You can reduce the risk of potentially harmful drug interactions and side effects with a little bit of knowledge and common sense.

Drug labels contain important information about ingredients, uses, warnings, and directions which you should take the time to read and understand. Labels also include warnings about possible drug interactions. Further, drug labels may change as new information becomes available. This is why it's especially important to read the label every time you use a medication. When your doctor prescribes a new drug, discuss all over-the-counter and prescription medications, dietary supplements, vitamins, botanicals, minerals and herbals you take as well as the foods you eat. Ask your pharmacist for the package insert for each prescription drug you take.

The package insert provides more information about potential drug interactions.

A Final Warning

At some point, you may hear of alternative medications from friends, relatives, or in the news media. Advertisements may suggest that certain alternative drugs can produce positive results for patients with hemorrhoids. Exercise caution--some of these drugs may have fraudulent claims, and others may actually hurt you. The Food and Drug Administration (FDA) is the official U.S. agency charged with discovering which medications are likely to improve the health of patients with hemorrhoids. The FDA warns patients to watch out for[34]:

- Secret formulas (real scientists share what they know)

- Amazing breakthroughs or miracle cures (real breakthroughs don't happen very often; when they do, real scientists do not call them amazing or miracles)

- Quick, painless, or guaranteed cures

- If it sounds too good to be true, it probably isn't true.

If you have any questions about any kind of medical treatment, the FDA may have an office near you. Look for their number in the blue pages of the phone book. You can also contact the FDA through its toll-free number, 1-888-INFO-FDA (1-888-463-6332), or on the World Wide Web at **www.fda.gov**.

General References

In addition to the resources provided earlier in this chapter, the following general references describe medications (sorted alphabetically by title; hyperlinks provide rankings, information and reviews at Amazon.com):

- **Drug Development: Molecular Targets for Gi Diseases** by Timothy S. Gaginella (Editor), Antonio Guglietta (Editor); Hardcover - 288 pages (December 1999), Humana Press; ISBN: 0896035891; http://www.amazon.com/exec/obidos/ASIN/0896035891/icongroupinterna

---

[34] This section has been adapted from **http://www.fda.gov/opacom/lowlit/medfraud.html**

- **Drug Therapy for Gastrointestinal and Liver Diseases** by Michael J.G. Farthing, M.D. (Editor), Anne B. Ballinger (Editor); Hardcover - 346 pages, 1st edition (August 15, 2001), Martin Dunitz Ltd.; ISBN: 1853177334; http://www.amazon.com/exec/obidos/ASIN/1853177334/icongroupinterna

- **Immunopharmacology of the Gastrointestinal System (Handbook of Immunopharmacology)** by John L. Wallace (Editor); Hardcover (October 1997), Academic Press; ISBN: 0127328602; http://www.amazon.com/exec/obidos/ASIN/0127328602/icongroupinterna

- **A Pharmacologic Approach to Gastrointestinal Disorders** by James H. Lewis, M.D. (Editor); Hardcover – (February 1994), Lippincott, Williams & Wilkins; ISBN: 0683049704; http://www.amazon.com/exec/obidos/ASIN/0683049704/icongroupinterna

Vocabulary Builder

The following vocabulary builder gives definitions of words used in this chapter that have not been defined in previous chapters:

Cetirizine: A potent second-generation histamine H1 antagonist that is effective in the treatment of allergic rhinitis, chronic urticaria, and pollen-induced asthma. Unlike many traditional antihistamines, it does not cause drowsiness or anticholinergic side effects. [NIH]

Estradiol: The most potent mammalian estrogenic hormone. It is produced in the ovary, placenta, testis, and possibly the adrenal cortex. [NIH]

Inhalation: The drawing of air or other substances into the lungs. [EU]

Ophthalmic: Pertaining to the eye. [EU]

Pharmacologic: Pertaining to pharmacology or to the properties and reactions of drugs. [EU]

Senna: Preparations of Cassia senna L. and C. angustifolia of the Leguminosae. They contain sennosides, which are anthraquinone type cathartics and are used in many different preparations as laxatives. [NIH]

APPENDIX B. RESEARCHING ALTERNATIVE MEDICINE

Overview

Complementary and alternative medicine (CAM) is one of the most contentious aspects of modern medical practice. You may have heard of these treatments on the radio or on television. Maybe you have seen articles written about these treatments in magazines, newspapers, or books. Perhaps your friends or doctor have mentioned alternatives.

In this chapter, we will begin by giving you a broad perspective on complementary and alternative therapies. Next, we will introduce you to official information sources on CAM relating to hemorrhoids. Finally, at the conclusion of this chapter, we will provide a list of readings on hemorrhoids from various authors. We will begin, however, with the National Center for Complementary and Alternative Medicine's (NCCAM) overview of complementary and alternative medicine.

What Is CAM?[35]

Complementary and alternative medicine (CAM) covers a broad range of healing philosophies, approaches, and therapies. Generally, it is defined as those treatments and healthcare practices which are not taught in medical schools, used in hospitals, or reimbursed by medical insurance companies. Many CAM therapies are termed "holistic," which generally means that the healthcare practitioner considers the whole person, including physical, mental, emotional, and spiritual health. Some of these therapies are also known as "preventive," which means that the practitioner educates and

---

[35] Adapted from the NCCAM: **http://nccam.nih.gov/nccam/fcp/faq/index.html#what-is**.

treats the person to prevent health problems from arising, rather than treating symptoms after problems have occurred.

People use CAM treatments and therapies in a variety of ways. Therapies are used alone (often referred to as alternative), in combination with other alternative therapies, or in addition to conventional treatment (sometimes referred to as complementary). Complementary and alternative medicine, or "integrative medicine," includes a broad range of healing philosophies, approaches, and therapies. Some approaches are consistent with physiological principles of Western medicine, while others constitute healing systems with non-Western origins. While some therapies are far outside the realm of accepted Western medical theory and practice, others are becoming established in mainstream medicine.

Complementary and alternative therapies are used in an effort to prevent illness, reduce stress, prevent or reduce side effects and symptoms, or control or cure disease. Some commonly used methods of complementary or alternative therapy include mind/body control interventions such as visualization and relaxation, manual healing including acupressure and massage, homeopathy, vitamins or herbal products, and acupuncture.

What Are the Domains of Alternative Medicine?[36]

The list of CAM practices changes continually. The reason being is that these new practices and therapies are often proved to be safe and effective, and therefore become generally accepted as "mainstream" healthcare practices. Today, CAM practices may be grouped within five major domains: (1) alternative medical systems, (2) mind-body interventions, (3) biologically-based treatments, (4) manipulative and body-based methods, and (5) energy therapies. The individual systems and treatments comprising these categories are too numerous to list in this sourcebook. Thus, only limited examples are provided within each.

Alternative Medical Systems

Alternative medical systems involve complete systems of theory and practice that have evolved independent of, and often prior to, conventional biomedical approaches. Many are traditional systems of medicine that are

[36] Adapted from the NCCAM: **http://nccam.nih.gov/nccam/fcp/classify/index.html**

practiced by individual cultures throughout the world, including a number of venerable Asian approaches.

Traditional oriental medicine emphasizes the balance or disturbances of qi (pronounced chi) or vital energy in health and disease, respectively. Traditional oriental medicine consists of a group of techniques and methods including acupuncture, herbal medicine, oriental massage, and qi gong (a form of energy therapy). Acupuncture involves stimulating specific anatomic points in the body for therapeutic purposes, usually by puncturing the skin with a thin needle.

Ayurveda is India's traditional system of medicine. Ayurvedic medicine (meaning "science of life") is a comprehensive system of medicine that places equal emphasis on body, mind, and spirit. Ayurveda strives to restore the innate harmony of the individual. Some of the primary Ayurvedic treatments include diet, exercise, meditation, herbs, massage, exposure to sunlight, and controlled breathing.

Other traditional healing systems have been developed by the world's indigenous populations. These populations include Native American, Aboriginal, African, Middle Eastern, Tibetan, and Central and South American cultures. Homeopathy and naturopathy are also examples of complete alternative medicine systems.

Homeopathic medicine is an unconventional Western system that is based on the principle that "like cures like," i.e., that the same substance that in large doses produces the symptoms of an illness, in very minute doses cures it. Homeopathic health practitioners believe that the more dilute the remedy, the greater its potency. Therefore, they use small doses of specially prepared plant extracts and minerals to stimulate the body's defense mechanisms and healing processes in order to treat illness.

Naturopathic medicine is based on the theory that disease is a manifestation of alterations in the processes by which the body naturally heals itself and emphasizes health restoration rather than disease treatment. Naturopathic physicians employ an array of healing practices, including the following: diet and clinical nutrition, homeopathy, acupuncture, herbal medicine, hydrotherapy (the use of water in a range of temperatures and methods of applications), spinal and soft-tissue manipulation, physical therapies (such as those involving electrical currents, ultrasound, and light), therapeutic counseling, and pharmacology.

Mind-Body Interventions

Mind-body interventions employ a variety of techniques designed to facilitate the mind's capacity to affect bodily function and symptoms. Only a select group of mind-body interventions having well-documented theoretical foundations are considered CAM. For example, patient education and cognitive-behavioral approaches are now considered "mainstream." On the other hand, complementary and alternative medicine includes meditation, certain uses of hypnosis, dance, music, and art therapy, as well as prayer and mental healing.

Biological-Based Therapies

This category of CAM includes natural and biological-based practices, interventions, and products, many of which overlap with conventional medicine's use of dietary supplements. This category includes herbal, special dietary, orthomolecular, and individual biological therapies.

Herbal therapy employs an individual herb or a mixture of herbs for healing purposes. An herb is a plant or plant part that produces and contains chemical substances that act upon the body. Special diet therapies, such as those proposed by Drs. Atkins, Ornish, Pritikin, and Weil, are believed to prevent and/or control illness as well as promote health. Orthomolecular therapies aim to treat disease with varying concentrations of chemicals such as magnesium, melatonin, and mega-doses of vitamins. Biological therapies include, for example, the use of laetrile and shark cartilage to treat cancer and the use of bee pollen to treat autoimmune and inflammatory diseases.

Manipulative and Body-Based Methods

This category includes methods that are based on manipulation and/or movement of the body. For example, chiropractors focus on the relationship between structure and function, primarily pertaining to the spine, and how that relationship affects the preservation and restoration of health. Chiropractors use manipulative therapy as an integral treatment tool.

In contrast, osteopaths place particular emphasis on the musculoskeletal system and practice osteopathic manipulation. Osteopaths believe that all of the body's systems work together and that disturbances in one system may have an impact upon function elsewhere in the body. Massage therapists manipulate the soft tissues of the body to normalize those tissues.

Energy Therapies

Energy therapies focus on energy fields originating within the body (biofields) or those from other sources (electromagnetic fields). Biofield therapies are intended to affect energy fields (the existence of which is not yet experimentally proven) that surround and penetrate the human body. Some forms of energy therapy manipulate biofields by applying pressure and/or manipulating the body by placing the hands in or through these fields. Examples include Qi gong, Reiki and Therapeutic Touch.

Qi gong is a component of traditional oriental medicine that combines movement, meditation, and regulation of breathing to enhance the flow of vital energy (qi) in the body, improve blood circulation, and enhance immune function. Reiki, the Japanese word representing Universal Life Energy, is based on the belief that, by channeling spiritual energy through the practitioner, the spirit is healed and, in turn, heals the physical body. Therapeutic Touch is derived from the ancient technique of "laying-on of hands." It is based on the premises that the therapist's healing force affects the patient's recovery and that healing is promoted when the body's energies are in balance. By passing their hands over the patient, these healers identify energy imbalances.

Bioelectromagnetic-based therapies involve the unconventional use of electromagnetic fields to treat illnesses or manage pain. These therapies are often used to treat asthma, cancer, and migraine headaches. Types of electromagnetic fields which are manipulated in these therapies include pulsed fields, magnetic fields, and alternating current or direct current fields.

Can Alternatives Affect My Treatment?

A critical issue in pursuing complementary alternatives mentioned thus far is the risk that these might have undesirable interactions with your medical treatment. It becomes all the more important to speak with your doctor who can offer advice on the use of alternatives. Official sources confirm this view. Though written for women, we find that the National Women's Health Information Center's advice on pursuing alternative medicine is appropriate for patients of both genders and all ages.[37]

---

[37] Adapted from **http://www.4woman.gov/faq/alternative.htm** .

Is It Okay to Want Both Traditional and Alternative Medicine?

Should you wish to explore non-traditional types of treatment, be sure to discuss all issues concerning treatments and therapies with your healthcare provider, whether a physician or practitioner of complementary and alternative medicine. Competent healthcare management requires knowledge of both conventional and alternative therapies you are taking for the practitioner to have a complete picture of your treatment plan.

The decision to use complementary and alternative treatments is an important one. Consider before selecting an alternative therapy, the safety and effectiveness of the therapy or treatment, the expertise and qualifications of the healthcare practitioner, and the quality of delivery. These topics should be considered when selecting any practitioner or therapy.

Finding CAM References on Hemorrhoids

Having read the previous discussion, you may be wondering which complementary or alternative treatments might be appropriate for hemorrhoids. For the remainder of this chapter, we will direct you to a number of official sources which can assist you in researching studies and publications. Some of these articles are rather technical, so some patience may be required.

The Combined Health Information Database

For a targeted search, The Combined Health Information Database is a bibliographic database produced by health-related agencies of the Federal Government (mostly from the National Institutes of Health). This database is updated four times a year at the end of January, April, July, and October. Check the titles, summaries, and availability of CAM-related information by using the "Simple Search" option at the following Web site: **http://chid.nih.gov/simple/simple.html**. In the drop box at the top, select "Complementary and Alternative Medicine." Then type "hemorrhoids" (or synonyms) in the second search box. We recommend that you select 100 "documents per page" and to check the "whole records" options. The following was extracted using this technique:

- **Hemorrhoids and Varicose Veins: A Review of Treatment Options**

  Source: Alternative Medicine Review. 6(2): 126-140. April 2001.

Summary: This journal article reviews the treatment options, including complementary and alternative therapies, for hemorrhoids and varicose veins. According to the author, conservative therapies such as diet, hydrotherapy, mechanical compression for varicose veins, topical agents for hemorrhoids, and lifestyle factors are the standard noninvasive approaches to these conditions. The next line of therapy involves the use of other nonsurgical modalities, including electrocoagulation, sclerotherapy, cryotherapy, photocoagulation, and diathermy. Oral dietary supplementation is another option for the treatment of hemorrhoids and varicose veins. The pathogenesis of both conditions is associated with a loss of vascular integrity. Several botanical extracts have been shown to improve microcirculation, capillary flow, and vascular tone, and to strengthen the connective tissue of the perivascular amorphous substrate. Oral supplementation with 'Aesculus hippocastanum,' 'Ruscus aculeatus,' 'Centella asiatica,' 'Hamamelis virginiana,' and bioflavonoids may be useful. The article has 3 figures, 1 table, and 70 references.

- **Phytotherapeutic Approaches to Common Dermatologic Conditions**

Source: Archives of Dermatology. 134: 1401-1404. 1998.

Summary: This journal article describes some herbal approaches to common skin conditions, and reviews recent studies that support their use. Preparations of marigold ('Calendula officinalis') flowers have long been used as topical remedies for burns, bruises, cuts, rashes, minor wounds, and leg ulcers. Chamomile ('Matricaria recutita') is used for the treatment of mild gastrointestinal tract conditions, irritation and inflammation of the oral mucosa, and minor irritations of the skin. Witch hazel ('Hamamelis virginiana') has a long history of use for the treatment of hemorrhoids, burns, cancer symptoms, tuberculosis, colds, and fever. Topical preparations also have been used for symptomatic relief of itching and minor skin irritation. However, the distilled witch hazel extracts available over-the-counter in the United States lack the tannins thought to be of use in dermatologic treatment. Licorice root commonly is used in traditional Chinese herbal medicine combinations for atopic dermatitis. Capsaicin (the pungent principle of cayenne pepper) and aloe have shown promise in the treatment of psoriasis. Lemon balm ('Melissa officinalis') has been shown to have antiviral activity against the herpes simplex 1 virus, and to help herpetic lesions heal faster. The article has 39 references.

- **Homeopathy for the Modern Pregnant Woman and Her Infant: A Therapeutic Practice Guidebook for Midwives, Physicians and Practitioners**

  Source: San Antonio, TX: Benchmark Homeopathic Publications. 1997. 415 p.

  Contact: Available from Benchmark Homeopathic Publications. 13526 George Road, Suite 101-F, San Antonio, TX 78230-3002. 210-493-0561, FAX: 210-493-0567. www.stic.net/users/benchmarkpub; benchmarkpub@stic.net. Price: $59.95. ISBN: 0965318702.

  Summary: This book is a therapeutic practice guide to homeopathy for pregnant women and infants. It is intended for use by midwives, physicians, and other practitioners with a working knowledge of the theory, principles, and practice of classical homeopathy. Chapter 1 provides an overview of homeopathy and its use in midwifery, including safety issues and general practice guidelines. Chapter 2 discusses the importance of nutrition and other lifestyle factors in prenatal care. Chapters 3 through 10 list remedies for specific conditions, including morning sickness, constipation, hemorrhoids, varicose veins, miscarriage from various causes, serious problems during pregnancy, problems during labor, postpartum difficulties, problems in the newborn, and breast and nursing problems. Chapter 11 provides quick keynote references to help the practitioner locate the needed remedy rapidly and easily in emergency situations. Appendices contain additional information about prenatal care, the midwifery remedy kit, organizations and associations, homeopathic pharmacies and remedy sources, educational institutions, literature sources, recommended readings, and names of remedies. This book also has a glossary, a list of references, and an index.

- **Herbs To Improve Digestion: Herbal Remedies for Stomach Pain, Constipation, Ulcers, Colitis and Other Gastrointestinal Problems**

  Source: New Canaan, CT: Keats Publishing, Inc. 1996. 90 p.

  Contact: Available from Keats Publishing, Inc., division of NTC/Contemporary. 203 Kitchawan Road, South Salem, NY 10590. 914-533-1175, FAX: 914-533-0035. Price: $4.95. ISBN: 087983742X.

  Summary: This book describes the use of herbs to improve digestion, including herbal remedies for stomach pain, constipation, ulcers, colitis, and other gastrointestinal problems. It provides an overview of the digestive system, including the digestive process and the role of bacteria. It discusses juicing, food sensitivities, digestive enzymes, and the role of exercise in improving digestion. It contains descriptions of frequently occurring digestive disorders such as colic, constipation, Crohn's disease, diarrhea, diverticulitis, flatulence, gastritis, heartburn, hemorrhoids, indigestion, irritable bowel syndrome, and ulcers. It provides suggestions on using herbs to treat these problems, and describes 12 steps to better digestion. This book contains a resource list and an index.

- **Topical Applications of Botanical Medicine: Aloe Vera and Other Medicinal Plants for Healing**

  Source: Alternative and Complementary Therapies. p. 241-244. July-August 1996.

  Summary: This journal article discusses topical applications of medical herbs. Aloe ('Aloe vera)' is a safe, effective treatment for mild burns and sunburns, frostbite, and minor, uncomplicated wounds. It also may help in treating radiation-induced dermatitis and mucous membrane ulcers. However, it is important to use the clear, mucilaginous gel found in the leaf center rather than the latex of the leaf base. Echinacea ('Echinacea purpurea') and comfrey ('Symphytum officinale') appear to be effective topical treatments for minor cuts and scrapes. Although comfrey causes liver damage when ingested, it is safe when used topically. St. John's wort ('Hypericum perforatum'), witch hazel ('Hamamelis virginiana)', and horse chestnut ('Aesculus hippocastanum') are astringent herbs that can be used to treat hemorrhoids, eczema, varicose veins, bruises, and chronic venous insufficiency. Tea tree ('Melaleuca alternifolia') oil recently has become popular as a antifungal topical, but it should not be applied to eczema. The essential oils of thyme ('Thymus vulgaris') and rosemary ('Rosimarinus officinalis') also may have some beneficial antiseptic actions on the skin. Eczema and other skin inflammations can be treated with soothing, antiallergic herbs such as white oak ('Quercus alba'), German chamomile ('Matricaria recutita'), and calendula ('Calendula officinalis'). The article has 3 tables and 20 references.

National Center for Complementary and Alternative Medicine

The National Center for Complementary and Alternative Medicine (NCCAM) of the National Institutes of Health (http://nccam.nih.gov) has created a link to the National Library of Medicine's databases to allow patients to search for articles that specifically relate to hemorrhoids and complementary medicine. To search the database, go to the following Web site: **www.nlm.nih.gov/nccam/camonpubmed.html**. Select "CAM on PubMed." Enter "hemorrhoids" (or synonyms) into the search box. Click "Go." The following references provide information on particular aspects of complementary and alternative medicine (CAM) that are related to hemorrhoids:

- **"Somatoanal" reflex or "thermosphincteric" reflex?**
  Author(s): Shafik A.
  Source: Diseases of the Colon and Rectum. 2000 May; 43(5): 726-8. No Abstract Available.
  http://www.ncbi.nlm.nih.gov:80/entrez/query.fcgi?cmd=Retrieve&db=PubMed&list_uids=10826442&dopt=Abstract

- **Ask the midwife. Prevention and care of hemorrhoids, including homeopathic remedies.**
  Author(s): Goldstein L.
  Source: Birth Gaz. 2000 Spring; 16(2): 13-6. No Abstract Available.
  http://www.ncbi.nlm.nih.gov:80/entrez/query.fcgi?cmd=Retrieve&db=PubMed&list_uids=11899340&dopt=Abstract

- **Combined traditional Chinese and western medicine sclerosing therapy in internal hemorrhoids.**
  Author(s): Ren CP.
  Source: Chin Med J (Engl). 1977 March; 3(2): 137-42. No Abstract Available.
  http://www.ncbi.nlm.nih.gov:80/entrez/query.fcgi?cmd=Retrieve&db=PubMed&list_uids=408110&dopt=Abstract

- **Direct current electrotherapy of internal hemorrhoids: an effective, safe, and painless outpatient approach.**
  Author(s): Norman DA, Newton R, Nicholas GV.
  Source: The American Journal of Gastroenterology. 1989 May; 84(5): 482-7.
  http://www.ncbi.nlm.nih.gov:80/entrez/query.fcgi?cmd=Retrieve&db=PubMed&list_uids=2785755&dopt=Abstract

- **Efficacy of an indigenous formulation in patients with bleeding piles: a preliminary clinical study.**
  Author(s): Paranjpe P, Patki P, Joshi N.
  Source: Fitoterapia. 2000 February; 71(1): 41-5.
  http://www.ncbi.nlm.nih.gov:80/entrez/query.fcgi?cmd=Retrieve&db=PubMed&list_uids=11449468&dopt=Abstract

- **He/Ne laser treatment of hemorrhoids.**
  Author(s): Trelles MA, Rotinen S.

Source: Acupunct Electrother Res. 1983; 8(3-4): 289-95.
http://www.ncbi.nlm.nih.gov:80/entrez/query.fcgi?cmd=Retrieve&db=
PubMed&list_uids=6145304&dopt=Abstract

- **Hemorrhoids and varicose veins: a review of treatment options.**
  Author(s): MacKay D.
  Source: Alternative Medicine Review : a Journal of Clinical Therapeutic.
  2001 April; 6(2): 126-40. Review.
  http://www.ncbi.nlm.nih.gov:80/entrez/query.fcgi?cmd=Retrieve&db=
  PubMed&list_uids=11302778&dopt=Abstract

- **Hemorrhoids, varicose veins and deep vein thrombosis: epidemiologic features and suggested causative factors.**
  Author(s): Burkitt DP.
  Source: Canadian Journal of Surgery. Journal Canadien De Chirurgie.
  1975 September; 18(5): 483-8. No Abstract Available.
  http://www.ncbi.nlm.nih.gov:80/entrez/query.fcgi?cmd=Retrieve&db=
  PubMed&list_uids=1175115&dopt=Abstract

- **High-fiber diet reduces bleeding and pain in patients with hemorrhoids: a double-blind trial of Vi-Siblin.**
  Author(s): Moesgaard F, Nielsen ML, Hansen JB, Knudsen JT.
  Source: Diseases of the Colon and Rectum. 1982 July-August; 25(5): 454-6.
  No Abstract Available.
  http://www.ncbi.nlm.nih.gov:80/entrez/query.fcgi?cmd=Retrieve&db=
  PubMed&list_uids=6284457&dopt=Abstract

- **Micronized purified flavonidic fraction compared favorably with rubber band ligation and fiber alone in the management of bleeding hemorrhoids: randomized controlled trial.**
  Author(s): Ho YH, Tan M, Seow-Choen F.
  Source: Diseases of the Colon and Rectum. 2000 January; 43(1): 66-9.
  http://www.ncbi.nlm.nih.gov:80/entrez/query.fcgi?cmd=Retrieve&db=
  PubMed&list_uids=10813126&dopt=Abstract

- **Piles. Ideas on how to reduce the pain from haemorrhoids.**
  Author(s): Hartley J.
  Source: Pract Midwife. 1999 April; 2(4): 12-3. No Abstract Available.
  http://www.ncbi.nlm.nih.gov:80/entrez/query.fcgi?cmd=Retrieve&db=
  PubMed&list_uids=10427282&dopt=Abstract

- **The biblical plague of "hemorrhoids". An outbreak of bilharziasis.**
  Author(s): Dirckx JH.
  Source: The American Journal of Dermatopathology. 1985 August; 7(4): 341-6. No Abstract Available.
  http://www.ncbi.nlm.nih.gov:80/entrez/query.fcgi?cmd=Retrieve&db=PubMed&list_uids=3939579&dopt=Abstract

Additional Web Resources

A number of additional Web sites offer encyclopedic information covering CAM and related topics. The following is a representative sample:

- Alternative Medicine Foundation, Inc.: **http://www.herbmed.org/**

- AOL: **http://search.aol.com/cat.adp?id=169&layer=&from=subcats**

- Chinese Medicine: **http://www.newcenturynutrition.com/**

- drkoop.com®:
  http://www.drkoop.com/InteractiveMedicine/IndexC.html

- Family Village: **http://www.familyvillage.wisc.edu/med_altn.htm**

- Google: **http://directory.google.com/Top/Health/Alternative/**

- Healthnotes: **http://www.thedacare.org/healthnotes/**

- Open Directory Project: **http://dmoz.org/Health/Alternative/**

- TPN.com: **http://www.tnp.com/**

- Yahoo.com: **http://dir.yahoo.com/Health/Alternative_Medicine/**

- WebMD®Health: **http://my.webmd.com/drugs_and_herbs**

- WellNet: **http://www.wellnet.ca/herbsa-c.htm**

- WholeHealthMD.com:
  http://www.wholehealthmd.com/reflib/0,1529,,00.html

The following is a specific Web list relating to hemorrhoids; please note that any particular subject below may indicate either a therapeutic use, or a contraindication (potential danger), and does not reflect an official recommendation:

- **General Overview**

  Hemorrhoids
  Source: Healthnotes, Inc.; www.healthnotes.com
  Hyperlink:
  http://www.thedacare.org/healthnotes/Concern/Hemorrhoids.htm

  Hemorrhoids
  Source: Integrative Medicine Communications; www.onemedicine.com
  Hyperlink:
  http://www.drkoop.com/InteractiveMedicine/ConsLookups/Uses/he
  morrhoids.html

  Hemorrhoids
  Source: Integrative Medicine Communications; www.onemedicine.com
  Hyperlink:
  http://www.drkoop.com/interactivemedicine/ConsConditions/Hemor
  rhoidscc.html

  Hemorrhoids
  Source: Prima Communications, Inc.
  Hyperlink: http://www.personalhealthzone.com/pg000292.html

- **Alternative Therapy**

  Ayurveda
  Source: WholeHealthMD.com, LLC.; www.wholehealthmd.com
  Hyperlink:
  http://www.wholehealthmd.com/refshelf/substances_view/0,1525,672,
  00.html

  Colon therapy
  Source: WholeHealthMD.com, LLC.; www.wholehealthmd.com
  Hyperlink:
  http://www.wholehealthmd.com/refshelf/substances_view/0,1525,682,
  00.html

  Hydrotherapy
  Source: WholeHealthMD.com, LLC.; www.wholehealthmd.com
  Hyperlink:
  http://www.wholehealthmd.com/refshelf/substances_view/0,1525,705,
  00.html

Osteopathy
Source: WholeHealthMD.com, LLC.; www.wholehealthmd.com
Hyperlink:
http://www.wholehealthmd.com/refshelf/substances_view/0,1525,724,
00.html

- ### Chinese Medicine

  ### Huanglian
  Alternative names: Golden Thread; Rhizoma Coptidis
  Source: Chinese Materia Medica
  Hyperlink: http://www.newcenturynutrition.com/

  ### Huhuanglian
  Alternative names: Figwortflower Picrorhiza Rhizome; Rhizoma
  Picrorhizae
  Source: Chinese Materia Medica
  Hyperlink: http://www.newcenturynutrition.com/

  ### Madouling
  Alternative names: Dutohmanspipe Fruit; Fructus Aristolochiae
  Source: Chinese Materia Medica
  Hyperlink: http://www.newcenturynutrition.com/

  ### Mangxiao
  Alternative names: Sodium Sulfate; Natrii Sulfas1
  Source: Chinese Materia Medica
  Hyperlink: http://www.newcenturynutrition.com/

  ### Mubiezi
  Alternative names: Cochinchina Momordica Seed; Semen Momordicae
  Source: Chinese Materia Medica
  Hyperlink: http://www.newcenturynutrition.com/

- ### Homeopathy

  ### Aesculus hippocastanum
  Source: Healthnotes, Inc.; www.healthnotes.com
  Hyperlink:
  http://www.thedacare.org/healthnotes/Homeo_Homeoix/Aesculus_hi
  ppocastanum.htm

Aloe
Source: Healthnotes, Inc.; www.healthnotes.com
Hyperlink:
http://www.thedacare.org/healthnotes/Homeo_Homeoix/Aloe.htm

Arnica
Source: Healthnotes, Inc.; www.healthnotes.com
Hyperlink:
http://www.thedacare.org/healthnotes/Homeo_Homeoix/Arnica.htm

Calcarea fluorica
Source: Healthnotes, Inc.; www.healthnotes.com
Hyperlink:
http://www.thedacare.org/healthnotes/Homeo_Homeoix/Calcarea_flu
orica.htm

Graphites
Source: Healthnotes, Inc.; www.healthnotes.com
Hyperlink:
http://www.thedacare.org/healthnotes/Homeo_Homeoix/Graphites.ht
m

Hamamelis
Source: Healthnotes, Inc.; www.healthnotes.com
Hyperlink:
http://www.thedacare.org/healthnotes/Homeo_Homeoix/Hamamelis.
htm

Ignatia
Source: Healthnotes, Inc.; www.healthnotes.com
Hyperlink:
http://www.thedacare.org/healthnotes/Homeo_Homeoix/Ignatia.htm

Pulsatilla
Source: Healthnotes, Inc.; www.healthnotes.com
Hyperlink:
http://www.thedacare.org/healthnotes/Homeo_Homeoix/Pulsatilla.ht
m

Sulphur
Source: Healthnotes, Inc.; www.healthnotes.com

Hyperlink:
http://www.thedacare.org/healthnotes/Homeo_Homeoix/Sulphur.ht
m

- **Herbs and Supplements**

    Achillea millefolium
    Source: Integrative Medicine Communications; www.onemedicine.com
    Hyperlink:
    http://www.drkoop.com/interactivemedicine/ConsHerbs/Yarrowch.ht
    ml

    Aesculus
    Alternative names: Horse Chestnut; Aesculus hippocastanum L.
    Source: Alternative Medicine Foundation, Inc.; www.amfoundation.org
    Hyperlink: http://www.herbmed.org/

    Agrimony
    Source: WholeHealthMD.com, LLC.; www.wholehealthmd.com
    Hyperlink:
    http://www.wholehealthmd.com/refshelf/substances_view/0,1525,833,
    00.html

    Aloe
    Alternative names: Aloe vera, Aloe barbadensis, Aloe ferox , Aloe Vera
    Source: Integrative Medicine Communications; www.onemedicine.com
    Hyperlink:
    http://www.drkoop.com/interactivemedicine/ConsHerbs/Aloech.html

    Aloe Vera
    Source: Integrative Medicine Communications; www.onemedicine.com
    Hyperlink:
    http://www.drkoop.com/interactivemedicine/ConsHerbs/Aloech.html

    Aortic Glycosaminoglycans
    Source: Prima Communications, Inc.
    Hyperlink: http://www.personalhealthzone.com/pg000096.html

    Aortic Glycosaminoglycans
    Source: Prima Communications, Inc.
    Hyperlink: http://www.personalhealthzone.com/pg000292.html

Bilberry
Alternative names: Vaccinium myrtillus, European Blueberry, Huckleberry
Source: Integrative Medicine Communications; www.onemedicine.com
Hyperlink:
http://www.drkoop.com/interactivemedicine/ConsHerbs/Bilberrych.html

Bilberry
Source: Prima Communications, Inc.
Hyperlink: http://www.personalhealthzone.com/pg000107.html

Bilberry
Source: WholeHealthMD.com, LLC.; www.wholehealthmd.com
Hyperlink:
http://www.wholehealthmd.com/refshelf/substances_view/0,1525,10007,00.html

Blackberry
Source: WholeHealthMD.com, LLC.; www.wholehealthmd.com
Hyperlink:
http://www.wholehealthmd.com/refshelf/substances_view/0,1525,837,00.html

Bromelain
Source: Prima Communications, Inc.
Hyperlink: http://www.personalhealthzone.com/pg000117.html

Bupleurum
Alternative names: Bupleurum chinense, Bupleurum falcatum
Source: Healthnotes, Inc.; www.healthnotes.com
Hyperlink:
http://www.thedacare.org/healthnotes/Herb/Bupleurum.htm

Butcher's Broom
Source: Prima Communications, Inc.
Hyperlink: http://www.personalhealthzone.com/pg000119.html

Butcher's Broom
Source: The Canadian Internet Directory for Holistic Help, WellNet, Health and Wellness Network; www.wellnet.ca
Hyperlink: http://www.wellnet.ca/herbsa-c.htm

Butcher's broom
Source: WholeHealthMD.com, LLC.; www.wholehealthmd.com
Hyperlink:
http://www.wholehealthmd.com/refshelf/substances_view/0,1525,100
10,00.html

Caffeine
Source: Integrative Medicine Communications; www.onemedicine.com
Hyperlink:
http://www.drkoop.com/interactivemedicine/ConsConditions/Hemor
rhoidscc.html

Calendula
Source: Prima Communications, Inc.
Hyperlink: http://www.personalhealthzone.com/pg000121.html

Cascara sagrada
Source: WholeHealthMD.com, LLC.; www.wholehealthmd.com
Hyperlink:
http://www.wholehealthmd.com/refshelf/substances_view/0,1525,100
13,00.html

Chamaemelum nobile
Source: Integrative Medicine Communications; www.onemedicine.com
Hyperlink:
http://www.drkoop.com/interactivemedicine/ConsHerbs/Chamomile
Romanch.html

Chamomile, German
Alternative names: Matricaria recutita
Source: Integrative Medicine Communications; www.onemedicine.com
Hyperlink:
http://www.drkoop.com/interactivemedicine/ConsHerbs/Chamomile
Germanch.html

Chamomile, Roman
Alternative names: Chamaemelum nobile
Source: Integrative Medicine Communications; www.onemedicine.com
Hyperlink:
http://www.drkoop.com/interactivemedicine/ConsHerbs/Chamomile
Romanch.html

Collinsonia
Source: Prima Communications, Inc.
Hyperlink: http://www.personalhealthzone.com/pg000292.html

Collinsonia
Source: The Canadian Internet Directory for Holistic Help, WellNet, Health and Wellness Network; www.wellnet.ca
Hyperlink: http://www.wellnet.ca/herbsa-c.htm

Comfrey
Source: Integrative Medicine Communications; www.onemedicine.com
Hyperlink:
http://www.drkoop.com/interactivemedicine/ConsConditions/Hemor rhoidscc.html

European Blueberry
Source: Integrative Medicine Communications; www.onemedicine.com
Hyperlink:
http://www.drkoop.com/interactivemedicine/ConsHerbs/Bilberrych.h tml

Evening Primrose
Alternative names: Oenothera biennis, Sun Drop
Source: Integrative Medicine Communications; www.onemedicine.com
Hyperlink:
http://www.drkoop.com/interactivemedicine/ConsHerbs/EveningPri mrosech.html

Fiber
Source: Healthnotes, Inc.; www.healthnotes.com
Hyperlink:
http://www.thedacare.org/healthnotes/Concern/Hemorrhoids.htm

Fiber
Source: Healthnotes, Inc.; www.healthnotes.com
Hyperlink: http://www.thedacare.org/healthnotes/Supp/Fiber.htm

Fiber
Source: Integrative Medicine Communications; www.onemedicine.com
Hyperlink:
http://www.drkoop.com/interactivemedicine/ConsConditions/Hemor rhoidscc.html

Fiber
Source: Integrative Medicine Communications; www.onemedicine.com
Hyperlink:
http://www.drkoop.com/interactivemedicine/ConsSupplements/Fiber
cs.html

Flavonoids
Source: Healthnotes, Inc.; www.healthnotes.com
Hyperlink:
http://www.thedacare.org/healthnotes/Supp/Flavonoids.htm

Flavonoids
Source: Healthnotes, Inc.; www.healthnotes.com
Hyperlink:
http://www.thedacare.org/healthnotes/Concern/Hemorrhoids.htm

Flavonoids
Source: Prima Communications, Inc.
Hyperlink: http://www.personalhealthzone.com/pg000292.html

Flavonoids
Source: WholeHealthMD.com, LLC.; www.wholehealthmd.com
Hyperlink:
http://www.wholehealthmd.com/refshelf/substances_view/0,1525,782,
00.html

German Chamomile
Alternative names: Matricaria recutita
Source: Integrative Medicine Communications; www.onemedicine.com
Hyperlink:
http://www.drkoop.com/interactivemedicine/ConsHerbs/Chamomile
Germanch.html

Gotu Kola
Source: Prima Communications, Inc.
Hyperlink: http://www.personalhealthzone.com/pg000172.html

Green Tea
Source: Integrative Medicine Communications; www.onemedicine.com
Hyperlink:
http://www.drkoop.com/interactivemedicine/ConsConditions/Hemor
rhoidscc.html

Horse Chestnut
Alternative names: Aesculus hippocastanum
Source: Healthnotes, Inc.; www.healthnotes.com
Hyperlink:
http://www.thedacare.org/healthnotes/Herb/Horse_Chestnut.htm

Horse Chestnut
Source: Healthnotes, Inc.; www.healthnotes.com
Hyperlink:
http://www.thedacare.org/healthnotes/Concern/Hemorrhoids.htm

Horse Chestnut
Source: Integrative Medicine Communications; www.onemedicine.com
Hyperlink:
http://www.drkoop.com/interactivemedicine/ConsConditions/Hemor
rhoidscc.html

Horse Chestnut
Source: Prima Communications, Inc.
Hyperlink: http://www.personalhealthzone.com/pg000182.html

Horse chestnut
Source: WholeHealthMD.com, LLC.; www.wholehealthmd.com
Hyperlink:
http://www.wholehealthmd.com/refshelf/substances_view/0,1525,100
37,00.html

Huckleberry
Source: Integrative Medicine Communications; www.onemedicine.com
Hyperlink:
http://www.drkoop.com/interactivemedicine/ConsHerbs/Bilberrych.h
tml

Hypericum perforatum
Source: Integrative Medicine Communications; www.onemedicine.com
Hyperlink:
http://www.drkoop.com/interactivemedicine/ConsHerbs/StJohnsWor
tch.html

Ispaghula
Source: Integrative Medicine Communications; www.onemedicine.com

Hyperlink:
http://www.drkoop.com/interactivemedicine/ConsSupplements/Psyll
iumcs.html

Klamathweed
Source: Integrative Medicine Communications; www.onemedicine.com
Hyperlink:
http://www.drkoop.com/interactivemedicine/ConsHerbs/StJohnsWor
tch.html

Matricaria recutita
Source: Integrative Medicine Communications; www.onemedicine.com
Hyperlink:
http://www.drkoop.com/interactivemedicine/ConsHerbs/Chamomile
Germanch.html

Mesoglycan
Source: Prima Communications, Inc.
Hyperlink: http://www.personalhealthzone.com/pg000292.html

Mullein
Source: Prima Communications, Inc.
Hyperlink: http://www.personalhealthzone.com/pg000210.html

Mullein flower
Source: WholeHealthMD.com, LLC.; www.wholehealthmd.com
Hyperlink:
http://www.wholehealthmd.com/refshelf/substances_view/0,1525,865,
00.html

Nettle
Source: WholeHealthMD.com, LLC.; www.wholehealthmd.com
Hyperlink:
http://www.wholehealthmd.com/refshelf/substances_view/0,1525,100
48,00.html

Oak
Alternative names: Quercus spp.
Source: Healthnotes, Inc.; www.healthnotes.com
Hyperlink: http://www.thedacare.org/healthnotes/Herb/Oak.htm

Oak bark
Source: WholeHealthMD.com, LLC.; www.wholehealthmd.com

Hyperlink:
http://www.wholehealthmd.com/refshelf/substances_view/0,1525,101
08,00.html

Oenothera biennis
Source: Integrative Medicine Communications; www.onemedicine.com
Hyperlink:
http://www.drkoop.com/interactivemedicine/ConsHerbs/EveningPri
mrosech.html

OPCs (Oligomeric Proanthocyanidins)
Source: Prima Communications, Inc.
Hyperlink: http://www.personalhealthzone.com/pg000173.html

Passiflora incarnata
Source: Integrative Medicine Communications; www.onemedicine.com
Hyperlink:
http://www.drkoop.com/interactivemedicine/ConsHerbs/Passionflow
erch.html

Passionflower
Alternative names: Passiflora incarnata
Source: Integrative Medicine Communications; www.onemedicine.com
Hyperlink:
http://www.drkoop.com/interactivemedicine/ConsHerbs/Passionflow
erch.html

Plantago isphagula
Source: Integrative Medicine Communications; www.onemedicine.com
Hyperlink:
http://www.drkoop.com/interactivemedicine/ConsSupplements/Psyll
iumcs.html

Plantago psyllium
Alternative names: Psyllium, Ispaghula; Plantago psyllium/ovata
Source: Alternative Medicine Foundation, Inc.; www.amfoundation.org
Hyperlink: http://www.herbmed.org/

Plantain
Alternative names: Plantago lanceolata, Plantago major
Source: Healthnotes, Inc.; www.healthnotes.com
Hyperlink: http://www.thedacare.org/healthnotes/Herb/Plantain.htm

Plantain
Source: The Canadian Internet Directory for Holistic Help, WellNet, Health and Wellness Network; www.wellnet.ca
Hyperlink: http://www.wellnet.ca/herbsp-r.htm

Potentilla
Alternative names: Cinquefoil, Silverweed; Potentilla sp.
Source: Alternative Medicine Foundation, Inc.; www.amfoundation.org
Hyperlink: http://www.herbmed.org/

Psyllium
Source: Healthnotes, Inc.; www.healthnotes.com
Hyperlink: http://www.thedacare.org/healthnotes/Drug/Psyllium.htm

Psyllium
Alternative names: Plantago ovata, Plantago ispaghula
Source: Healthnotes, Inc.; www.healthnotes.com
Hyperlink: http://www.thedacare.org/healthnotes/Herb/Psyllium.htm

Psyllium
Source: Healthnotes, Inc.; www.healthnotes.com
Hyperlink:
http://www.thedacare.org/healthnotes/Concern/Hemorrhoids.htm

Psyllium
Alternative names: Ispaghula,Plantago isphagula
Source: Integrative Medicine Communications; www.onemedicine.com
Hyperlink:
http://www.drkoop.com/interactivemedicine/ConsSupplements/Psyll
iumcs.html

Psyllium
Source: Integrative Medicine Communications; www.onemedicine.com
Hyperlink:
http://www.drkoop.com/interactivemedicine/ConsConditions/Hemor
rhoidscc.html

Psyllium
Source: WholeHealthMD.com, LLC.; www.wholehealthmd.com
Hyperlink:
http://www.wholehealthmd.com/refshelf/substances_view/0,1525,814,
00.html

Red Elm
Source: Integrative Medicine Communications; www.onemedicine.com
Hyperlink:
http://www.drkoop.com/interactivemedicine/ConsHerbs/SlipperyElm
ch.html

Roman Chamomile
Alternative names: Chamaemelum nobile
Source: Integrative Medicine Communications; www.onemedicine.com
Hyperlink:
http://www.drkoop.com/interactivemedicine/ConsHerbs/Chamomile
Romanch.html

Slippery Elm
Alternative names: Ulmus fulva, Red Elm, Sweet Elm
Source: Integrative Medicine Communications; www.onemedicine.com
Hyperlink:
http://www.drkoop.com/interactivemedicine/ConsHerbs/SlipperyElm
ch.html

Slippery Elm
Source: Prima Communications, Inc.
Hyperlink: http://www.personalhealthzone.com/pg000236.html

St. John's Wort
Alternative names: Hypericum perforatum, Klamathweed
Source: Integrative Medicine Communications; www.onemedicine.com
Hyperlink:
http://www.drkoop.com/interactivemedicine/ConsHerbs/StJohnsWor
tch.html

St. John's wort
Source: WholeHealthMD.com, LLC.; www.wholehealthmd.com
Hyperlink:
http://www.wholehealthmd.com/refshelf/substances_view/0,1525,824,
00.html

Sun Drop
Source: Integrative Medicine Communications; www.onemedicine.com
Hyperlink:
http://www.drkoop.com/interactivemedicine/ConsHerbs/EveningPri
mrosech.html

Sweet Annie
Alternative names: Artemisia annua
Source: Healthnotes, Inc.; www.healthnotes.com
Hyperlink:
http://www.thedacare.org/healthnotes/Herb/Sweet_Annie.htm

Sweet Elm
Source: Integrative Medicine Communications; www.onemedicine.com
Hyperlink:
http://www.drkoop.com/interactivemedicine/ConsHerbs/SlipperyElm
ch.html

Ulmus fulva
Source: Integrative Medicine Communications; www.onemedicine.com
Hyperlink:
http://www.drkoop.com/interactivemedicine/ConsHerbs/SlipperyElm
ch.html

Vaccinium myrtillus
Source: Integrative Medicine Communications; www.onemedicine.com
Hyperlink:
http://www.drkoop.com/interactivemedicine/ConsHerbs/Bilberrych.h
tml

Witch Hazel
Alternative names: Hamamelis virginiana
Source: Healthnotes, Inc.; www.healthnotes.com
Hyperlink:
http://www.thedacare.org/healthnotes/Herb/Witch_Hazel.htm

Yarrow
Alternative names: Achillea millefolium, Milfoil
Source: Integrative Medicine Communications; www.onemedicine.com
Hyperlink:
http://www.drkoop.com/interactivemedicine/ConsHerbs/Yarrowch.ht
ml

Zanthoxylum
Alternative names: Prickly Ash; Zanthoxylum sp.
Source: Alternative Medicine Foundation, Inc.; www.amfoundation.org
Hyperlink: http://www.herbmed.org/

- **Related Conditions**

  Cancer, Colorectal
  Source: Integrative Medicine Communications; www.onemedicine.com
  Hyperlink:
  http://www.drkoop.com/interactivemedicine/ConsConditions/Cancer
  Colorectalcc.html

  Colorectal Cancer
  Source: Integrative Medicine Communications; www.onemedicine.com
  Hyperlink:
  http://www.drkoop.com/interactivemedicine/ConsConditions/Cancer
  Colorectalcc.html

  Iron-Deficiency Anemia
  Source: Healthnotes, Inc.; www.healthnotes.com
  Hyperlink:
  http://www.thedacare.org/healthnotes/Concern/Iron_Deficiency.htm

  Peripheral Vascular Disease
  Source: Healthnotes, Inc.; www.healthnotes.com
  Hyperlink:
  http://www.thedacare.org/healthnotes/Concern/Peripheral_Vascular_
  Disease.htm

  Varicose Veins
  Source: Healthnotes, Inc.; www.healthnotes.com
  Hyperlink:
  http://www.thedacare.org/healthnotes/Concern/Varicose_Veins.htm

  Varicose Veins
  Source: Prima Communications, Inc.
  Hyperlink: http://www.personalhealthzone.com/pg000303.html

General References

A good place to find general background information on CAM is the National Library of Medicine. It has prepared within the MEDLINEplus system an information topic page dedicated to complementary and alternative medicine. To access this page, go to the MEDLINEplus site at: **www.nlm.nih.gov/medlineplus/alternativemedicine.html.** This Web site provides a general overview of various topics and can lead to a number of general sources. The following additional references describe, in broad terms, alternative and complementary medicine (sorted alphabetically by title; hyperlinks provide rankings, information, and reviews at Amazon.com):

- **Gastrointestinal Disorders and Nutrition** by Tonia Reinhard; Paperback - 192 pages (January 24, 2002), McGraw-Hill Professional Publishing; ISBN: 0737303611;
  http://www.amazon.com/exec/obidos/ASIN/0737303611/icongroupinterna

- **Healthy Digestion the Natural Way: Preventing and Healing Heartburn, Constipation, Gas, Diarrhea, Inflammatory Bowel and Gallbladder Diseases, Ulcers, Irritable Bowel Syndrome, and More** by D. Lindsey Berkson, et al; Paperback - 256 pages, 1st edition (February 2000), John Wiley & Sons; ISBN: 0471349623;
  http://www.amazon.com/exec/obidos/ASIN/0471349623/icongroupinterna

- **No More Heartburn: Stop the Pain in 30 Days--Naturally!: The Safe, Effective Way to Prevent and Heal Chronic Gastrointestinal Disorders** by Sherry A. Rogers, M.D.; Paperback - 320 pages (February 2000), Kensington Publishing Corp.; ISBN: 1575665107;
  http://www.amazon.com/exec/obidos/ASIN/1575665107/icongroupinterna

For additional information on complementary and alternative medicine, ask your doctor or write to:

National Institutes of Health
National Center for Complementary and Alternative Medicine Clearinghouse
P. O. Box 8218
Silver Spring, MD 20907-8218

Vocabulary Builder

The following vocabulary builder gives definitions of words used in this chapter that have not been defined in previous chapters:

Antiallergic: Counteracting allergy or allergic conditions. [EU]

Antiseptic: An agent that kills bacteria. Alcohol is a common antiseptic. Before injecting insulin, many people use alcohol to clean their skin to avoid infection. [NIH]

Atopic: Pertaining to an atopen or to atopy; allergic. [EU]

Dermatology: A medical specialty concerned with the skin, its structure, functions, diseases, and treatment. [NIH]

Echinacea: A genus of perennial herbs used topically and internally. It contains echinacoside, glycosides, inulin, isobutyl amides, resin, and sesquiterpenes. [NIH]

Eczema: A pruritic papulovesicular dermatitis occurring as a reaction to many endogenous and exogenous agents, characterized in the acute stage by erythema, edema associated with a serous exudate between the cells of the epidermis (spongiosis) and an inflammatory infiltrate in the dermis, oozing and vesiculation, and crusting and scaling; and in the more chronic stages by lichenification or thickening or both, signs of excoriations, and hyperpigmentation or hypopigmentation or both. Atopic dermatitis is the most common type of dermatitis. Called also eczematous dermatitis. [EU]

Frostbite: Damage to tissues as the result of low environmental temperatures. [NIH]

Herpes: Any inflammatory skin disease caused by a herpesvirus and characterized by the formation of clusters of small vesicles. When used alone, the term may refer to herpes simplex or to herpes zoster. [EU]

Midwifery: The practice of assisting women in childbirth. [NIH]

Prenatal: Existing or occurring before birth, with reference to the fetus. [EU]

Psoriasis: A common genetically determined, chronic, inflammatory skin disease characterized by rounded erythematous, dry, scaling patches. The lesions have a predilection for nails, scalp, genitalia, extensor surfaces, and the lumbosacral region. Accelerated epidermopoiesis is considered to be the fundamental pathologic feature in psoriasis. [NIH]

Reflex: 1; reflected. 2. a reflected action or movement; the sum total of any particular involuntary activity. [EU]

Sunburn: An injury to the skin causing erythema, tenderness, and sometimes blistering and resulting from excessive exposure to the sun. The reaction is produced by the ultraviolet radiation in sunlight. [NIH]

Tuberculosis: Any of the infectious diseases of man and other animals caused by species of mycobacterium. [NIH]

APPENDIX C. RESEARCHING NUTRITION

Overview

Since the time of Hippocrates, doctors have understood the importance of diet and nutrition to patients' health and well-being. Since then, they have accumulated an impressive archive of studies and knowledge dedicated to this subject. Based on their experience, doctors and healthcare providers may recommend particular dietary supplements to patients with hemorrhoids. Any dietary recommendation is based on a patient's age, body mass, gender, lifestyle, eating habits, food preferences, and health condition. It is therefore likely that different patients with hemorrhoids may be given different recommendations. Some recommendations may be directly related to hemorrhoids, while others may be more related to the patient's general health. These recommendations, themselves, may differ from what official sources recommend for the average person.

In this chapter we will begin by briefly reviewing the essentials of diet and nutrition that will broadly frame more detailed discussions of hemorrhoids. We will then show you how to find studies dedicated specifically to nutrition and hemorrhoids.

Food and Nutrition: General Principles

What Are Essential Foods?

Food is generally viewed by official sources as consisting of six basic elements: (1) fluids, (2) carbohydrates, (3) protein, (4) fats, (5) vitamins, and (6) minerals. Consuming a combination of these elements is considered to be a healthy diet:

- **Fluids** are essential to human life as 80-percent of the body is composed of water. Water is lost via urination, sweating, diarrhea, vomiting, diuretics (drugs that increase urination), caffeine, and physical exertion.

- **Carbohydrates** are the main source for human energy (thermoregulation) and the bulk of typical diets. They are mostly classified as being either simple or complex. Simple carbohydrates include sugars which are often consumed in the form of cookies, candies, or cakes. Complex carbohydrates consist of starches and dietary fibers. Starches are consumed in the form of pastas, breads, potatoes, rice, and other foods. Soluble fibers can be eaten in the form of certain vegetables, fruits, oats, and legumes. Insoluble fibers include brown rice, whole grains, certain fruits, wheat bran and legumes.

- **Proteins** are eaten to build and repair human tissues. Some foods that are high in protein are also high in fat and calories. Food sources for protein include nuts, meat, fish, cheese, and other dairy products.

- **Fats** are consumed for both energy and the absorption of certain vitamins. There are many types of fats, with many general publications recommending the intake of unsaturated fats or those low in cholesterol.

Vitamins and minerals are fundamental to human health, growth, and, in some cases, disease prevention. Most are consumed in your diet (exceptions being vitamins K and D which are produced by intestinal bacteria and sunlight on the skin, respectively). Each vitamin and mineral plays a different role in health. The following outlines essential vitamins:

- **Vitamin A** is important to the health of your eyes, hair, bones, and skin; sources of vitamin A include foods such as eggs, carrots, and cantaloupe.

- **Vitamin B^1**, also known as thiamine, is important for your nervous system and energy production; food sources for thiamine include meat, peas, fortified cereals, bread, and whole grains.

- **Vitamin B^2**, also known as riboflavin, is important for your nervous system and muscles, but is also involved in the release of proteins from nutrients; food sources for riboflavin include dairy products, leafy vegetables, meat, and eggs.

- **Vitamin B^3**, also known as niacin, is important for healthy skin and helps the body use energy; food sources for niacin include peas, peanuts, fish, and whole grains

- **Vitamin B^6**, also known as pyridoxine, is important for the regulation of cells in the nervous system and is vital for blood formation; food sources for pyridoxine include bananas, whole grains, meat, and fish.

- **Vitamin B^{12}** is vital for a healthy nervous system and for the growth of red blood cells in bone marrow; food sources for vitamin B^{12} include yeast, milk, fish, eggs, and meat.

- **Vitamin C** allows the body's immune system to fight various diseases, strengthens body tissue, and improves the body's use of iron; food sources for vitamin C include a wide variety of fruits and vegetables.

- **Vitamin D** helps the body absorb calcium which strengthens bones and teeth; food sources for vitamin D include oily fish and dairy products.

- **Vitamin E** can help protect certain organs and tissues from various degenerative diseases; food sources for vitamin E include margarine, vegetables, eggs, and fish.

- **Vitamin K** is essential for bone formation and blood clotting; common food sources for vitamin K include leafy green vegetables.

- **Folic Acid** maintains healthy cells and blood and, when taken by a pregnant woman, can prevent her fetus from developing neural tube defects; food sources for folic acid include nuts, fortified breads, leafy green vegetables, and whole grains.

It should be noted that one can overdose on certain vitamins which become toxic if consumed in excess (e.g. vitamin A, D, E and K).

Like vitamins, minerals are chemicals that are required by the body to remain in good health. Because the human body does not manufacture these chemicals internally, we obtain them from food and other dietary sources. The more important minerals include:

- **Calcium** is needed for healthy bones, teeth, and muscles, but also helps the nervous system function; food sources for calcium include dry beans, peas, eggs, and dairy products.

- **Chromium** is helpful in regulating sugar levels in blood; food sources for chromium include egg yolks, raw sugar, cheese, nuts, beets, whole grains, and meat.

- **Fluoride** is used by the body to help prevent tooth decay and to reinforce bone strength; sources of fluoride include drinking water and certain brands of toothpaste.

- **Iodine** helps regulate the body's use of energy by synthesizing into the hormone thyroxine; food sources include leafy green vegetables, nuts, egg yolks, and red meat.

- **Iron** helps maintain muscles and the formation of red blood cells and certain proteins; food sources for iron include meat, dairy products, eggs, and leafy green vegetables.

- **Magnesium** is important for the production of DNA, as well as for healthy teeth, bones, muscles, and nerves; food sources for magnesium include dried fruit, dark green vegetables, nuts, and seafood.

- **Phosphorous** is used by the body to work with calcium to form bones and teeth; food sources for phosphorous include eggs, meat, cereals, and dairy products.

- **Selenium** primarily helps maintain normal heart and liver functions; food sources for selenium include wholegrain cereals, fish, meat, and dairy products.

- **Zinc** helps wounds heal, the formation of sperm, and encourage rapid growth and energy; food sources include dried beans, shellfish, eggs, and nuts.

The United States government periodically publishes recommended diets and consumption levels of the various elements of food. Again, your doctor may encourage deviations from the average official recommendation based on your specific condition. To learn more about basic dietary guidelines, visit the Web site: **http://www.health.gov/dietaryguidelines/**. Based on these guidelines, many foods are required to list the nutrition levels on the food's packaging. Labeling Requirements are listed at the following site maintained by the Food and Drug Administration: **http://www.cfsan.fda.gov/~dms/lab-cons.html**. When interpreting these requirements, the government recommends that consumers become familiar with the following abbreviations before reading FDA literature:[38]

- **DVs (Daily Values):** A new dietary reference term that will appear on the food label. It is made up of two sets of references, DRVs and RDIs.

- **DRVs (Daily Reference Values):** A set of dietary references that applies to fat, saturated fat, cholesterol, carbohydrate, protein, fiber, sodium, and potassium.

---

[38] Adapted from the FDA: **http://www.fda.gov/fdac/special/foodlabel/dvs.html**.

- **RDIs (Reference Daily Intakes):** A set of dietary references based on the Recommended Dietary Allowances for essential vitamins and minerals and, in selected groups, protein. The name "RDI" replaces the term "U.S. RDA."

- **RDAs (Recommended Dietary Allowances):** A set of estimated nutrient allowances established by the National Academy of Sciences. It is updated periodically to reflect current scientific knowledge.

What Are Dietary Supplements?[39]

Dietary supplements are widely available through many commercial sources, including health food stores, grocery stores, pharmacies, and by mail. Dietary supplements are provided in many forms including tablets, capsules, powders, gel-tabs, extracts, and liquids. Historically in the United States, the most prevalent type of dietary supplement was a multivitamin/mineral tablet or capsule that was available in pharmacies, either by prescription or "over the counter." Supplements containing strictly herbal preparations were less widely available. Currently in the United States, a wide array of supplement products are available, including vitamin, mineral, other nutrients, and botanical supplements as well as ingredients and extracts of animal and plant origin.

The Office of Dietary Supplements (ODS) of the National Institutes of Health is the official agency of the United States which has the expressed goal of acquiring "new knowledge to help prevent, detect, diagnose, and treat disease and disability, from the rarest genetic disorder to the common cold."[40] According to the ODS, dietary supplements can have an important impact on the prevention and management of disease and on the maintenance of health.[41] The ODS notes that considerable research on the effects of dietary supplements has been conducted in Asia and Europe where the use of plant products, in particular, has a long tradition. However, the

---

[39] This discussion has been adapted from the NIH:
http://ods.od.nih.gov/whatare/whatare.html.

[40] Contact: The Office of Dietary Supplements, National Institutes of Health, Building 31, Room 1B29, 31 Center Drive, MSC 2086, Bethesda, Maryland 20892-2086, Tel: (301) 435-2920, Fax: (301) 480-1845, E-mail: **ods@nih.gov**.

[41] Adapted from **http://ods.od.nih.gov/about/about.html**. The Dietary Supplement Health and Education Act defines dietary supplements as "a product (other than tobacco) intended to supplement the diet that bears or contains one or more of the following dietary ingredients: a vitamin, mineral, amino acid, herb or other botanical; or a dietary substance for use to supplement the diet by increasing the total dietary intake; or a concentrate, metabolite, constituent, extract, or combination of any ingredient described above; and intended for ingestion in the form of a capsule, powder, softgel, or gelcap, and not represented as a conventional food or as a sole item of a meal or the diet."

overwhelming majority of supplements have not been studied scientifically. To explore the role of dietary supplements in the improvement of health care, the ODS plans, organizes, and supports conferences, workshops, and symposia on scientific topics related to dietary supplements. The ODS often works in conjunction with other NIH Institutes and Centers, other government agencies, professional organizations, and public advocacy groups.

To learn more about official information on dietary supplements, visit the ODS site at **http://ods.od.nih.gov/whatare/whatare.html**. Or contact:

> The Office of Dietary Supplements
> National Institutes of Health
> Building 31, Room 1B29
> 31 Center Drive, MSC 2086
> Bethesda, Maryland 20892-2086
> Tel: (301) 435-2920
> Fax: (301) 480-1845
> E-mail: ods@nih.gov

Finding Studies on Hemorrhoids

The NIH maintains an office dedicated to patient nutrition and diet. The National Institutes of Health's Office of Dietary Supplements (ODS) offers a searchable bibliographic database called the IBIDS (International Bibliographic Information on Dietary Supplements). The IBIDS contains over 460,000 scientific citations and summaries about dietary supplements and nutrition as well as references to published international, scientific literature on dietary supplements such as vitamins, minerals, and botanicals.[42] IBIDS is available to the public free of charge through the ODS Internet page: **http://ods.od.nih.gov/databases/ibids.html**.

After entering the search area, you have three choices: (1) IBIDS Consumer Database, (2) Full IBIDS Database, or (3) Peer Reviewed Citations Only. We recommend that you start with the Consumer Database. While you may not find references for the topics that are of most interest to you, check back periodically as this database is frequently updated. More studies can be

---

[42] Adapted from **http://ods.od.nih.gov**. IBIDS is produced by the Office of Dietary Supplements (ODS) at the National Institutes of Health to assist the public, healthcare providers, educators, and researchers in locating credible, scientific information on dietary supplements. IBIDS was developed and will be maintained through an interagency partnership with the Food and Nutrition Information Center of the National Agricultural Library, U.S. Department of Agriculture.

found by searching the Full IBIDS Database. Healthcare professionals and researchers generally use the third option, which lists peer-reviewed citations. In all cases, we suggest that you take advantage of the "Advanced Search" option that allows you to retrieve up to 100 fully explained references in a comprehensive format. Type "hemorrhoids" (or synonyms) into the search box. To narrow the search, you can also select the "Title" field.

The following information is typical of that found when using the "Full IBIDS Database" when searching using "hemorrhoids" (or a synonym):

- **Clinical trial of oral diosmin (Daflon) in the treatment of hemorrhoids.**
  Author(s): Department of Surgery, Faculty of Medicine, Chulalongkorn University, Bangkok, Thailand.
  Source: Thanapongsathorn, W Vajrabukka, T Dis-Colon-Rectum. 1992 November; 35(11): 1085-8 0012-3706

- **Doppler sonographic diagnostics and treatment control of symptomatic first-degree hemorrhoids. Preliminary report and results.**
  Author(s): Second Department of Internal Medicine, Stadtisches Klinikum Fulda, Academic Hospital of the University of Marburg, Germany.
  Source: Jaspersen, D Dig-Dis-Sci. 1993 July; 38(7): 1329-32 0163-2116

- **Double-blind, placebo-controlled evaluation of clinical activity and safety of Daflon 500 mg in the treatment of acute hemorrhoids.**
  Author(s): Dipartimento di Scienze Chirurgiche e Anatomiche, Universita di Palermo, Italy.
  Source: Cospite, M Angiology. 1994 June; 45(6 Pt 2): 566-73 0003-3197

- **Double-blind, randomized clinical trial of troxerutin-carbazochrome in patients with hemorrhoids.**
  Author(s): Istituto di Farmacologia, Servizio di Farmacologia Clinica, Universita degli Studi di Messina, Italy.
  Source: Squadrito, F Altavilla, D Oliaro Bosso, S Eur-Rev-Med-Pharmacol-Sci. 2000 Jan-April; 4(1-2): 21-4

- **Effect of fiber supplements on internal bleeding hemorrhoids.**
  Author(s): Gastroenterology Department, Hospital de Ia Princesa, Universidad Autonoma de Madrid, Spain.
  Source: Perez Miranda, M Gomez Cedenilla, A Leon Colombo, T Pajares, J Mate Jimenez, J Hepatogastroenterology. 1996 Nov-December; 43(12): 1504-7 0172-6390

- **Efficacy of an indigenous formulation in patients with bleeding piles: a preliminary clinical study.**
Author(s): Medinova Diagnostic Services, 1319, Jungli Maharaj Road, Pune 411005, India.
Source: Paranjpe, P Patki, P Joshi, N Fitoterapia. 2000 February; 71(1): 41-5 0367-326X

- **Hemorrhoids and varicose veins: a review of treatment options.**
Author(s): Thorne Research, 4616 SE 30th, Portland, OR 97202, USA. mackaynd@earthlink.net
Source: MacKay, D Altern-Med-Revolume 2001 April; 6(2): 126-40 1089-5159

- **Hemorrhoids. A review of current techniques and management.**
Source: Smith, L E Gastroenterol-Clin-North-Am. 1987 March; 16(1): 79-91 0889-8553

- **Long-term results of large-dose, single-session phenol injection sclerotherapy for hemorrhoids.**
Author(s): University Department of Surgery, Royal Free Hospital and School of Medicine, London, United Kingdom.
Source: Santos, G Novell, J R Khoury, G Winslet, M C Lewis, A A Dis-Colon-Rectum. 1993 October; 36(10): 958-61 0012-3706

- **Micronized flavonoid therapy in internal hemorrhoids of pregnancy.**
Author(s): Department of Obstetrics and Gynaecology, All India Institute of Medical Sciences, New Delhi, India.
Source: Buckshee, K Takkar, D Aggarwal, N Int-J-Gynaecol-Obstet. 1997 May; 57(2): 145-51 0020-7292

- **Micronized purified flavonidic fraction compared favorably with rubber band ligation and fiber alone in the management of bleeding hemorrhoids: randomized controlled trial.**
Author(s): Department of Colorectal Surgery, Singapore General Hospital, Singapore.
Source: Ho, Y H Tan, M Seow Choen, F Dis-Colon-Rectum. 2000 January; 43(1): 66-9 0012-3706

Federal Resources on Nutrition

In addition to the IBIDS, the United States Department of Health and Human Services (HHS) and the United States Department of Agriculture (USDA) provide many sources of information on general nutrition and health. Recommended resources include:

- healthfinder®, HHS's gateway to health information, including diet and nutrition:
  http://www.healthfinder.gov/scripts/SearchContext.asp?topic=238&page=0

- The United States Department of Agriculture's Web site dedicated to nutrition information: **www.nutrition.gov**

- The Food and Drug Administration's Web site for federal food safety information: **www.foodsafety.gov**

- The National Action Plan on Overweight and Obesity sponsored by the United States Surgeon General:
  http://www.surgeongeneral.gov/topics/obesity/

- The Center for Food Safety and Applied Nutrition has an Internet site sponsored by the Food and Drug Administration and the Department of Health and Human Services: **http://vm.cfsan.fda.gov/**

- Center for Nutrition Policy and Promotion sponsored by the United States Department of Agriculture: **http://www.usda.gov/cnpp/**

- Food and Nutrition Information Center, National Agricultural Library sponsored by the United States Department of Agriculture: **http://www.nal.usda.gov/fnic/**

- Food and Nutrition Service sponsored by the United States Department of Agriculture: **http://www.fns.usda.gov/fns/**

Additional Web Resources

A number of additional Web sites offer encyclopedic information covering food and nutrition. The following is a representative sample:

- AOL: **http://search.aol.com/cat.adp?id=174&layer=&from=subcats**

- Family Village: **http://www.familyvillage.wisc.edu/med_nutrition.html**

- Google: **http://directory.google.com/Top/Health/Nutrition/**

- Healthnotes: **http://www.thedacare.org/healthnotes/**

- Open Directory Project: **http://dmoz.org/Health/Nutrition/**

- Yahoo.com: **http://dir.yahoo.com/Health/Nutrition/**

- WebMD®Health: **http://my.webmd.com/nutrition**

- WholeHealthMD.com:
  http://www.wholehealthmd.com/reflib/0,1529,,00.html

Vocabulary Builder

The following vocabulary builder defines words used in the references in this chapter that have not been defined in previous chapters:

Degenerative: Undergoing degeneration : tending to degenerate; having the character of or involving degeneration; causing or tending to cause degeneration. [EU]

Diosmin: A bioflavonoid that strengthens vascular walls. [NIH]

Iodine: A nonmetallic element of the halogen group that is represented by the atomic symbol I, atomic number 53, and atomic weight of 126.90. It is a nutritionally essential element, especially important in thyroid hormone synthesis. In solution, it has anti-infective properties and is used topically. [NIH]

Neural: 1. pertaining to a nerve or to the nerves. 2. situated in the region of the spinal axis, as the neutral arch. [EU]

Niacin: Water-soluble vitamin of the B complex occurring in various animal and plant tissues. Required by the body for the formation of coenzymes NAD and NADP. Has pellagra-curative, vasodilating, and antilipemic properties. [NIH]

Overdose: 1. to administer an excessive dose. 2. an excessive dose. [EU]

Riboflavin: Nutritional factor found in milk, eggs, malted barley, liver, kidney, heart, and leafy vegetables. The richest natural source is yeast. It occurs in the free form only in the retina of the eye, in whey, and in urine; its principal forms in tissues and cells are as FMN and FAD. [NIH]

Selenium: An element with the atomic symbol Se, atomic number 34, and atomic weight 78.96. It is an essential micronutrient for mammals and other animals but is toxic in large amounts. Selenium protects intracellular structures against oxidative damage. It is an essential component of glutathione peroxidase. [NIH]

Thyroxine: An amino acid of the thyroid gland which exerts a stimulating effect on thyroid metabolism. [NIH]

APPENDIX D. FINDING MEDICAL LIBRARIES

Overview

At a medical library you can find medical texts and reference books, consumer health publications, specialty newspapers and magazines, as well as medical journals. In this Appendix, we show you how to quickly find a medical library in your area.

Preparation

Before going to the library, highlight the references mentioned in this sourcebook that you find interesting. Focus on those items that are not available via the Internet, and ask the reference librarian for help with your search. He or she may know of additional resources that could be helpful to you. Most importantly, your local public library and medical libraries have Interlibrary Loan programs with the National Library of Medicine (NLM), one of the largest medical collections in the world. According to the NLM, most of the literature in the general and historical collections of the National Library of Medicine is available on interlibrary loan to any library. NLM's interlibrary loan services are only available to libraries. If you would like to access NLM medical literature, then visit a library in your area that can request the publications for you.[43]

---

[43] Adapted from the NLM: **http://www.nlm.nih.gov/psd/cas/interlibrary.html**

Finding a Local Medical Library

The quickest method to locate medical libraries is to use the Internet-based directory published by the National Network of Libraries of Medicine (NN/LM). This network includes 4626 members and affiliates that provide many services to librarians, health professionals, and the public. To find a library in your area, simply visit **http://nnlm.gov/members/adv.html** or call 1-800-338-7657.

Medical Libraries Open to the Public

In addition to the NN/LM, the National Library of Medicine (NLM) lists a number of libraries that are generally open to the public and have reference facilities. The following is the NLM's list plus hyperlinks to each library Web site. These Web pages can provide information on hours of operation and other restrictions. The list below is a small sample of libraries recommended by the National Library of Medicine (sorted alphabetically by name of the U.S. state or Canadian province where the library is located):[44]

- **Alabama:** Health InfoNet of Jefferson County (Jefferson County Library Cooperative, Lister Hill Library of the Health Sciences), **http://www.uab.edu/infonet/**

- **Alabama:** Richard M. Scrushy Library (American Sports Medicine Institute), **http://www.asmi.org/LIBRARY.HTM**

- **Arizona:** Samaritan Regional Medical Center: The Learning Center (Samaritan Health System, Phoenix, Arizona), **http://www.samaritan.edu/library/bannerlibs.htm**

- **California:** Kris Kelly Health Information Center (St. Joseph Health System), **http://www.humboldt1.com/~kkhic/index.html**

- **California:** Community Health Library of Los Gatos (Community Health Library of Los Gatos), **http://www.healthlib.org/orgresources.html**

- **California:** Consumer Health Program and Services (CHIPS) (County of Los Angeles Public Library, Los Angeles County Harbor-UCLA Medical Center Library) - Carson, CA, **http://www.colapublib.org/services/chips.html**

- **California:** Gateway Health Library (Sutter Gould Medical Foundation)

- **California:** Health Library (Stanford University Medical Center), **http://www-med.stanford.edu/healthlibrary/**

---

[44] Abstracted from **http://www.nlm.nih.gov/medlineplus/libraries.html**.

- **California:** Patient Education Resource Center - Health Information and Resources (University of California, San Francisco), **http://sfghdean.ucsf.edu/barnett/PERC/default.asp**

- **California:** Redwood Health Library (Petaluma Health Care District), **http://www.phcd.org/rdwdlib.html**

- **California:** San José PlaneTree Health Library, **http://planetreesanjose.org/**

- **California:** Sutter Resource Library (Sutter Hospitals Foundation), **http://go.sutterhealth.org/comm/resc-library/sac-resources.html**

- **California:** University of California, Davis. Health Sciences Libraries

- **California:** ValleyCare Health Library & Ryan Comer Cancer Resource Center (ValleyCare Health System), **http://www.valleycare.com/library.html**

- **California:** Washington Community Health Resource Library (Washington Community Health Resource Library), **http://www.healthlibrary.org/**

- **Colorado:** William V. Gervasini Memorial Library (Exempla Healthcare), **http://www.exempla.org/conslib.htm**

- **Connecticut:** Hartford Hospital Health Science Libraries (Hartford Hospital), **http://www.harthosp.org/library/**

- **Connecticut:** Healthnet: Connecticut Consumer Health Information Center (University of Connecticut Health Center, Lyman Maynard Stowe Library), **http://library.uchc.edu/departm/hnet/**

- **Connecticut:** Waterbury Hospital Health Center Library (Waterbury Hospital), **http://www.waterburyhospital.com/library/consumer.shtml**

- **Delaware:** Consumer Health Library (Christiana Care Health System, Eugene du Pont Preventive Medicine & Rehabilitation Institute), **http://www.christianacare.org/health_guide/health_guide_pmri_health _info.cfm**

- **Delaware:** Lewis B. Flinn Library (Delaware Academy of Medicine), **http://www.delamed.org/chls.html**

- **Georgia:** Family Resource Library (Medical College of Georgia), **http://cmc.mcg.edu/kids_families/fam_resources/fam_res_lib/frl.htm**

- **Georgia:** Health Resource Center (Medical Center of Central Georgia), **http://www.mccg.org/hrc/hrchome.asp**

- **Hawaii:** Hawaii Medical Library: Consumer Health Information Service (Hawaii Medical Library), **http://hml.org/CHIS/**

- **Idaho:** DeArmond Consumer Health Library (Kootenai Medical Center), http://www.nicon.org/DeArmond/index.htm

- **Illinois:** Health Learning Center of Northwestern Memorial Hospital (Northwestern Memorial Hospital, Health Learning Center), http://www.nmh.org/health_info/hlc.html

- **Illinois:** Medical Library (OSF Saint Francis Medical Center), http://www.osfsaintfrancis.org/general/library/

- **Kentucky:** Medical Library - Services for Patients, Families, Students & the Public (Central Baptist Hospital), http://www.centralbap.com/education/community/library.htm

- **Kentucky:** University of Kentucky - Health Information Library (University of Kentucky, Chandler Medical Center, Health Information Library), http://www.mc.uky.edu/PatientEd/

- **Louisiana:** Alton Ochsner Medical Foundation Library (Alton Ochsner Medical Foundation), http://www.ochsner.org/library/

- **Louisiana:** Louisiana State University Health Sciences Center Medical Library-Shreveport, http://lib-sh.lsuhsc.edu/

- **Maine:** Franklin Memorial Hospital Medical Library (Franklin Memorial Hospital), http://www.fchn.org/fmh/lib.htm

- **Maine:** Gerrish-True Health Sciences Library (Central Maine Medical Center), http://www.cmmc.org/library/library.html

- **Maine:** Hadley Parrot Health Science Library (Eastern Maine Healthcare), http://www.emh.org/hll/hpl/guide.htm

- **Maine:** Maine Medical Center Library (Maine Medical Center), http://www.mmc.org/library/

- **Maine:** Parkview Hospital, http://www.parkviewhospital.org/communit.htm#Library

- **Maine:** Southern Maine Medical Center Health Sciences Library (Southern Maine Medical Center), http://www.smmc.org/services/service.php3?choice=10

- **Maine:** Stephens Memorial Hospital Health Information Library (Western Maine Health), http://www.wmhcc.com/hil_frame.html

- **Manitoba, Canada:** Consumer & Patient Health Information Service (University of Manitoba Libraries), http://www.umanitoba.ca/libraries/units/health/reference/chis.html

- **Manitoba, Canada:** J.W. Crane Memorial Library (Deer Lodge Centre), http://www.deerlodge.mb.ca/library/libraryservices.shtml

- **Maryland:** Health Information Center at the Wheaton Regional Library (Montgomery County, Md., Dept. of Public Libraries, Wheaton Regional Library), **http://www.mont.lib.md.us/healthinfo/hic.asp**

- **Massachusetts:** Baystate Medical Center Library (Baystate Health System), **http://www.baystatehealth.com/1024/**

- **Massachusetts:** Boston University Medical Center Alumni Medical Library (Boston University Medical Center), **http://med-libwww.bu.edu/library/lib.html**

- **Massachusetts:** Lowell General Hospital Health Sciences Library (Lowell General Hospital), **http://www.lowellgeneral.org/library/HomePageLinks/WWW.htm**

- **Massachusetts:** Paul E. Woodard Health Sciences Library (New England Baptist Hospital), **http://www.nebh.org/health_lib.asp**

- **Massachusetts:** St. Luke's Hospital Health Sciences Library (St. Luke's Hospital), **http://www.southcoast.org/library/**

- **Massachusetts:** Treadwell Library Consumer Health Reference Center (Massachusetts General Hospital), **http://www.mgh.harvard.edu/library/chrcindex.html**

- **Massachusetts:** UMass HealthNet (University of Massachusetts Medical School), **http://healthnet.umassmed.edu/**

- **Michigan:** Botsford General Hospital Library - Consumer Health (Botsford General Hospital, Library & Internet Services), **http://www.botsfordlibrary.org/consumer.htm**

- **Michigan:** Helen DeRoy Medical Library (Providence Hospital and Medical Centers), **http://www.providence-hospital.org/library/**

- **Michigan:** Marquette General Hospital - Consumer Health Library (Marquette General Hospital, Health Information Center), **http://www.mgh.org/center.html**

- **Michigan:** Patient Education Resouce Center - University of Michigan Cancer Center (University of Michigan Comprehensive Cancer Center), **http://www.cancer.med.umich.edu/learn/leares.htm**

- **Michigan:** Sladen Library & Center for Health Information Resources - Consumer Health Information, **http://www.sladen.hfhs.org/library/consumer/index.html**

- **Montana:** Center for Health Information (St. Patrick Hospital and Health Sciences Center), **http://www.saintpatrick.org/chi/librarydetail.php3?ID=41**

- **National:** Consumer Health Library Directory (Medical Library Association, Consumer and Patient Health Information Section), http://caphis.mlanet.org/directory/index.html

- **National:** National Network of Libraries of Medicine (National Library of Medicine) - provides library services for health professionals in the United States who do not have access to a medical library, http://nnlm.gov/

- **National:** NN/LM List of Libraries Serving the Public (National Network of Libraries of Medicine), http://nnlm.gov/members/

- **Nevada:** Health Science Library, West Charleston Library (Las Vegas Clark County Library District), http://www.lvccld.org/special_collections/medical/index.htm

- **New Hampshire:** Dartmouth Biomedical Libraries (Dartmouth College Library), http://www.dartmouth.edu/~biomed/resources.htmld/conshealth.htmld/

- **New Jersey:** Consumer Health Library (Rahway Hospital), http://www.rahwayhospital.com/library.htm

- **New Jersey:** Dr. Walter Phillips Health Sciences Library (Englewood Hospital and Medical Center), http://www.englewoodhospital.com/links/index.htm

- **New Jersey:** Meland Foundation (Englewood Hospital and Medical Center), http://www.geocities.com/ResearchTriangle/9360/

- **New York:** Choices in Health Information (New York Public Library) - NLM Consumer Pilot Project participant, http://www.nypl.org/branch/health/links.html

- **New York:** Health Information Center (Upstate Medical University, State University of New York), http://www.upstate.edu/library/hic/

- **New York:** Health Sciences Library (Long Island Jewish Medical Center), http://www.lij.edu/library/library.html

- **New York:** ViaHealth Medical Library (Rochester General Hospital), http://www.nyam.org/library/

- **Ohio:** Consumer Health Library (Akron General Medical Center, Medical & Consumer Health Library), http://www.akrongeneral.org/hwlibrary.htm

- **Oklahoma:** Saint Francis Health System Patient/Family Resource Center (Saint Francis Health System), http://www.sfh-tulsa.com/patientfamilycenter/default.asp

- **Oregon:** Planetree Health Resource Center (Mid-Columbia Medical Center), **http://www.mcmc.net/phrc/**

- **Pennsylvania:** Community Health Information Library (Milton S. Hershey Medical Center), **http://www.hmc.psu.edu/commhealth/**

- **Pennsylvania:** Community Health Resource Library (Geisinger Medical Center), **http://www.geisinger.edu/education/commlib.shtml**

- **Pennsylvania:** HealthInfo Library (Moses Taylor Hospital), **http://www.mth.org/healthwellness.html**

- **Pennsylvania:** Hopwood Library (University of Pittsburgh, Health Sciences Library System), **http://www.hsls.pitt.edu/chi/hhrcinfo.html**

- **Pennsylvania:** Koop Community Health Information Center (College of Physicians of Philadelphia), **http://www.collphyphil.org/kooppg1.shtml**

- **Pennsylvania:** Learning Resources Center - Medical Library (Susquehanna Health System), **http://www.shscares.org/services/lrc/index.asp**

- **Pennsylvania:** Medical Library (UPMC Health System), **http://www.upmc.edu/passavant/library.htm**

- **Quebec, Canada:** Medical Library (Montreal General Hospital), **http://ww2.mcgill.ca/mghlib/**

- **South Dakota:** Rapid City Regional Hospital - Health Information Center (Rapid City Regional Hospital, Health Information Center), **http://www.rcrh.org/education/LibraryResourcesConsumers.htm**

- **Texas:** Houston HealthWays (Houston Academy of Medicine-Texas Medical Center Library), **http://hhw.library.tmc.edu/**

- **Texas:** Matustik Family Resource Center (Cook Children's Health Care System), **http://www.cookchildrens.com/Matustik_Library.html**

- **Washington:** Community Health Library (Kittitas Valley Community Hospital), **http://www.kvch.com/**

- **Washington:** Southwest Washington Medical Center Library (Southwest Washington Medical Center), **http://www.swmedctr.com/Home/**

APPENDIX E. YOUR RIGHTS AND INSURANCE

Overview

Any patient with hemorrhoids faces a series of issues related more to the healthcare industry than to the medical condition itself. This appendix covers two important topics in this regard: your rights and responsibilities as a patient, and how to get the most out of your medical insurance plan.

Your Rights as a Patient

The President's Advisory Commission on Consumer Protection and Quality in the Healthcare Industry has created the following summary of your rights as a patient.[45]

Information Disclosure

Consumers have the right to receive accurate, easily understood information. Some consumers require assistance in making informed decisions about health plans, health professionals, and healthcare facilities. Such information includes:

- *Health plans.* Covered benefits, cost-sharing, and procedures for resolving complaints, licensure, certification, and accreditation status, comparable measures of quality and consumer satisfaction, provider network composition, the procedures that govern access to specialists and emergency services, and care management information.

---

[45] Adapted from Consumer Bill of Rights and Responsibilities: http://www.hcqualitycommission.gov/press/cbor.html#head1.

- *Health professionals.* Education, board certification, and recertification, years of practice, experience performing certain procedures, and comparable measures of quality and consumer satisfaction.

- *Healthcare facilities.* Experience in performing certain procedures and services, accreditation status, comparable measures of quality, worker, and consumer satisfaction, and procedures for resolving complaints.

- *Consumer assistance programs.* Programs must be carefully structured to promote consumer confidence and to work cooperatively with health plans, providers, payers, and regulators. Desirable characteristics of such programs are sponsorship that ensures accountability to the interests of consumers and stable, adequate funding.

Choice of Providers and Plans

Consumers have the right to a choice of healthcare providers that is sufficient to ensure access to appropriate high-quality healthcare. To ensure such choice, the Commission recommends the following:

- *Provider network adequacy.* All health plan networks should provide access to sufficient numbers and types of providers to assure that all covered services will be accessible without unreasonable delay -- including access to emergency services 24 hours a day and 7 days a week. If a health plan has an insufficient number or type of providers to provide a covered benefit with the appropriate degree of specialization, the plan should ensure that the consumer obtains the benefit outside the network at no greater cost than if the benefit were obtained from participating providers.

- *Women's health services.* Women should be able to choose a qualified provider offered by a plan -- such as gynecologists, certified nurse midwives, and other qualified healthcare providers -- for the provision of covered care necessary to provide routine and preventative women's healthcare services.

- *Access to specialists.* Consumers with complex or serious medical conditions who require frequent specialty care should have direct access to a qualified specialist of their choice within a plan's network of providers. Authorizations, when required, should be for an adequate number of direct access visits under an approved treatment plan.

- *Transitional care.* Consumers who are undergoing a course of treatment for a chronic or disabling condition (or who are in the second or third trimester of a pregnancy) at the time they involuntarily change health plans or at a time when a provider is terminated by a plan for other than cause should be able to continue seeing their current specialty providers for up to 90 days (or through completion of postpartum care) to allow for transition of care.

- *Choice of health plans.* Public and private group purchasers should, wherever feasible, offer consumers a choice of high-quality health insurance plans.

Access to Emergency Services

Consumers have the right to access emergency healthcare services when and where the need arises. Health plans should provide payment when a consumer presents to an emergency department with acute symptoms of sufficient severity--including severe pain--such that a "prudent layperson" could reasonably expect the absence of medical attention to result in placing that consumer's health in serious jeopardy, serious impairment to bodily functions, or serious dysfunction of any bodily organ or part.

Participation in Treatment Decisions

Consumers have the right and responsibility to fully participate in all decisions related to their healthcare. Consumers who are unable to fully participate in treatment decisions have the right to be represented by parents, guardians, family members, or other conservators. Physicians and other health professionals should:

- Provide patients with sufficient information and opportunity to decide among treatment options consistent with the informed consent process.

- Discuss all treatment options with a patient in a culturally competent manner, including the option of no treatment at all.

- Ensure that persons with disabilities have effective communications with members of the health system in making such decisions.

- Discuss all current treatments a consumer may be undergoing.

- Discuss all risks, benefits, and consequences to treatment or nontreatment.

- Give patients the opportunity to refuse treatment and to express preferences about future treatment decisions.

- Discuss the use of advance directives -- both living wills and durable powers of attorney for healthcare -- with patients and their designated family members.

- Abide by the decisions made by their patients and/or their designated representatives consistent with the informed consent process.

Health plans, health providers, and healthcare facilities should:

- Disclose to consumers factors -- such as methods of compensation, ownership of or interest in healthcare facilities, or matters of conscience -- that could influence advice or treatment decisions.

- Assure that provider contracts do not contain any so-called "gag clauses" or other contractual mechanisms that restrict healthcare providers' ability to communicate with and advise patients about medically necessary treatment options.

- Be prohibited from penalizing or seeking retribution against healthcare professionals or other health workers for advocating on behalf of their patients.

Respect and Nondiscrimination

Consumers have the right to considerate, respectful care from all members of the healthcare industry at all times and under all circumstances. An environment of mutual respect is essential to maintain a quality healthcare system. To assure that right, the Commission recommends the following:

- Consumers must not be discriminated against in the delivery of healthcare services consistent with the benefits covered in their policy, or as required by law, based on race, ethnicity, national origin, religion, sex, age, mental or physical disability, sexual orientation, genetic information, or source of payment.

- Consumers eligible for coverage under the terms and conditions of a health plan or program, or as required by law, must not be discriminated against in marketing and enrollment practices based on race, ethnicity, national origin, religion, sex, age, mental or physical disability, sexual orientation, genetic information, or source of payment.

Confidentiality of Health Information

Consumers have the right to communicate with healthcare providers in confidence and to have the confidentiality of their individually identifiable healthcare information protected. Consumers also have the right to review and copy their own medical records and request amendments to their records.

Complaints and Appeals

Consumers have the right to a fair and efficient process for resolving differences with their health plans, healthcare providers, and the institutions that serve them, including a rigorous system of internal review and an independent system of external review. A free copy of the Patient's Bill of Rights is available from the American Hospital Association.[46]

Patient Responsibilities

Treatment is a two-way street between you and your healthcare providers. To underscore the importance of finance in modern healthcare as well as your responsibility for the financial aspects of your care, the President's Advisory Commission on Consumer Protection and Quality in the Healthcare Industry has proposed that patients understand the following "Consumer Responsibilities."[47] In a healthcare system that protects consumers' rights, it is reasonable to expect and encourage consumers to assume certain responsibilities. Greater individual involvement by the consumer in his or her care increases the likelihood of achieving the best outcome and helps support a quality-oriented, cost-conscious environment. Such responsibilities include:

- Take responsibility for maximizing healthy habits such as exercising, not smoking, and eating a healthy diet.

- Work collaboratively with healthcare providers in developing and carrying out agreed-upon treatment plans.

- Disclose relevant information and clearly communicate wants and needs.

- Use your health insurance plan's internal complaint and appeal processes to address your concerns.

- Avoid knowingly spreading disease.

---

[46] To order your free copy of the Patient's Bill of Rights, telephone 312-422-3000 or visit the American Hospital Association's Web site: **http://www.aha.org**. Click on "Resource Center," go to "Search" at bottom of page, and then type in "Patient's Bill of Rights." The Patient's Bill of Rights is also available from Fax on Demand, at 312-422-2020, document number 471124.

[47] Adapted from **http://www.hcqualitycommission.gov/press/cbor.html#head1**.

- Recognize the reality of risks, the limits of the medical science, and the human fallibility of the healthcare professional.

- Be aware of a healthcare provider's obligation to be reasonably efficient and equitable in providing care to other patients and the community.

- Become knowledgeable about your health plan's coverage and options (when available) including all covered benefits, limitations, and exclusions, rules regarding use of network providers, coverage and referral rules, appropriate processes to secure additional information, and the process to appeal coverage decisions.

- Show respect for other patients and health workers.

- Make a good-faith effort to meet financial obligations.

- Abide by administrative and operational procedures of health plans, healthcare providers, and Government health benefit programs.

Choosing an Insurance Plan

There are a number of official government agencies that help consumers understand their healthcare insurance choices.[48] The U.S. Department of Labor, in particular, recommends ten ways to make your health benefits choices work best for you.[49]

1. Your options are important. There are many different types of health benefit plans. Find out which one your employer offers, then check out the plan, or plans, offered. Your employer's human resource office, the health plan administrator, or your union can provide information to help you match your needs and preferences with the available plans. The more information you have, the better your healthcare decisions will be.

2. Reviewing the benefits available. Do the plans offered cover preventive care, well-baby care, vision or dental care? Are there deductibles? Answers to these questions can help determine the out-of-pocket expenses you may face. Matching your needs and those of your family members will result in the best possible benefits. Cheapest may not always be best. Your goal is high quality health benefits.

---

[48] More information about quality across programs is provided at the following AHRQ Web site:
http://www.ahrq.gov/consumer/qntascii/qnthplan.htm .
[49] Adapted from the Department of Labor:
http://www.dol.gov/dol/pwba/public/pubs/health/top10-text.html.

3. Look for quality. The quality of healthcare services varies, but quality can be measured. You should consider the quality of healthcare in deciding among the healthcare plans or options available to you. Not all health plans, doctors, hospitals and other providers give the highest quality care. Fortunately, there is quality information you can use right now to help you compare your healthcare choices. Find out how you can measure quality. Consult the U.S. Department of Health and Human Services publication "Your Guide to Choosing Quality Health Care" on the Internet at **www.ahcpr.gov/consumer**.

4. Your plan's summary plan description (SPD) provides a wealth of information. Your health plan administrator can provide you with a copy of your plan's SPD. It outlines your benefits and your legal rights under the Employee Retirement Income Security Act (ERISA), the federal law that protects your health benefits. It should contain information about the coverage of dependents, what services will require a co-pay, and the circumstances under which your employer can change or terminate a health benefits plan. Save the SPD and all other health plan brochures and documents, along with memos or correspondence from your employer relating to health benefits.

5. Assess your benefit coverage as your family status changes. Marriage, divorce, childbirth or adoption, and the death of a spouse are all life events that may signal a need to change your health benefits. You, your spouse and dependent children may be eligible for a special enrollment period under provisions of the Health Insurance Portability and Accountability Act (HIPAA). Even without life-changing events, the information provided by your employer should tell you how you can change benefits or switch plans, if more than one plan is offered. If your spouse's employer also offers a health benefits package, consider coordinating both plans for maximum coverage.

6. Changing jobs and other life events can affect your health benefits. Under the Consolidated Omnibus Budget Reconciliation Act (COBRA), you, your covered spouse, and your dependent children may be eligible to purchase extended health coverage under your employer's plan if you lose your job, change employers, get divorced, or upon occurrence of certain other events. Coverage can range from 18 to 36 months depending on your situation. COBRA applies to most employers with 20 or more workers and requires your plan to notify you of your rights. Most plans require eligible individuals to make their COBRA election within 60 days of the plan's notice. Be sure to follow up with your plan sponsor if you don't receive notice, and make sure you respond within the allotted time.

7. HIPAA can also help if you are changing jobs, particularly if you have a medical condition. HIPAA generally limits pre-existing condition exclusions to a maximum of 12 months (18 months for late enrollees). HIPAA also requires this maximum period to be reduced by the length of time you had prior "creditable coverage." You should receive a certificate documenting your prior creditable coverage from your old plan when coverage ends.

8. Plan for retirement. Before you retire, find out what health benefits, if any, extend to you and your spouse during your retirement years. Consult with your employer's human resources office, your union, the plan administrator, and check your SPD. Make sure there is no conflicting information among these sources about the benefits you will receive or the circumstances under which they can change or be eliminated. With this information in hand, you can make other important choices, like finding out if you are eligible for Medicare and Medigap insurance coverage.

9. Know how to file an appeal if your health benefits claim is denied. Understand how your plan handles grievances and where to make appeals of the plan's decisions. Keep records and copies of correspondence. Check your health benefits package and your SPD to determine who is responsible for handling problems with benefit claims. Contact PWBA for customer service assistance if you are unable to obtain a response to your complaint.

10. You can take steps to improve the quality of the healthcare and the health benefits you receive. Look for and use things like Quality Reports and Accreditation Reports whenever you can. Quality reports may contain consumer ratings -- how satisfied consumers are with the doctors in their plan, for instance-- and clinical performance measures -- how well a healthcare organization prevents and treats illness. Accreditation reports provide information on how accredited organizations meet national standards, and often include clinical performance measures. Look for these quality measures whenever possible. Consult "Your Guide to Choosing Quality Health Care" on the Internet at **www.ahcpr.gov/consumer**.

Medicare and Medicaid

Illness strikes both rich and poor families. For low-income families, Medicaid is available to defer the costs of treatment. The Health Care Financing Administration (HCFA) administers Medicare, the nation's largest health insurance program, which covers 39 million Americans. In the following pages, you will learn the basics about Medicare insurance as well as useful contact information on how to find more in-depth information about Medicaid.[50]

Who is Eligible for Medicare?

Generally, you are eligible for Medicare if you or your spouse worked for at least 10 years in Medicare-covered employment and you are 65 years old and a citizen or permanent resident of the United States. You might also qualify for coverage if you are under age 65 but have a disability or End-Stage Renal disease (permanent kidney failure requiring dialysis or transplant). Here are some simple guidelines:

You can get Part A at age 65 without having to pay premiums if:

- You are already receiving retirement benefits from Social Security or the Railroad Retirement Board.

- You are eligible to receive Social Security or Railroad benefits but have not yet filed for them.

- You or your spouse had Medicare-covered government employment.

If you are under 65, you can get Part A without having to pay premiums if:

- You have received Social Security or Railroad Retirement Board disability benefit for 24 months.

- You are a kidney dialysis or kidney transplant patient.

Medicare has two parts:

- Part A (Hospital Insurance). Most people do not have to pay for Part A.
- Part B (Medical Insurance). Most people pay monthly for Part B.

Part A (Hospital Insurance)

Helps Pay For: Inpatient hospital care, care in critical access hospitals (small facilities that give limited outpatient and inpatient services to people in rural areas) and skilled nursing facilities, hospice care, and some home healthcare.

---

[50] This section has been adapted from the Official U.S. Site for Medicare Information: **http://www.medicare.gov/Basics/Overview.asp**.

Cost: Most people get Part A automatically when they turn age 65. You do not have to pay a monthly payment called a premium for Part A because you or a spouse paid Medicare taxes while you were working.

If you (or your spouse) did not pay Medicare taxes while you were working and you are age 65 or older, you still may be able to buy Part A. If you are not sure you have Part A, look on your red, white, and blue Medicare card. It will show "Hospital Part A" on the lower left corner of the card. You can also call the Social Security Administration toll free at 1-800-772-1213 or call your local Social Security office for more information about buying Part A. If you get benefits from the Railroad Retirement Board, call your local RRB office or 1-800-808-0772. For more information, call your Fiscal Intermediary about Part A bills and services. The phone number for the Fiscal Intermediary office in your area can be obtained from the following Web site: **http://www.medicare.gov/Contacts/home.asp**.

Part B (Medical Insurance)

Helps Pay For: Doctors, services, outpatient hospital care, and some other medical services that Part A does not cover, such as the services of physical and occupational therapists, and some home healthcare. Part B helps pay for covered services and supplies when they are medically necessary.

Cost: As of 2001, you pay the Medicare Part B premium of $50.00 per month. In some cases this amount may be higher if you did not choose Part B when you first became eligible at age 65. The cost of Part B may go up 10% for each 12-month period that you were eligible for Part B but declined coverage, except in special cases. You will have to pay the extra 10% cost for the rest of your life.

Enrolling in Part B is your choice. You can sign up for Part B anytime during a 7-month period that begins 3 months before you turn 65. Visit your local Social Security office, or call the Social Security Administration at 1-800-772-1213 to sign up. If you choose to enroll in Part B, the premium is usually taken out of your monthly Social Security, Railroad Retirement, or Civil Service Retirement payment. If you do not receive any of the above payments, Medicare sends you a bill for your part B premium every 3 months. You should receive your Medicare premium bill in the mail by the 10th of the month. If you do not, call the Social Security Administration at 1-800-772-1213, or your local Social Security office. If you get benefits from the Railroad Retirement Board, call your local RRB office or 1-800-808-0772. For more information, call your Medicare carrier about bills and services. The phone number for the Medicare carrier in your area can be found at the following Web site: **http://www.medicare.gov/Contacts/home.asp**. You may have choices in how you get your healthcare including the Original Medicare Plan, Medicare Managed Care Plans (like HMOs), and Medicare Private Fee-for-Service Plans.

Medicaid

Medicaid is a joint federal and state program that helps pay medical costs for some people with low incomes and limited resources. Medicaid programs vary from state to state. People on Medicaid may also get coverage for nursing home care and outpatient prescription drugs which are not covered by Medicare. You can find more information about Medicaid on the HCFA.gov Web site at **http://www.hcfa.gov/medicaid/medicaid.htm**.

States also have programs that pay some or all of Medicare's premiums and may also pay Medicare deductibles and coinsurance for certain people who have Medicare and a low income. To qualify, you must have:

- Part A (Hospital Insurance),

- Assets, such as bank accounts, stocks, and bonds that are not more than $4,000 for a single person, or $6,000 for a couple, and

- A monthly income that is below certain limits.

For more information on these programs, look at the Medicare Savings Programs brochure, **http://www.medicare.gov/Library/PDFNavigation/PDFInterim.asp?Langua ge=English&Type=Pub&PubID=10126**. There are also Prescription Drug Assistance Programs available. Find information on these programs which offer discounts or free medications to individuals in need at **http://www.medicare.gov/Prescription/Home.asp**.

NORD's Medication Assistance Programs

Finally, the National Organization for Rare Disorders, Inc. (NORD) administers medication programs sponsored by humanitarian-minded pharmaceutical and biotechnology companies to help uninsured or under-insured individuals secure life-saving or life-sustaining drugs.[51] NORD

---

[51] Adapted from NORD: **http://www.rarediseases.org/cgi-bin/nord/progserv#patient?id=rPIzL9oD&mv_pc=30**.

programs ensure that certain vital drugs are available "to those individuals whose income is too high to qualify for Medicaid but too low to pay for their prescribed medications." The program has standards for fairness, equity, and unbiased eligibility. It currently covers some 14 programs for nine pharmaceutical companies. NORD also offers early access programs for investigational new drugs (IND) under the approved "Treatment INDs" programs of the Food and Drug Administration (FDA). In these programs, a limited number of individuals can receive investigational drugs that have yet to be approved by the FDA. These programs are generally designed for rare diseases or disorders. For more information, visit **www.rarediseases.org**.

Additional Resources

In addition to the references already listed in this chapter, you may need more information on health insurance, hospitals, or the healthcare system in general. The NIH has set up an excellent guidance Web site that addresses these and other issues. Topics include:[52]

- Health Insurance:
  http://www.nlm.nih.gov/medlineplus/healthinsurance.html

- Health Statistics:
  http://www.nlm.nih.gov/medlineplus/healthstatistics.html

- HMO and Managed Care:
  http://www.nlm.nih.gov/medlineplus/managedcare.html

- Hospice Care: **http://www.nlm.nih.gov/medlineplus/hospicecare.html**

- Medicaid: **http://www.nlm.nih.gov/medlineplus/medicaid.html**

- Medicare: **http://www.nlm.nih.gov/medlineplus/medicare.html**

- Nursing Homes and Long-term Care:
  http://www.nlm.nih.gov/medlineplus/nursinghomes.html

- Patient's Rights, Confidentiality, Informed Consent, Ombudsman Programs, Privacy and Patient Issues:
  http://www.nlm.nih.gov/medlineplus/patientissues.html

---

[52] You can access this information at:
http://www.nlm.nih.gov/medlineplus/healthsystem.html.

ONLINE GLOSSARIES

The Internet provides access to a number of free-to-use medical dictionaries and glossaries. The National Library of Medicine has compiled the following list of online dictionaries:

- ADAM Medical Encyclopedia (A.D.A.M., Inc.), comprehensive medical reference: **http://www.nlm.nih.gov/medlineplus/encyclopedia.html**

- MedicineNet.com Medical Dictionary (MedicineNet, Inc.): **http://www.medterms.com/Script/Main/hp.asp**

- Merriam-Webster Medical Dictionary (Inteli-Health, Inc.): **http://www.intelihealth.com/IH/**

- Multilingual Glossary of Technical and Popular Medical Terms in Eight European Languages (European Commission) - Danish, Dutch, English, French, German, Italian, Portuguese, and Spanish: **http://allserv.rug.ac.be/~rvdstich/eugloss/welcome.html**

- On-line Medical Dictionary (CancerWEB): **http://www.graylab.ac.uk/omd/**

- Technology Glossary (National Library of Medicine) - Health Care Technology: **http://www.nlm.nih.gov/nichsr/ta101/ta10108.htm**

- Terms and Definitions (Office of Rare Diseases): **http://rarediseases.info.nih.gov/ord/glossary_a-e.html**

Beyond these, MEDLINEplus contains a very user-friendly encyclopedia covering every aspect of medicine (licensed from A.D.A.M., Inc.). The ADAM Medical Encyclopedia Web site address is **http://www.nlm.nih.gov/medlineplus/encyclopedia.html**. ADAM is also available on commercial Web sites such as Web MD (**http://my.webmd.com/adam/asset/adam_disease_articles/a_to_z/a**) and drkoop.com (**http://www.drkoop.com/**). Topics of interest can be researched by using keywords before continuing elsewhere, as these basic definitions and concepts will be useful in more advanced areas of research. You may choose to print various pages specifically relating to hemorrhoids and keep them on file. The NIH, in particular, suggests that patients with hemorrhoids visit the following Web sites in the ADAM Medical Encyclopedia:

- **Basic Guidelines for Hemorrhoids**

  Hemorrhoids
  Web site:
  http://www.nlm.nih.gov/medlineplus/ency/article/000292.htm

- **Signs & Symptoms for Hemorrhoids**

  Blood in the stool
  Web site:
  http://www.nlm.nih.gov/medlineplus/ency/article/003130.htm

  Constipation
  Web site:
  http://www.nlm.nih.gov/medlineplus/ency/article/003125.htm

  Incontinence
  Web site:
  http://www.nlm.nih.gov/medlineplus/ency/article/003142.htm

  Itching
  Web site:
  http://www.nlm.nih.gov/medlineplus/ency/article/003217.htm

  Pruritus
  Web site:
  http://www.nlm.nih.gov/medlineplus/ency/article/003217.htm

  Swelling
  Web site:
  http://www.nlm.nih.gov/medlineplus/ency/article/003103.htm

- **Diagnostics and Tests for Hemorrhoids**

  Anoscopy
  Web site:
  http://www.nlm.nih.gov/medlineplus/ency/article/003890.htm

  Digital rectal exam
  Web site:
  http://www.nlm.nih.gov/medlineplus/ency/article/007069.htm

Proctoscopy
Web site:
http://www.nlm.nih.gov/medlineplus/ency/article/003885.htm

Sigmoidoscopy
Web site:
http://www.nlm.nih.gov/medlineplus/ency/article/003885.htm

Stool guaiac
Web site:
http://www.nlm.nih.gov/medlineplus/ency/article/003393.htm

- **Nutrition for Hemorrhoids**

Fiber
Web site:
http://www.nlm.nih.gov/medlineplus/ency/article/002470.htm

Fiber diet
Web site:
http://www.nlm.nih.gov/medlineplus/ency/article/002470.htm

High-fiber
Web site:
http://www.nlm.nih.gov/medlineplus/ency/article/002470.htm

- **Surgery and Procedures for Hemorrhoids**

Hemorrhoidectomy
Web site:
http://www.nlm.nih.gov/medlineplus/ency/article/002939.htm

Laser surgery
Web site:
http://www.nlm.nih.gov/medlineplus/ency/article/002958.htm

- **Background Topics for Hemorrhoids**

Acute
Web site:
http://www.nlm.nih.gov/medlineplus/ency/article/002215.htm

Chronic
Web site:
http://www.nlm.nih.gov/medlineplus/ency/article/002312.htm

Incidence
Web site:
http://www.nlm.nih.gov/medlineplus/ency/article/002387.htm

Online Dictionary Directories

The following are additional online directories compiled by the National Library of Medicine, including a number of specialized medical dictionaries and glossaries:

- Medical Dictionaries: Medical & Biological (World Health Organization):
  http://www.who.int/hlt/virtuallibrary/English/diction.htm#Medical

- MEL-Michigan Electronic Library List of Online Health and Medical Dictionaries (Michigan Electronic Library):
  http://mel.lib.mi.us/health/health-dictionaries.html

- Patient Education: Glossaries (DMOZ Open Directory Project):
  http://dmoz.org/Health/Education/Patient_Education/Glossaries/

- Web of Online Dictionaries (Bucknell University):
  http://www.yourdictionary.com/diction5.html#medicine

HEMORRHOIDS GLOSSARY

The following is a complete glossary of terms used in this sourcebook. The definitions are derived from official public sources including the National Institutes of Health [NIH] and the European Union [EU]. After this glossary, we list a number of additional hardbound and electronic glossaries and dictionaries that you may wish to consult.

Abdomen: That portion of the body that lies between the thorax and the pelvis. [NIH]

Abdominal: Pertaining to the abdomen. [EU]

Acetaminophen: Analgesic antipyretic derivative of acetanilide. It has weak anti-inflammatory properties and is used as a common analgesic, but may cause liver, blood cell, and kidney damage. [NIH]

Acne: An inflammatory disease of the pilosebaceous unit, the specific type usually being indicated by a modifying term; frequently used alone to designate common acne, or acne vulgaris. [EU]

Adhesions: Pathological processes consisting of the union of the opposing surfaces of a wound. [NIH]

Adverse: Harmful. [EU]

Aerobic: 1. having molecular oxygen present. 2. growing, living, or occurring in the presence of molecular oxygen. 3. requiring oxygen for respiration. [EU]

Aetiology: Study of the causes of disease. [EU]

Algorithms: A procedure consisting of a sequence of algebraic formulas and/or logical steps to calculate or determine a given task. [NIH]

Alimentary: Pertaining to food or nutritive material, or to the organs of digestion. [EU]

Aluminum: A metallic element that has the atomic number 13, atomic symbol Al, and atomic weight 26.98. [NIH]

Anaerobic: 1. lacking molecular oxygen. 2. growing, living, or occurring in the absence of molecular oxygen; pertaining to an anaerobe. [EU]

Analgesic: An agent that alleviates pain without causing loss of consciousness. [EU]

Anatomical: Pertaining to anatomy, or to the structure of the organism. [EU]

Anemia: A reduction in the number of circulating erythrocytes or in the quantity of hemoglobin. [NIH]

Anesthesia: A state characterized by loss of feeling or sensation. This depression of nerve function is usually the result of pharmacologic action and is induced to allow performance of surgery or other painful procedures. [NIH]

Anesthetics: Agents that are capable of inducing a total or partial loss of sensation, especially tactile sensation and pain. They may act to induce general anesthesia, in which an unconscious state is achieved, or may act locally to induce numbness or lack of sensation at a targeted site. [NIH]

Angiodysplasia: Degenerative, acquired lesions consisting of distorted, dilated, thin-walled vessels lined by vascular endothelium. This pathological state is seen especially in the gastrointestinal tract and is frequently a cause of upper and lower gastrointestinal hemorrhage in the elderly. [NIH]

Angiography: Radiography of blood vessels after injection of a contrast medium. [NIH]

Angiotensinogen: An alpha-globulin of which a fragment of 14 amino acids is converted by renin to angiotensin I, the inactive precursor of angiotensin II. It is a member of the serpin superfamily. [NIH]

Angiotensins: Oligopeptides ranging in size from angiotensin precursors with 14 amino acids to the active vasoconstrictor angiotensin II with 8 amino acids, or their analogs or derivatives. The amino acid content varies with the species and changes in that content produce antagonistic or inactive compounds. [NIH]

Anomalies: Birth defects; abnormalities. [NIH]

Anorectal: Pertaining to the anus and rectum or to the junction region between the two. [EU]

Anorexia: Lack or loss of the appetite for food. [EU]

Antiallergic: Counteracting allergy or allergic conditions. [EU]

Antibiotic: A chemical substance produced by a microorganism which has the capacity, in dilute solutions, to inhibit the growth of or to kill other microorganisms. Antibiotics that are sufficiently nontoxic to the host are used as chemotherapeutic agents in the treatment of infectious diseases of man, animals and plants. [EU]

Antibody: An immunoglobulin molecule that has a specific amino acid sequence by virtue of which it interacts only with the antigen that induced its synthesis in cells of the lymphoid series (especially plasma cells), or with antigen closely related to it. Antibodies are classified according to their ode of action as agglutinins, bacteriolysins, haemolysins, opsonins, precipitins, etc. [EU]

Antifungal: Destructive to fungi, or suppressing their reproduction or growth; effective against fungal infections. [EU]

Antigens: Substances that cause an immune response in the body. The body "sees" the antigens as harmful or foreign. To fight them, the body produces antibodies, which attack and try to eliminate the antigens. [NIH]

Antipruritic: Relieving or preventing itching. [EU]

Antiseptic: An agent that kills bacteria. Alcohol is a common antiseptic. Before injecting insulin, many people use alcohol to clean their skin to avoid infection. [NIH]

Antiviral: Destroying viruses or suppressing their replication. [EU]

Anus: The distal or terminal orifice of the alimentary canal. [EU]

Appendicitis: Acute inflammation of the vermiform appendix. [NIH]

Arterial: Pertaining to an artery or to the arteries. [EU]

Arteries: The vessels carrying blood away from the heart. [NIH]

Arteriolar: Pertaining to or resembling arterioles. [EU]

Arterioles: The smallest divisions of the arteries located between the muscular arteries and the capillaries. [NIH]

Arteriovenous: Both arterial and venous; pertaining to or affecting an artery and a vein. [EU]

Aspiration: The act of inhaling. [EU]

Assay: Determination of the amount of a particular constituent of a mixture, or of the biological or pharmacological potency of a drug. [EU]

Astringent: Causing contraction, usually locally after topical application. [EU]

Atopic: Pertaining to an atopen or to atopy; allergic. [EU]

Bacteria: Unicellular prokaryotic microorganisms which generally possess rigid cell walls, multiply by cell division, and exhibit three principal forms: round or coccal, rodlike or bacillary, and spiral or spirochetal. [NIH]

Bacteriophages: Viruses whose host is a bacterial cell. [NIH]

Barium: An element of the alkaline earth group of metals. It has an atomic symbol Ba, atomic number 56, and atomic weight 138. All of its acid-soluble salts are poisonous. [NIH]

Baths: The immersion or washing of the body or any of its parts in water or other medium for cleansing or medical treatment. It includes bathing for personal hygiene as well as for medical purposes with the addition of therapeutic agents, such as alkalines, antiseptics, oil, etc. [NIH]

Benign: Not malignant; not recurrent; favourable for recovery. [EU]

Bezoars: Concretions of swallowed hair, fruit or vegetable fibers, or similar substances found in the alimentary canal. [NIH]

Biliary: Pertaining to the bile, to the bile ducts, or to the gallbladder. [EU]

Biochemical: Relating to biochemistry; characterized by, produced by, or involving chemical reactions in living organisms. [EU]

Biopharmaceutics: The study of the physical and chemical properties of a drug and its dosage form as related to the onset, duration, and intensity of its action. [NIH]

Biopsy: The removal and examination, usually microscopic, of tissue from the living body, performed to establish precise diagnosis. [EU]

Bupivacaine: A widely used local anesthetic agent. [NIH]

Campylobacter: A genus of bacteria found in the reproductive organs, intestinal tract, and oral cavity of animals and man. Some species are pathogenic. [NIH]

Capillary: Any one of the minute vessels that connect the arterioles and venules, forming a network in nearly all parts of the body. Their walls act as semipermeable membranes for the interchange of various substances, including fluids, between the blood and tissue fluid; called also vas capillare. [EU]

Capsules: Hard or soft soluble containers used for the oral administration of medicine. [NIH]

Carbohydrate: An aldehyde or ketone derivative of a polyhydric alcohol, particularly of the pentahydric and hexahydric alcohols. They are so named because the hydrogen and oxygen are usually in the proportion to form water, $(CH_2O)n$. The most important carbohydrates are the starches, sugars, celluloses, and gums. They are classified into mono-, di-, tri-, poly- and heterosaccharides. [EU]

Carcinoma: A malignant new growth made up of epithelial cells tending to infiltrate the surrounding tissues and give rise to metastases. [EU]

Cardiac: Pertaining to the heart. [EU]

Cardiovascular: Pertaining to the heart and blood vessels. [EU]

Catheter: A tubular, flexible, surgical instrument for withdrawing fluids from (or introducing fluids into) a cavity of the body, especially one for introduction into the bladder through the urethra for the withdraw of urine. [EU]

Cetirizine: A potent second-generation histamine H1 antagonist that is effective in the treatment of allergic rhinitis, chronic urticaria, and pollen-induced asthma. Unlike many traditional antihistamines, it does not cause drowsiness or anticholinergic side effects. [NIH]

Cholangitis: Inflammation of a bile duct. [EU]

Cholecystitis: Inflammation of the gallbladder. [EU]

Cholelithiasis: The presence or formation of gallstones. [EU]

Cholera: An acute diarrheal disease endemic in India and Southeast Asia whose causative agent is vibrio cholerae. This condition can lead to severe dehydration in a matter of hours unless quickly treated. [NIH]

Chronic: Persisting over a long period of time. [EU]

Cirrhosis: Liver disease characterized pathologically by loss of the normal microscopic lobular architecture, with fibrosis and nodular regeneration. The term is sometimes used to refer to chronic interstitial inflammation of any organ. [EU]

Clostridium: A genus of motile or nonmotile gram-positive bacteria of the family bacillaceae. Many species have been identified with some being pathogenic. They occur in water, soil, and in the intestinal tract of humans and lower animals. [NIH]

Coagulation: 1. the process of clot formation. 2. in colloid chemistry, the solidification of a sol into a gelatinous mass; an alteration of a disperse phase or of a dissolved solid which causes the separation of the system into a liquid phase and an insoluble mass called the clot or curd. Coagulation is usually irreversible. 3. in surgery, the disruption of tissue by physical means to form an amorphous residuum, as in electrocoagulation and photocoagulation. [EU]

Colic: Paroxysms of pain. This condition usually occurs in the abdominal region but may occur in other body regions as well. [NIH]

Colitis: Inflammation of the colon. [EU]

Colonoscopy: Endoscopic examination, therapy or surgery of the luminal surface of the colon. [NIH]

Colorectal: Pertaining to or affecting the colon and rectum. [EU]

Concomitant: Accompanying; accessory; joined with another. [EU]

Congestion: Excessive or abnormal accumulation of blood in a part. [EU]

Constipation: Infrequent or difficult evacuation of the faeces. [EU]

Constriction: The act of constricting. [NIH]

Contamination: The soiling or pollution by inferior material, as by the introduction of organisms into a wound, or sewage into a stream. [EU]

Contracture: A condition of fixed high resistance to passive stretch of a muscle, resulting from fibrosis of the tissues supporting the muscles or the joints, or from disorders of the muscle fibres. [EU]

Convalescence: The stage of recovery following an attack of disease, a surgical operation, or an injury. [EU]

Cortex: The outer layer of an organ or other body structure, as distinguished from the internal substance. [EU]

Cryosurgery: The use of freezing as a special surgical technique to destroy or excise tissue. [NIH]

Curative: Tending to overcome disease and promote recovery. [EU]

Cyclic: Pertaining to or occurring in a cycle or cycles; the term is applied to chemical compounds that contain a ring of atoms in the nucleus. [EU]

Cytokines: Non-antibody proteins secreted by inflammatory leukocytes and some non-leukocytic cells, that act as intercellular mediators. They differ from classical hormones in that they are produced by a number of tissue or cell types rather than by specialized glands. They generally act locally in a paracrine or autocrine rather than endocrine manner. [NIH]

Cytotoxic: Pertaining to or exhibiting cytotoxicity. [EU]

Cytotoxins: Substances elaborated by microorganisms, plants or animals that are specifically toxic to individual cells; they may be involved in immunity or may be contained in venoms. [NIH]

Defecation: The normal process of elimination of fecal material from the RECTUM. [NIH]

Degenerative: Undergoing degeneration : tending to degenerate; having the character of or involving degeneration; causing or tending to cause degeneration. [EU]

Dehydration: The condition that results from excessive loss of body water. Called also anhydration, deaquation and hypohydration. [EU]

Dermatitis: Inflammation of the skin. [EU]

Dermatology: A medical specialty concerned with the skin, its structure, functions, diseases, and treatment. [NIH]

Diarrhea: Passage of excessively liquid or excessively frequent stools. [NIH]

Diathermy: Heating of the body tissues due to their resistance to the passage of high-frequency electromagnetic radiation, electric currents, or ultrasonic waves. In medical d. (thermopenetration) the tissues are warmed but not damaged; in surgical d. (electrocoagulation) tissue is destroyed. [EU]

Dilatation: The condition, as of an orifice or tubular structure, of being dilated or stretched beyond the normal dimensions. [EU]

Diosmin: A bioflavonoid that strengthens vascular walls. [NIH]

Distal: Remote; farther from any point of reference; opposed to proximal. In dentistry, used to designate a position on the dental arch farther from the median line of the jaw. [EU]

Diverticulitis: Inflammation of a diverticulum, especially inflammation related to colonic diverticula, which may undergo perforation with abscess formation. Sometimes called left-sided or L-sides appendicitis. [EU]

Diverticulum: A pathological condition manifested as a pouch or sac opening from a tubular or sacular organ. [NIH]

Dysentery: Any of various disorders marked by inflammation of the intestines, especially of the colon, and attended by pain in the abdomen, tenesmus, and frequent stools containing blood and mucus. Causes include chemical irritants, bacteria, protozoa, or parasitic worms. [EU]

Dyspareunia: Difficult or painful coitus. [EU]

Dyspepsia: Impairment of the power of function of digestion; usually applied to epigastric discomfort following meals. [EU]

Echinacea: A genus of perennial herbs used topically and internally. It contains echinacoside, glycosides, inulin, isobutyl amides, resin, and sesquiterpenes. [NIH]

Eczema: A pruritic papulovesicular dermatitis occurring as a reaction to many endogenous and exogenous agents, characterized in the acute stage by erythema, edema associated with a serous exudate between the cells of the epidermis (spongiosis) and an inflammatory infiltrate in the dermis, oozing and vesiculation, and crusting and scaling; and in the more chronic stages by lichenification or thickening or both, signs of excoriations, and hyperpigmentation or hypopigmentation or both. Atopic dermatitis is the most common type of dermatitis. Called also eczematous dermatitis. [EU]

Edema: Excessive amount of watery fluid accumulated in the intercellular spaces, most commonly present in subcutaneous tissue. [NIH]

Elastic: Susceptible of resisting and recovering from stretching, compression or distortion applied by a force. [EU]

Embryo: In animals, those derivatives of the fertilized ovum that eventually become the offspring, during their period of most rapid development, i.e., after the long axis appears until all major structures are represented. In man, the developing organism is an embryo from about two weeks after fertilization to the end of seventh or eighth week. [EU]

Endocrinology: A subspecialty of internal medicine concerned with the metabolism, physiology, and disorders of the endocrine system. [NIH]

Endocytosis: Cellular uptake of extracellular materials within membrane-limited vacuoles or microvesicles. Endosomes play a central role in endocytosis. [NIH]

Endoscopy: Visual inspection of any cavity of the body by means of an endoscope. [EU]

Endothelium: The layer of epithelial cells that lines the cavities of the heart and of the blood and lymph vessels, and the serous cavities of the body, originating from the mesoderm. [EU]

Enema: A clyster or injection; a liquid injected or to be injected into the rectum. [EU]

Entamoeba: A genus of ameboid protozoa characterized by the presence of beaded chromatin on the inner surface of the nuclear membrane. Its organisms are parasitic in invertebrates and vertebrates, including humans. [NIH]

Enteritis: Inflammation of the intestine, applied chiefly to inflammation of the small intestine; see also enterocolitis. [EU]

Enterocolitis: Inflammation involving both the small intestine and the colon; see also enteritis. [EU]

Enzyme: A protein molecule that catalyses chemical reactions of other substances without itself being destroyed or altered upon completion of the reactions. Enzymes are classified according to the recommendations of the Nomenclature Committee of the International Union of Biochemistry. Each enzyme is assigned a recommended name and an Enzyme Commission (EC) number. They are divided into six main groups; oxidoreductases, transferases, hydrolases, lyases, isomerases, and ligases. [EU]

Epinephrine: The active sympathomimetic hormone from the adrenal medulla in most species. It stimulates both the alpha- and beta- adrenergic systems, causes systemic vasoconstriction and gastrointestinal relaxation, stimulates the heart, and dilates bronchi and cerebral vessels. It is used in asthma and cardiac failure and to delay absorption of local anesthetics. [NIH]

Escherichia: A genus of gram-negative, facultatively anaerobic, rod-shaped bacteria whose organisms occur in the lower part of the intestine of warm-blooded animals. The species are either nonpathogenic or opportunistic pathogens. [NIH]

Esophagitis: Inflammation, acute or chronic, of the esophagus caused by bacteria, chemicals, or trauma. [NIH]

Estradiol: The most potent mammalian estrogenic hormone. It is produced in the ovary, placenta, testis, and possibly the adrenal cortex. [NIH]

Fatal: Causing death, deadly; mortal; lethal. [EU]

Fats: One of the three main classes of foods and a source of energy in the body. Fats help the body use some vitamins and keep the skin healthy. They also serve as energy stores for the body. In food, there are two types of fats: saturated and unsaturated. [NIH]

Fibrin: The insoluble protein formed from fibrinogen by the proteolytic action of thrombin during normal clotting of blood. Fibrin forms the essential portion of the blood clot. [EU]

Fibrinolytic: Pertaining to, characterized by, or causing the dissolution of fibrin by enzymatic action [EU]

Filtration: The passage of a liquid through a filter, accomplished by gravity, pressure, or vacuum (suction). [EU]

Fissure: Any cleft or groove, normal or otherwise; especially a deep fold in the cerebral cortex which involves the entire thickness of the brain wall. [EU]

Flatulence: The presence of excessive amounts of air or gases in the stomach or intestine, leading to distention of the organs. [EU]

Fluoroscopy: Production of an image when x-rays strike a fluorescent screen. [NIH]

Frostbite: Damage to tissues as the result of low environmental temperatures. [NIH]

Gastritis: Inflammation of the stomach. [EU]

Gastroenteritis: An acute inflammation of the lining of the stomach and intestines, characterized by anorexia, nausea, diarrhoea, abdominal pain, and weakness, which has various causes, including food poisoning due to infection with such organisms as Escherichia coli, Staphylococcus aureus, and Salmonella species; consumption of irritating food or drink; or psychological factors such as anger, stress, and fear. Called also enterogastritis. [EU]

Gastrointestinal: Pertaining to or communicating with the stomach and intestine, as a gastrointestinal fistula. [EU]

Gastroscopy: Endoscopic examination, therapy or surgery of the interior of the stomach. [NIH]

Gelatin: A product formed from skin, white connective tissue, or bone collagen. It is used as a protein food adjuvant, plasma substitute, hemostatic, suspending agent in pharmaceutical preparations, and in the manufacturing of capsules and suppositories. [NIH]

Genital: Pertaining to the genitalia. [EU]

Genotype: The genetic constitution of the individual; the characterization of the genes. [NIH]

Glomerular: Pertaining to or of the nature of a glomerulus, especially a renal glomerulus. [EU]

Gout: Hereditary metabolic disorder characterized by recurrent acute arthritis, hyperuricemia and deposition of sodium urate in and around the joints, sometimes with formation of uric acid calculi. [NIH]

Gynecology: A medical-surgical specialty concerned with the physiology and disorders primarily of the female genital tract, as well as female endocrinology and reproductive physiology. [NIH]

Haemorrhoid: A varicose dilatation of a vein of the superior or inferior haemorrhoidal plexus, resulting from a persistent increase in venous pressure. [EU]

Heartburn: Substernal pain or burning sensation, usually associated with regurgitation of gastric juice into the esophagus. [NIH]

Helicobacter: A genus of gram-negative, spiral-shaped bacteria that is pathogenic and has been isolated from the intestinal tract of mammals, including humans. [NIH]

Helminthiasis: Infestation with parasitic worms of the helminth class. [NIH]

Hematology: A subspecialty of internal medicine concerned with morphology, physiology, and pathology of the blood and blood-forming tissues. [NIH]

Hemorrhage: Bleeding or escape of blood from a vessel. [NIH]

Hemorrhoids: Varicosities of the hemorrhoidal venous plexuses. [NIH]

Hepatic: Pertaining to the liver. [EU]

Hepatitis: Inflammation of the liver. [EU]

Heredity: 1. the genetic transmission of a particular quality or trait from parent to offspring. 2. the genetic constitution of an individual. [EU]

Hernia: (he protrusion of a loop or knuckle of an organ or tissue through an abnormal opening. [EU]

Herpes: Any inflammatory skin disease caused by a herpesvirus and characterized by the formation of clusters of small vesicles. When used alone, the term may refer to herpes simplex or to herpes zoster. [EU]

Hiccup: A spasm of the diaphragm that causes a sudden inhalation followed by rapid closure of the glottis which produces a sound. [NIH]

Hormonal: Pertaining to or of the nature of a hormone. [EU]

Humoral: Of, relating to, proceeding from, or involving a bodily humour - now often used of endocrine factors as opposed to neural or somatic. [EU]

Hygienic: Pertaining to hygiene, or conducive to health. [EU]

Hypercholesterolemia: Abnormally high levels of cholesterol in the blood. [NIH]

Hyperplasia: The abnormal multiplication or increase in the number of normal cells in normal arrangement in a tissue. [EU]

Hypertension: Persistently high arterial blood pressure. Various criteria for its threshold have been suggested, ranging from 140 mm. Hg systolic and 90 mm. Hg diastolic to as high as 200 mm. Hg systolic and 110 mm. Hg diastolic. Hypertension may have no known cause (essential or idiopathic h.) or be associated with other primary diseases (secondary h.). [EU]

Hypertrophy: Nutrition) the enlargement or overgrowth of an organ or part due to an increase in size of its constituent cells. [EU]

Hypogonadism: A condition resulting from or characterized by abnormally decreased functional activity of the gonads, with retardation of growth and sexual development. [EU]

Hypothyroidism: Deficiency of thyroid activity. In adults, it is most common in women and is characterized by decrease in basal metabolic rate, tiredness and lethargy, sensitivity to cold, and menstrual disturbances. If untreated, it progresses to full-blown myxoedema. In infants, severe hypothyroidism leads to cretinism. In juveniles, the manifestations are intermediate, with less severe mental and developmental retardation and only mild symptoms of the adult form. When due to pituitary deficiency of thyrotropin secretion it is called secondary hypothyroidism. [EU]

Hypoxia: Reduction of oxygen supply to tissue below physiological levels despite adequate perfusion of the tissue by blood. [EU]

Idiopathic: Of the nature of an idiopathy; self-originated; of unknown causation. [EU]

Ileostomy: Surgical creation of an external opening into the ileum for fecal diversion or drainage. Loop or tube procedures are most often employed. [NIH]

Ileus: Obstruction of the intestines. [EU]

Immunity: The condition of being immune; the protection against infectious disease conferred either by the immune response generated by immunization or previous infection or by other nonimmunologic factors (innate i.). [EU]

Immunization: The induction of immunity. [EU]

Immunoassay: Immunochemical assay or detection of a substance by serologic or immunologic methods. Usually the substance being studied serves as antigen both in antibody production and in measurement of antibody by the test substance. [NIH]

Incision: 1. cleft, cut, gash. 2. an act or action of incising. [EU]

Incontinence: Inability to control excretory functions, as defecation (faecal i.) or urination (urinary i.). [EU]

Induction: The act or process of inducing or causing to occur, especially the production of a specific morphogenetic effect in the developing embryo through the influence of evocators or organizers, or the production of anaesthesia or unconsciousness by use of appropriate agents. [EU]

Inflammation: A pathological process characterized by injury or destruction of tissues caused by a variety of cytologic and chemical reactions. It is usually manifested by typical signs of pain, heat, redness, swelling, and loss of function. [NIH]

Influenza: An acute viral infection involving the respiratory tract. It is marked by inflammation of the nasal mucosa, the pharynx, and conjunctiva, and by headache and severe, often generalized, myalgia. [NIH]

Ingestion: The act of taking food, medicines, etc., into the body, by mouth. [EU]

Inguinal: Pertaining to the inguen, or groin. [EU]

Inhalation: The drawing of air or other substances into the lungs. [EU]

Intestines: The section of the alimentary canal from the stomach to the anus. It includes the large intestine and small intestine. [NIH]

Iodine: A nonmetallic element of the halogen group that is represented by the atomic symbol I, atomic number 53, and atomic weight of 126.90. It is a nutritionally essential element, especially important in thyroid hormone synthesis. In solution, it has anti-infective properties and is used topically. [NIH]

Jaundice: A clinical manifestation of hyperbilirubinemia, consisting of deposition of bile pigments in the skin, resulting in a yellowish staining of the skin and mucous membranes. [NIH]

Lesion: Any pathological or traumatic discontinuity of tissue or loss of function of a part. [EU]

Ligation: Application of a ligature to tie a vessel or strangulate a part. [NIH]

Lipid: Any of a heterogeneous group of flats and fatlike substances characterized by being water-insoluble and being extractable by nonpolar (or fat) solvents such as alcohol, ether, chloroform, benzene, etc. All contain as a major constituent aliphatic hydrocarbons. The lipids, which are easily stored in the body, serve as a source of fuel, are an important constituent of cell structure, and serve other biological functions. Lipids may be considered to include fatty acids, neutral fats, waxes, and steroids. Compound lipids comprise the glycolipids, lipoproteins, and phospholipids. [EU]

Liquifilm: A thin liquid layer of coating. [EU]

Localization: 1. the determination of the site or place of any process or lesion. 2. restriction to a circumscribed or limited area. 3. prelocalization. [EU]

Malabsorption: Impaired intestinal absorption of nutrients. [EU]

Malformation: A morphologic defect resulting from an intrinsically abnormal developmental process. [EU]

Mediator: An object or substance by which something is mediated, such as (1) a structure of the nervous system that transmits impulses eliciting a specific response; (2) a chemical substance (transmitter substance) that induces activity in an excitable tissue, such as nerve or muscle; or (3) a substance released from cells as the result of the interaction of antigen with antibody or by the action of antigen with a sensitized lymphocyte. [EU]

Megacolon: An abnormally large or dilated colon; the condition may be congenital or acquired, acute or chronic. [EU]

Membrane: A thin layer of tissue which covers a surface, lines a cavity or divides a space or organ. [EU]

Metabolite: Any substance produced by metabolism or by a metabolic process. [EU]

Methylcellulose: Methylester of cellulose. Methylcellulose is used as an emulsifying and suspending agent in cosmetics, pharmaceutics and the chemical industry. It is used therapeutically as a bulk laxative. [NIH]

Microbiology: The study of microorganisms such as fungi, bacteria, algae, archaea, and viruses. [NIH]

Microcirculation: The flow of blood in the entire system of finer vessels (100 microns or less in diameter) of the body (the microvasculature). [EU]

Microvilli: Minute projections of cell membranes which greatly increase the surface area of the cell. [NIH]

Midwifery: The practice of assisting women in childbirth. [NIH]

Mobility: Capability of movement, of being moved, or of flowing freely. [EU]

Molecular: Of, pertaining to, or composed of molecules : a very small mass of matter. [EU]

Motility: The ability to move spontaneously. [EU]

Mucus: The free slime of the mucous membranes, composed of secretion of the glands, along with various inorganic salts, desquamated cells, and leucocytes. [EU]

Myxedema: A condition characterized by a dry, waxy type of swelling with abnormal deposits of mucin in the skin and other tissues. It is produced by a functional insufficiency of the thyroid gland, resulting in deficiency of thyroid hormone. The skin becomes puffy around the eyes and on the cheeks and the face is dull and expressionless with thickened nose and lips. The congenital form of the disease is cretinism. [NIH]

Narcotic: 1. pertaining to or producing narcosis. 2. an agent that produces insensibility or stupor, applied especially to the opioids, i.e. to any natural or synthetic drug that has morphine-like actions. [EU]

Nasal: Pertaining to the nose. [EU]

Nausea: An unpleasant sensation, vaguely referred to the epigastrium and abdomen, and often culminating in vomiting. [EU]

Necrosis: The sum of the morphological changes indicative of cell death and caused by the progressive degradative action of enzymes; it may affect groups of cells or part of a structure or an organ. [EU]

Neonatal: Pertaining to the first four weeks after birth. [EU]

Neoplasms: New abnormal growth of tissue. Malignant neoplasms show a greater degree of anaplasia and have the properties of invasion and metastasis, compared to benign neoplasms. [NIH]

Neural: 1. pertaining to a nerve or to the nerves. 2. situated in the region of the spinal axis, as the neutral arch. [EU]

Niacin: Water-soluble vitamin of the B complex occurring in various animal and plant tissues. Required by the body for the formation of coenzymes NAD and NADP. Has pellagra-curative, vasodilating, and antilipemic properties. [NIH]

Nicotine: Nicotine is highly toxic alkaloid. It is the prototypical agonist at nicotinic cholinergic receptors where it dramatically stimulates neurons and ultimately blocks synaptic transmission. Nicotine is also important medically because of its presence in tobacco smoke. [NIH]

Nitroglycerin: A highly volatile organic nitrate that acts as a dilator of arterial and venous smooth muscle and is used in the treatment of angina. It provides relief through improvement of the balance between myocardial oxygen supply and demand. Although total coronary blood flow is not increased, there is redistribution of blood flow in the heart when partial occlusion of coronary circulation is effected. [NIH]

Obstetrics: A medical-surgical specialty concerned with management and care of women during pregnancy, parturition, and the puerperium. [NIH]

Occult: Obscure; concealed from observation, difficult to understand. [EU]

Ointments: Semisolid preparations used topically for protective emollient effects or as a vehicle for local administration of medications. Ointment bases are various mixtures of fats, waxes, animal and plant oils and solid and liquid hydrocarbons. [NIH]

Ophthalmic: Pertaining to the eye. [EU]

Oral: Pertaining to the mouth, taken through or applied in the mouth, as an oral medication or an oral thermometer. [EU]

Organelles: Specific particles of membrane-bound organized living substances present in eukaryotic cells, such as the mitochondria; the golgi apparatus; endoplasmic reticulum; lysomomes; plastids; and vacuoles. [NIH]

Osteoporosis: Reduction in the amount of bone mass, leading to fractures after minimal trauma. [EU]

Overdosage: 1. the administration of an excessive dose. 2. the condition resulting from an excessive dose. [EU]

Pacemaker: An object or substance that influences the rate at which a certain phenomenon occurs; often used alone to indicate the natural cardiac pacemaker or an artificial cardiac pacemaker. In biochemistry, a substance whose rate of reaction sets the pace for a series of interrelated reactions. [EU]

Palliative: 1. affording relief, but not cure. 2. an alleviating medicine. [EU]

Pancreas: An organ behind the lower part of the stomach that is about the size of a hand. It makes insulin so that the body can use glucose (sugar) for energy. It also makes enzymes that help the body digest food. Spread all over the pancreas are areas called the islets of Langerhans. The cells in these areas each have a special purpose. The alpha cells make glucagon, which raises the level of glucose in the blood; the beta cells make insulin; the delta cells make somatostatin. There are also the PP cells and the D1 cells, about which little is known. [NIH]

Pancreatitis: Inflammation (pain, tenderness) of the pancreas; it can make the pancreas stop working. It is caused by drinking too much alcohol, by disease in the gallbladder, or by a virus. [NIH]

Parenteral: Not through the alimentary canal but rather by injection through some other route, as subcutaneous, intramuscular, intraorbital, intracapsular, intraspinal, intrasternal, intravenous, etc. [EU]

Pathologic: 1. indicative of or caused by a morbid condition. 2. pertaining to pathology (= branch of medicine that treats the essential nature of the disease, especially the structural and functional changes in tissues and organs of the body caused by the disease). [EU]

Pediatrics: A medical specialty concerned with maintaining health and providing medical care to children from birth to adolescence. [NIH]

Pelvic: Pertaining to the pelvis. [EU]

Peptic: Pertaining to pepsin or to digestion; related to the action of gastric juices. [EU]

Perianal: Located around the anus. [EU]

Perioperative: Pertaining to the period extending from the time of hospitalization for surgery to the time of discharge. [EU]

Peristalsis: The wormlike movement by which the alimentary canal or other tubular organs provided with both longitudinal and circular muscle fibres propel their contents. It consists of a wave of contraction passing along the tube for variable distances. [EU]

Peritonitis: Inflammation of the peritoneum; a condition marked by exudations in the peritoneum of serum, fibrin, cells, and pus. It is attended by abdominal pain and tenderness, constipation, vomiting, and moderate fever. [EU]

Perivascular: Situated around a vessel. [EU]

Pernicious: Tending to a fatal issue. [EU]

Petroleum: Naturally occurring complex liquid hydrocarbons which, after distillation, yield combustible fuels, petrochemicals, and lubricants. [NIH]

Pharmacist: A person trained to prepare and distribute medicines and to give information about them. [NIH]

Pharmacologic: Pertaining to pharmacology or to the properties and reactions of drugs. [EU]

Phenotype: The outward appearance of the individual. It is the product of interactions between genes and between the genotype and the environment. This includes the killer phenotype, characteristic of yeasts. [NIH]

Photocoagulation: Using a special strong beam of light (laser) to seal off bleeding blood vessels such as in the eye. The laser can also burn away blood vessels that should not have grown in the eye. This is the main treatment for diabetic retinopathy. [NIH]

Placenta: A highly vascular fetal organ through which the fetus absorbs oxygen and other nutrients and excretes carbon dioxide and other wastes. It begins to form about the eighth day of gestation when the blastocyst adheres to the decidua. [NIH]

Plague: An acute infectious disease caused by yersinia pestis that affects humans, wild rodents, and their ectoparasites. This condition persists due to its firm entrenchment in sylvatic rodent-flea ecosystems throughout the world. Bubonic plague is the most common form. [NIH]

Plexus: A network or tangle; a general term for a network of lymphatic vessels, nerves, or veins. [EU]

Poisoning: A condition or physical state produced by the ingestion, injection or inhalation of, or exposure to a deleterious agent. [NIH]

Postoperative: Occurring after a surgical operation. [EU]

Potassium: An element that is in the alkali group of metals. It has an atomic symbol K, atomic number 19, and atomic weight 39.10. It is the chief cation in the intracellular fluid of muscle and other cells. Potassium ion is a strong electrolyte and it plays a significant role in the regulation of fluid volume and maintenance of the water-electrolyte balance. [NIH]

Preclinical: Before a disease becomes clinically recognizable. [EU]

Preeclampsia: A condition that some women with diabetes have during the late stages of pregnancy. Two signs of this condition are high blood pressure and swelling because the body cells are holding extra water. [NIH]

Prenatal: Existing or occurring before birth, with reference to the fetus. [EU]

Preoperative: Preceding an operation. [EU]

Prevalence: The number of people in a given group or population who are reported to have a disease. [NIH]

Proctitis: Inflammation of the rectum. [EU]

Proctoscopy: Endoscopic examination, therapy or surgery of the rectum.

[NIH]

Progressive: Advancing; going forward; going from bad to worse; increasing in scope or severity. [EU]

Prolapse: 1. the falling down, or sinking, of a part or viscus; procidentia. 2. to undergo such displacement. [EU]

Prophylaxis: The prevention of disease; preventive treatment. [EU]

Prostate: A gland in males that surrounds the neck of the bladder and the urethra. It secretes a substance that liquifies coagulated semen. It is situated in the pelvic cavity behind the lower part of the pubic symphysis, above the deep layer of the triangular ligament, and rests upon the rectum. [NIH]

Proteins: Polymers of amino acids linked by peptide bonds. The specific sequence of amino acids determines the shape and function of the protein. [NIH]

Proximal: Nearest; closer to any point of reference; opposed to distal. [EU]

Proxy: A person authorized to decide or act for another person, for example, a person having durable power of attorney. [NIH]

Pruritus: Itching skin; may be a symptom of diabetes. [NIH]

Psoriasis: A common genetically determined, chronic, inflammatory skin disease characterized by rounded erythematous, dry, scaling patches. The lesions have a predilection for nails, scalp, genitalia, extensor surfaces, and the lumbosacral region. Accelerated epidermopoiesis is considered to be the fundamental pathologic feature in psoriasis. [NIH]

Purpura: Purplish or brownish red discoloration, easily visible through the epidermis, caused by hemorrhage into the tissues. [NIH]

Quiescent: Marked by a state of inactivity or repose. [EU]

Reagent: A substance employed to produce a chemical reaction so as to detect, measure, produce, etc., other substances. [EU]

Receptor: 1. a molecular structure within a cell or on the surface characterized by (1) selective binding of a specific substance and (2) a specific physiologic effect that accompanies the binding, e.g., cell-surface receptors for peptide hormones, neurotransmitters, antigens, complement fragments, and immunoglobulins and cytoplasmic receptors for steroid hormones. 2. a sensory nerve terminal that responds to stimuli of various kinds. [EU]

Recurrence: The return of a sign, symptom, or disease after a remission. [NIH]

Renin: An enzyme of the hydrolase class that catalyses cleavage of the leucine-leucine bond in angiotensin to generate angiotensin. 1. The enzyme is synthesized as inactive prorenin in the kidney and released into the blood in the active form in response to various metabolic stimuli. Not to be confused with rennin (chymosin). [EU]

Retrograde: 1. moving backward or against the usual direction of flow. 2. degenerating, deteriorating, or catabolic. [EU]

Riboflavin: Nutritional factor found in milk, eggs, malted barley, liver, kidney, heart, and leafy vegetables. The richest natural source is yeast. It occurs in the free form only in the retina of the eye, in whey, and in urine; its principal forms in tissues and cells are as FMN and FAD. [NIH]

Saline: Salty; of the nature of a salt; containing a salt or salts. [EU]

Salmonella: A genus of gram-negative, facultatively anaerobic, rod-shaped bacteria that utilizes citrate as a sole carbon source. It is pathogenic for humans, causing enteric fevers, gastroenteritis, and bacteremia. Food poisoning is the most common clinical manifestation. Organisms within this genus are separated on the basis of antigenic characteristics, sugar fermentation patterns, and bacteriophage susceptibility. [NIH]

Sclerotherapy: Treatment of varicose veins, hemorrhoids, gastric and esophageal varices, and peptic ulcer hemorrhage by injection or infusion of chemical agents which cause localized thrombosis and eventual fibrosis and obliteration of the vessels. [NIH]

Secretion: 1. the process of elaborating a specific product as a result of the activity of a gland; this activity may range from separating a specific substance of the blood to the elaboration of a new chemical substance. 2. any substance produced by secretion. [EU]

Sedentary: 1. sitting habitually; of inactive habits. 2. pertaining to a sitting posture. [EU]

Selenium: An element with the atomic symbol Se, atomic number 34, and atomic weight 78.96. It is an essential micronutrient for mammals and other animals but is toxic in large amounts. Selenium protects intracellular structures against oxidative damage. It is an essential component of glutathione peroxidase. [NIH]

Semisynthetic: Produced by chemical manipulation of naturally occurring substances. [EU]

Senna: Preparations of Cassia senna L. and C. angustifolia of the Leguminosae. They contain sennosides, which are anthraquinone type cathartics and are used in many different preparations as laxatives. [NIH]

Septic: Produced by or due to decomposition by microorganisms; putrefactive. [EU]

Septicemia: Systemic disease associated with the presence and persistence of pathogenic microorganisms or their toxins in the blood. Called also blood poisoning. [EU]

Sigmoid: 1. shaped like the letter S or the letter C. 2. the sigmoid colon. [EU]

Sigmoidoscopy: Endoscopic examination, therapy or surgery of the sigmoid flexure. [NIH]

Species: A taxonomic category subordinate to a genus (or subgenus) and superior to a subspecies or variety, composed of individuals possessing common characters distinguishing them from other categories of individuals of the same taxonomic level. In taxonomic nomenclature, species are designated by the genus name followed by a Latin or Latinized adjective or noun. [EU]

Spectrum: A charted band of wavelengths of electromagnetic vibrations obtained by refraction and diffraction. By extension, a measurable range of activity, such as the range of bacteria affected by an antibiotic (antibacterial s.) or the complete range of manifestations of a disease. [EU]

Sphincter: A ringlike band of muscle fibres that constricts a passage or closes a natural orifice; called also musculus sphincter. [EU]

Stasis: A word termination indicating the maintenance of (or maintaining) a constant level; preventing increase or multiplication. [EU]

Stenosis: Narrowing or stricture of a duct or canal. [EU]

Stomach: An organ of digestion situated in the left upper quadrant of the abdomen between the termination of the esophagus and the beginning of the duodenum. [NIH]

Stomatitis: Inflammation of the oral mucosa, due to local or systemic factors which may involve the buccal and labial mucosa, palate, tongue, floor of the mouth, and the gingivae. [EU]

Sucralfate: A basic aluminum complex of sulfated sucrose. It is advocated in the therapy of peptic, duodenal, and prepyloric ulcers, gastritis, reflux esophagitis, and other gastrointestinal irritations. It acts primarily at the ulcer site, where it has cytoprotective, pepsinostatic, antacid, and bile acid-binding properties. The drug is only slightly absorbed by the digestive mucosa, which explains the absence of systemic effects and toxicity. [NIH]

Sulfur: An element that is a member of the chalcogen family. It has an atomic symbol S, atomic number 16, and atomic weight 32.066. It is found in the amino acids cysteine and methionine. [NIH]

Sunburn: An injury to the skin causing erythema, tenderness, and sometimes blistering and resulting from excessive exposure to the sun. The reaction is produced by the ultraviolet radiation in sunlight. [NIH]

Suppository: A medicated mass adapted for introduction into the rectal, vaginal, or urethral orifice of the body, suppository bases are solid at room temperature but melt or dissolve at body temperature. Commonly used bases are cocoa butter, glycerinated gelatin, hydrogenated vegetable oils, polyethylene glycols of various molecular weights, and fatty acid esters of polyethylene glycol. [EU]

Symptomatic: 1. pertaining to or of the nature of a symptom. 2. indicative (of a particular disease or disorder). 3. exhibiting the symptoms of a particular disease but having a different cause. 4. directed at the allying of symptoms, as symptomatic treatment. [EU]

Systemic: Pertaining to or affecting the body as a whole. [EU]

Tears: The fluid secreted by the lacrimal glands. This fluid moistens the conjunctiva and cornea. [NIH]

Tenesmus: Straining, especially ineffectual and painful straining at stool or in urination. [EU]

Thermal: Pertaining to or characterized by heat. [EU]

Thrombocytopenia: Decrease in the number of blood platelets. [EU]

Thrombosis: The formation, development, or presence of a thrombus. [EU]

Thrombus: An aggregation of blood factors, primarily platelets and fibrin with entrapment of cellular elements, frequently causing vascular obstruction at the point of its formation. Some authorities thus differentiate thrombus formation from simple coagulation or clot formation. [EU]

Thyroxine: An amino acid of the thyroid gland which exerts a stimulating effect on thyroid metabolism. [NIH]

Tone: 1. the normal degree of vigour and tension; in muscle, the resistance to passive elongation or stretch; tonus. 2. a particular quality of sound or of voice. 3. to make permanent, or b change, the colour of silver stain by chemical treatment, usually with a heavy metal. [EU]

Topical: Pertaining to a particular surface area, as a topical anti-infective applied to a certain area of the skin and affecting only the area to which it is applied. [EU]

Toxicity: The quality of being poisonous, especially the degree of virulence of a toxic microbe or of a poison. [EU]

Toxicology: The science concerned with the detection, chemical composition, and pharmacologic action of toxic substances or poisons and the treatment and prevention of toxic manifestations. [NIH]

Toxin: A poison; frequently used to refer specifically to a protein produced by some higher plants, certain animals, and pathogenic bacteria, which is highly toxic for other living organisms. Such substances are differentiated from the simple chemical poisons and the vegetable alkaloids by their high molecular weight and antigenicity. [EU]

Transdermal: Entering through the dermis, or skin, as in administration of a drug applied to the skin in ointment or patch form. [EU]

Transfusion: The introduction of whole blood or blood component directly into the blood stream. [EU]

Trophoblast: The outer layer of cells of the blastocyst which works its way into the endometrium during ovum implantation and grows rapidly, later combining with mesoderm. [NIH]

Tuberculosis: Any of the infectious diseases of man and other animals caused by species of mycobacterium. [NIH]

Ulceration: 1. the formation or development of an ulcer. 2. an ulcer. [EU]

Urinary: Pertaining to the urine; containing or secreting urine. [EU]

Urology: A surgical specialty concerned with the study, diagnosis, and treatment of diseases of the urinary tract in both sexes and the genital tract in the male. It includes the specialty of andrology which addresses both male genital diseases and male infertility. [NIH]

Vaccine: A suspension of attenuated or killed microorganisms (bacteria, viruses, or rickettsiae), administered for the prevention, amelioration or treatment of infectious diseases. [EU]

Vaginal: 1. of the nature of a sheath; ensheathing. 2. pertaining to the vagina. 3. pertaining to the tunica vaginalis testis. [EU]

Valerian: Valeriana officinale, an ancient, sedative herb of the large family Valerianaceae. The roots were formerly used to treat hysterias and other neurotic states and are presently used to treat sleep disorders. [NIH]

Vascular: Pertaining to blood vessels or indicative of a copious blood supply. [EU]

Vasoactive: Exerting an effect upon the calibre of blood vessels. [EU]

Veins: The vessels carrying blood toward the heart. [NIH]

Virulence: The degree of pathogenicity within a group or species of microorganisms or viruses as indicated by case fatality rates and/or the ability of the organism to invade the tissues of the host. [NIH]

Viscera: Any of the large interior organs in any one of the three great cavities of the body, especially in the abdomen. [NIH]

Viscosity: A physical property of fluids that determines the internal resistance to shear forces. [EU]

Warfarin: An anticoagulant that acts by inhibiting the synthesis of vitamin K-dependent coagulation factors. Warfarin is indicated for the prophylaxis and/or treatment of venous thrombosis and its extension, pulmonary embolism, and atrial fibrillation with embolization. It is also used as an adjunct in the prophylaxis of systemic embolism after myocardial infarction. Warfarin is also used as a rodenticide. [NIH]

Warts: Benign epidermal proliferations or tumors; some are viral in origin. [NIH]

Yersinia: A genus of gram-negative, facultatively anaerobic rod- to coccobacillus-shaped bacteria that occurs in a broad spectrum of habitats. [NIH]

General Dictionaries and Glossaries

While the above glossary is essentially complete, the dictionaries listed here cover virtually all aspects of medicine, from basic words and phrases to more advanced terms (sorted alphabetically by title; hyperlinks provide rankings, information and reviews at Amazon.com):

- **Dictionary of Medical Acronymns & Abbreviations** by Stanley Jablonski (Editor), Paperback, 4th edition (2001), Lippincott Williams & Wilkins Publishers, ISBN: 1560534605,
  http://www.amazon.com/exec/obidos/ASIN/1560534605/icongroupinterna

- **Dictionary of Medical Terms : For the Nonmedical Person (Dictionary of Medical Terms for the Nonmedical Person, Ed 4)** by Mikel A. Rothenberg, M.D, et al, Paperback - 544 pages, 4th edition (2000), Barrons Educational Series, ISBN: 0764112015,
  http://www.amazon.com/exec/obidos/ASIN/0764112015/icongroupinterna

- **A Dictionary of the History of Medicine** by A. Sebastian, CD-Rom edition (2001), CRC Press-Parthenon Publishers, ISBN: 185070368X,
  http://www.amazon.com/exec/obidos/ASIN/185070368X/icongroupinterna

- **Dorland's Illustrated Medical Dictionary (Standard Version)** by Dorland, et al, Hardcover - 2088 pages, 29th edition (2000), W B Saunders Co, ISBN: 0721662544,
  http://www.amazon.com/exec/obidos/ASIN/0721662544/icongroupinterna

- **Dorland's Electronic Medical Dictionary** by Dorland, et al, Software, 29th Book & CD-Rom edition (2000), Harcourt Health Sciences, ISBN: 0721694934,
  http://www.amazon.com/exec/obidos/ASIN/0721694934/icongroupinterna

- **Dorland's Pocket Medical Dictionary (Dorland's Pocket Medical Dictionary, 26th Ed)** Hardcover - 912 pages, 26th edition (2001), W B Saunders Co, ISBN: 0721682812,
  http://www.amazon.com/exec/obidos/ASIN/0721682812/icongroupinterna /103-4193558-7304618

- **Melloni's Illustrated Medical Dictionary (Melloni's Illustrated Medical Dictionary, 4th Ed)** by Melloni, Hardcover, 4th edition (2001), CRC Press-Parthenon Publishers, ISBN: 85070094X,
  http://www.amazon.com/exec/obidos/ASIN/85070094X/icongroupinterna

- **Stedman's Electronic Medical Dictionary Version 5.0 (CD-ROM for Windows and Macintosh, Individual)** by Stedmans, CD-ROM edition (2000), Lippincott Williams & Wilkins Publishers, ISBN: 0781726328, http://www.amazon.com/exec/obidos/ASIN/0781726328/icongroupinterna

- **Stedman's Medical Dictionary** by Thomas Lathrop Stedman, Hardcover - 2098 pages, 27th edition (2000), Lippincott, Williams & Wilkins, ISBN: 068340007X, http://www.amazon.com/exec/obidos/ASIN/068340007X/icongroupinterna

- **Tabers Cyclopedic Medical Dictionary (Thumb Index)** by Donald Venes (Editor), et al, Hardcover - 2439 pages, 19th edition (2001), F A Davis Co, ISBN: 0803606540, http://www.amazon.com/exec/obidos/ASIN/0803606540/icongroupinterna

INDEX

Printed in the United States
112389LV00003B/22/A